Teachers' voices for school change

The increased importance of research in academic institutions has not only strengthened the view that the role of teachers is to implement theories and recommendations imposed from above, but has also increased the divide between theory and practice so that theory is perceived exclusively as the domain of the university and practice as that of the school.

Teachers' voices for school change challenges this view of the teacher role as well as the division of theory and practice by describing an alternative approach to research, Educative Research. This approach enables teachers to speak out and also allows them to protest at the way school structures, educational beliefs and teacher actions contribute to distorted notions of education which limit and constrain those who have been pushed to the margins of our society.

Also in the Investigating Schooling series

Studying Teachers' Lives
Edited by Ivor F. Goodson

Teachers' voices for school change

An introduction to educative research

A. Gitlin
K. Bringhurst
M. Burns
V. Cooley
B. Myers
K. Price
R. Russell
P. Tiess

TEACHERS COLLEGE PRESS

Teachers College, Columbia University
New York and London

Published by Teachers College Press, 1234 Amsterdam Avenue,
New York, NY 10027

Printed in Great Britain

Library of Congress Cataloging-in-Publication Data
Teachers' voices for school change: an introduction to educative
    research/A. Gitlin . . . [et al.].
    p. cm.
    Includes bibliographical references (p.) and index.
    ISBN 0–8077–3181–1 (alk. paper). – ISBN 0–8077–3180–3
    (pbk.: alk. paper)
    1. Education – Research – Methodology. 2. Experiential research –
    United States. I. Gitlin, Andrew David.
    LB1028.T368   1992
    370′.7′8 dc20   92-4403
                                                                  CIP

ISBN 0–8077–3181–1
      0–8077–3180–3

For those working in the classrooms of our schools

Contents

Acknowledgements

It is difficult to imagine how this text could have become a reality without the help of many others. First, we would like to thank the other members of the Salt Lake Master's cooperative who struggled with us to help shape this approach, but could not participate in the writing of the text. Their actions and concerns throughout the first two years of the project were central to our understanding of Educative Research. In particular, the endless patience and insight of Deborah Mohrman and Theresa Cryns, the teaching assistants for the cooperative, helped to keep the process going when it looked like we might not make it through another week. Two other members, Lawrence Burton and Kate Moulton, were also very helpful in giving feedback on initial drafts of the book and providing help with our library searches. Another important contributor to the cooperative was the Salt Lake City School District office. This office provided funds for two national conferences and additional monies for substitute teachers enabling members to participate more fully in the Educative Research Project. Without their support we would not be able to speak out to a larger audience and more fully examine our stories. In much the same way, the University of Utah played an important role in facilitating our work. Not only did the Educational Studies Department contribute funds for conferences and substitutes, but they also provided the opportunity to shape the cooperative around the concept of Educative Research.

As the writing of the text proceeded, we wanted to get feedback from practicing teachers. Two teachers, Judy Thomas and Carol Randell, gave us invaluable feedback. Their insights helped us reconsider both the organization of the text and a number of sections that were overly jargonistic. Finally, this manuscript would not have been possible without the help of Robyn Turner. Robyn not only put the chapters together and made chapter corrections, but importantly helped shape the style of the manuscript, including the pages that separated the sections of the book and the table of contents.

Part I
What is Educative Research?

1 Protest and silence

Continuing erosion of teachers' salaries and support for education in general in the state of Utah prompted a few brave teachers in a suburban Salt Lake high school to stage a wild cat strike. While teachers played a primary role in organizing this action, as the strike spread, other groups such as the student association from the University of Utah added their support by scheduling a rally in which a number of university professors were invited to speak. The speakers at the rally focused on the plight of professors and how their salaries were not competitive with others in comparable institutions. They also talked about how the relative decline in professor salaries would adversely affect the quality of education offered at the university. Little mention was made of the plight of public school teachers or the common interests held by university professors and teachers.

The following day the Education Department at the university organized a seminar in which public school teachers were to speak on the wild cat strike. Only a few professors attended and those that did were all from the Education Department. As the discussion raged in the media over the next few days, lobbyists were spinning a consistent tale: given a finite amount of money to be apportioned, what teachers get in salary raises will decrease the amount available for university professors and vice versa.

This event reflects a tension common to many educational communities: the interests of university professors are seen as oppositional to those who work in schools. Unfortunately, these opposing interests can not be overcome simply by fostering more cooperative relations between academics and teachers or providing new funding formulas for education that do not pit higher education against the public schools. Instead, the problem goes much deeper, and is related to a historical struggle concerning questions about who should be seen as expert and what is legitimate knowledge.

Over the last several decades, university professors have approached this struggle by devoting more and more time to research. Because research knowledge is generally seen as legitimate, this emphasis has enhanced their claims of expertise. Teachers, on the other hand, have continued to base their knowledge on experience. They have done so both because many believe this is an important source of knowledge and also because they have been denied opportunities to produce other sorts of knowledge. Their continued emphasis on experiential knowledge, however, has come at a cost: they are often discredited as experts and have for the most part been denied a say in fundamental matters of educational policy. If we are to contest this hierarchy and encourage the development of educational communities that value multiple forms of legitimate knowledge and corresponding notions of expertise, one important area of concern is research methods. This is so because research methods set the standards which help determine who is considered expert. And it is this perceived expertise that allows certain groups to have extended opportunities and receive an unequal share of the communities' resources.

The purpose of this book is to explore the possibilities of an alternative approach to research, Educative Research, that values both experiential knowledge and knowledge produced through systematic inquiry and therefore attempts to broaden notions of expertise. In particular, we want to raise the following issues. Is it possible to foster a more community-based type of inquiry that values different forms of knowing and expertise? And, what difference if any would this sort of method make? For example, would teachers' voices be heard, and, if so, would these voices encourage school change and challenge the narrow and oppressive features of our school system?

To address these issues, we will trace our attempt to understand and practice Educative Research. In many ways this journey begins with the personal history of the university professor, Andrew Gitlin, who initially worked on the outline for Educative Research. While Educative Research is a collaborative endeavor that was developed by a group struggling to practice this method, the initial assumptions embedded in this process are related to a set of experiences and events which shaped the thinking of this professor. By beginning with his history, we can describe the assumptions underlying this method and provide an authentic account of how the journey began with the voice of the researcher and then attempted to include others who have been traditionally silenced.

RESEARCHER AS PERSON

As was true of most students who went to college in the 1960s, the political fervor of this period was hard to escape. However, I did not enter college with much concern about politics. Like most of my fellow students in 1967, I wore my hair short and my socks white. On my way to class, not long after arriving at the University of Wisconsin-Madison, I encountered a group of people marching in the hallway of the Commerce building. My first inclination was to steer clear and make sure I was on time for class. But, my curiosity got the better of me and I asked one of the protesters what all the fuss was about. One participant explained that Dow Chemical was recruiting on campus while at the same time they were making napalm for Vietnam. Given my liberal upbringing his argument seemed more than reasonable, but surely not so compelling that I would miss class. As I walked off, however, a loud voice pierced the corridor informing all that they must leave the building in five minutes. After no more than thirty seconds someone in the group shouted, 'Link arms!' There I was trapped in the middle of this angry crowd. Moments later I saw police unleash a curtain of violence that was beyond my imagination. Blood was everywhere, people were screaming, and I remember thinking, 'They even hit the girls.' My jingoistic view of America was crushed. While I wasn't hurt, something in me changed. To understand politics better, I began to study Marx and others and became active in Students for a Democratic Society. I did maintain my pre-med classwork, but my vocational orientation to university work was altered. Anyway, what did I have to lose? I always knew my family would take care of me if things got rough. And the economy was going so well that I figured I could get some sort of job.

Graduation from the University of Wisconsin-Madison in 1971 was an emotional time. I did get several interviews for admission into medical school, but none resulted in an acceptance. The interview at New York University, in particular, stands out.

I walked into the New York University medical building feeling very self-conscious. Why was I going though this med school thing if it conflicted with all my activism of the past few years? Why did I agree to cut my hair for the interview? And why was I wearing a tie? The wait for my interview was short and before I could compose myself, I was rushed into an imposing room with a large desk. In a formal way the man behind the desk welcomed me. His first comment was that he, too, had gone to Wisconsin. Before I could say anything he launched into an analysis of my grades and test scores: 'Why did you take all these science courses pass/fail?' This was definitely one of those questions to which he already had an answer, because it was common knowledge for those who had followed the activities on the Madison campus that science courses could not be taken pass/fail except in the 1969–1970 academic year when Students for a Democratic Society had shut down the university. As part of an amnesty agreement those who decided to join the protest could take the courses pass/fail. And so my interviewer was quite aware that the pass/fail grade signified my political commitments. At first I could not speak. Should I try to get around this question or just tell him? With a touch of defiance in my voice, I told him about my political activities and added that I would do the same in the future. I don't remember much of what followed, but as I walked to the street at the end of the interview, I cursed my attempt to enter the establishment.

Shortly after this interview, my parents came to Wisconsin to attend my graduation. After the ceremony we all went out to eat at a local pizzeria. After a few slices my dad asked, 'What do you plan to do if you don't get into medical school?' Much to my surprise I had an answer, 'Teach.' As I looked over at my mother, I could see the disappointment in her eyes and she said quite openly, 'That's a job for women; surely you could do something more with your life.'

I did become a teacher and taught for six years. During this time my intent was to carry on the political vision that I had developed over the past four years. I taught in ghetto schools with large minority populations and tried to make a difference. Over time, however, my original intent was transformed. Instead of working in the community and trying to provide a political education for students that directly addressed racism and class issues, my attention was directed more and more to the discipline of the class and the development of basic skills. I found myself viewing students as disadvantaged. I began to champion equal opportunity when only a few years earlier I had strongly argued with other teachers about the distortions of a disadvantaged view and the limits of equalizing opportunities without equalizing economic realities. At about the same time that the gap between my intentions and practice became clear, I received an offer to be a teaching assistant in the Education Department at the University of Wisconsin. Without much hesitation I left teaching and returned to the academy.

After two years in the doctoral program I found myself spending every Friday afternoon in a critical theory seminar that in many ways helped shape the educational positions I hold today. The discussions for the most part focused on Marxist concepts related to the economy and the state. But, on one particular Friday, the reading being discussed had a more psychological bent and argued that reconstruction started with the self and should include the writing of autobiographical sketches. This view was adamantly crushed as we returned quickly to our focus on issues of cultural and economic reproduction and the new sociology of knowledge.

Several years later, upon finishing my dissertation, I took a job at the University of Utah. By this time my emphasis was less on political action than political theory. I wanted to fight it out with other academics about the reproductive nature of schooling and, in particular, argue that schools deskilled and oppressed teachers. My writing skills were limited at best, but I did produce a few manuscripts and looked for a forum to present them. One senior faculty member, who was informally acting as a mentor, suggested I try the Curriculum Theorizing Conference. I put in a proposal and it was accepted. Without knowing it, I had stepped back into the debate about autobiography that we had in the Friday seminar several years earlier. One group at the conference was clearly arguing for the importance of the autobiographical method, while many of those who considered themselves neo-Marxists were talking about cultural and economic reproduction.

The autobiographical method, while powerful in many respects, did not have an immediate effect on my work; I continued to focus on issues of proletarianization and reproduction. However, subtle changes began taking place and surfaced quite a few years later when I was asked to give a seminar at the University of Utah. In this seminar, I presented some work on how teacher dialogue could encourage school change. The response to my talk was quick and pointed. One group argued that to give teachers a chance to influence policy through dialogue was like allowing 'the blind to lead the blind.' The radicals on the staff, on the other hand, pointed out that this process might encourage teachers to change, but that the change was unlikely to be progressive given the 'interests' of these practitioners.

After the seminar my emotions were running high. I could understand why some of the staff, who viewed themselves as experts disseminating educational truths, felt a need to view teachers as inexpert. I was mystified, however, by the responses from those on the left. Weren't teachers oppressed as both women and workers? Wasn't this a group worth fighting for, or were they simply facilitators of inequality? I left the office late that night with a pain in my stomach and a feeling of ambiguity about the direction of my scholarship.

As I reflect back on these selected events, it appears that my educational philosophy was greatly influenced by two competing trends: one came out of the neo-Marxist tradition and the other from a more personal approach that focused on how cultural norms and economic priorities are experienced and mediated by particular actors. This may explain why the initial conception of Educative Research focused both on personal knowledge and the political arguments of critical theorists. It is also apparent that I identified with teachers and had a great deal more faith in their 'interests' and abilities than many other academics. Not surprisingly, what research did to teachers and their relationship to academics (researchers) became one of my important concerns.

The start of a Cooperative Masters of Education program provided an opportunity for me to shape a course around these assumptions and concerns. From this rather typical structure I started a journey with twenty-two

teachers to discover what is Educative Research and consider its importance for teachers, schooling and educational change.

AIMS OF EDUCATIVE RESEARCH

Whatever else may be said about this journey, there can be no doubt that it
has been a struggle. Many times what became the Educative Research
Project (ERP) was on the verge of collapse. Many times we slipped into
roles which were oppressive to others in the group, and many times we
simply started to wilt under the pressure of trying to tell our story and keep
a balance between our public and private lives. At the core of our struggle
was an attempt to deal with difference.

Some differences are created and then associated with a set of privileges,
opportunities and material rewards. For example, who is seen as 'expert' is
related to a set of work conditions which allows academics to engage in
certain types of inquiry that are difficult, if not impossible, for teachers to
attempt, given the intensification of their work (Apple, 1986). Because
teachers cannot effectively make claims of expertise, they tend to get fewer
privileges, opportunities and economic rewards when compared to
academics. The difference between academics and teachers, therefore, is
created, it is not based not on merit, but primarily on the opportunity to
engage in certain forms of inquiry.

On the other hand, sometimes important differences get obscured such
that those residing on the lower ends of a hierarchy must conform to
standards imposed from above if they want to get ahead. Tannen argues that
this type of result often occurs between men and women.

> Denying real differences can only compound the confusion that is
> already widespread in this era of shifting and re-forming relationships
> between women and men. Pretending that women and men are the same
> hurts women, because the ways they are treated are based on the norms
> for men.

(Tannen, 1990, p.16)

Both these trends, the creation of differences that set up hierarchies, and the
obscuring of important differences that make it necessary for groups to blur
their identity to get ahead, are processes against which we have struggled.

Our primary focus has been to challenge the creation of hierarchical
differences within the educational community between teachers and
academics. We have struggled against this hierarchy because it leaves
teachers silenced and limits reform efforts by excluding the concerns and
insights of those who are best informed about the everyday workings of
schools. Our actions, however, are not simply directed at finding ways for

teachers to collaborate with those researchers housed in the university. Instead, we are attempting to challenge the narrow standards on which expertise is based as well as the material results of such standards. Questions of what is legitimate knowledge, the working conditions of those living in our schools, and the distribution of community resources are central to our alternative beliefs and practices.

In the process of challenging these exaggerated differences, we have also tried to honor and respect authentic differences. Our aim is not, for example, to make all teachers teacher/researchers, even if resources and material working conditions could be changed to encourage such an alteration in the teaching role. This sort of change is condescending to teachers and suggests that there is something lacking about being 'only' a teacher. Our intent is not to force all teachers into a common mold, but to embrace a more varied, wide-ranging notion of what is legitimate knowledge that allows those traditionally silenced to enter into policy debates.

While our struggle over difference has not produced an answer or a final solution, it has created a bond that has allowed us to name our relation to the community: the Educative Research Project. But, why do we signify ourselves with such a combination of terms: educative and research? One reason we do so is that the university professor introduced this phrase in his opening remarks as part of the masters class. However, it would be misleading to think that this fully explains our use of the term because when the term was introduced it was vague to both the teachers and the university professor. Only through constant interaction did the ERP take on a particular meaning and enable *us* to see more fully our relation to the community.

The meaning we attach to Educative Research may, at first glance, seem elusive. Isn't it the case that research of all kinds is educative in some sense of the word? And if this is so, how does Educative Research differ from our common notions of what is research? We are using the term educative to refer to a process that, in the ideal, brings individuals together in such a fashion that all participants have a say in setting the agenda or topic and all have the potential to benefit and learn from the experience. When looked at from this point of view, it is clear that most research is anything but educative. For while research usually brings participants together, the 'subjects' are not involved in determining the research question and often are not expected to learn or benefit from the experience in any direct way. Underlying our notion of educative, therefore, is a certain politic that suggests the importance of issues of reciprocity and equity. It is not enough to say that research is educative simply because something has been learned, for this position ignores who determines what is studied, and who is involved in the learning process. Given that teachers and others have historically been excluded from the research process, both because of their work conditions and assumptions about their role, leaving out questions about who is involved in research allows their silence to seem natural and to continue.

Our notion of educative research also differs from the more commonly held view in that learning is not limited to a reflective process, but also embraces an active moment. Educative Research attempts to enhance participants' understanding of the educational world as well as their ability to **act** on that world. While most if not all research has a reflective component, at least for the researcher, action is often something that comes later, as policy makers digest the 'truths' embedded in the research studies. In contrast, our notion of educative links reflection and action and therefore is based on a politic that encourages participants both to examine and to remake schooling.

To clarify how we have come to this position, this text is divided into three parts. The first looks at the process of Educative Research and considers the relation between this process and the research context. The second provides case studies of four of those involved in the project, and the third captures our reflections on the ERP and possible future directions.

In particular, Chapter 1 gives a brief overview of how we practiced Educative Research. Viewed from the perspective of both the teachers and the university professor, this description emphasizes the significant events that shaped this approach. The described events are then used as a text to consider the underlying assumptions of Educative Research. These assumptions, in turn, help clarify how this approach differs from traditional methods and builds on a number of current alternative trends. Included in this discussion is a consideration of the role of dialogue in research, an examination of what is legitimate knowledge and an elaboration of the notion of voice, a central aim of Educative Research.

Chapter 3 provides a more indepth description of Educative Research by focusing on two central aspects of this process: the creation of school and personal histories. We begin with an overview of how these histories were developed and then use this description to compare our method with others that focus on the self and context. An abbreviated example of a school and personal history follows this comparison and gives a sense of what these histories can look like and what part they can play in Educative Research.

Chapter 4 centers on another important aspect of Educative Research, the use of Horizontal Evaluation. We describe this dialogical process, clarify its relation to the Educative Research process, and consider its underlying assumptions. An extended final section uses actual dialogue to show how this form of evaluation can enable participants to examine the connection between their research questions and classroom practices.

In many ways Chapter 5 is a critique of the previous descriptions of Educative Research because it points to the limits of looking only at method as a way to alter relations and schooling. Based on a historical sketch of institutions of higher education and their relationship to public schools, we argue that part of the larger project of Educative Research is the restructuring of the research context. Our claim is that altering the relationship between researchers and those studied requires changes in our research methods, as well as changes in the conditions under which teachers work and commonly held notions about legitimate knowledge.

The second part of the book moves to case studies of Educative Research. These case studies provide exemplars of the Educative Research process, illuminate the types of insights that can be encouraged by the process, and provide a text which exposes the limits and tensions within the process. Written by four teachers within the ERP, these case studies make it possible for these practitioners to tell their stories to a larger audience.

Chapter 6 traces Robyn's attempt to develop her voice and encourage other teachers in her school to do the same. By initiating teacher dialogue sessions in her school, she uncovers her own difficulties in dealing with issues of control, the established priorities of her peers functioning in an intensified, complex job, and the structural and hierarchical barriers inherent in the educational system. Robyn also discovers new partners in silence, such as students and parents, who deserve an opportunity to speak out and be heard.

In Chapter 7, Karen, a Special Education teacher, takes us on an experiential journey to define success in school. By confronting her own feelings of dissatisfaction, and lack of success as a teacher, she discovers that the role of 'expert' has not helped her develop the type of student/teacher relationships she desires. As she begins to let go of this role and listen to students, she discovers that many of her underlying assumptions about them are at the very core of her own misunderstandings. While Karen never defines success, she sees that developing successful relationships with students requires an approach to teaching that allows teachers to learn from students, as well as having students learn from teachers.

In Chapter 8, we witness the transformation in thinking that occurs as Pat, a fourth grade teacher, examines the role of computers in education. At the beginning of the project, Pat feels confident in her belief that computers will solve the problems of classroom practice. Over time, however, she encounters challenges to her belief system and becomes aware of how issues of computing are related to a set of political concerns. In particular, Pat is struck by the possibility that her own practice, and that of her colleagues, may be furthering gender distinctions. After re-examining the importance of gender issues in her own personal history, she is determined to look critically at the use of computers in her classroom and in her school.

Chapter 9 documents Kathy's use of personal histories with elementary students. With the writing of her own personal history and the insights gained through Horizontal Evaluation, Kathy comes to realize how little she knows about the lives of her students. Having tried with little success, a variety of approaches to teach a group of non-reading second graders, she decides to explore the possibility of using student autobiographies to build a sense of trust and community. What follows is a vivid account of Jacob, the most difficult student in the group and the influence of autobiographies on his role and relations with others in the classroom.

In the third part of the book, Chapter 10 gives an overview of the meaning of Educative Research from the point of view of the participants in the ERP. Based on a discussion audio-taped at one of the ERP meetings, this chapter focuses on three questions: what significance did Educative Research have for the participants?; in what ways, if any, did Educative Research reshape the roles of those involved in the ERP?; and what influence, if any, did Educative Research have in forming more collective relations? Consideration of these questions allows some of the central concerns of Educative Research to unfold, including our attempt to confront hierarchical differences while recognizing important differences between individuals, the development of voice, and the influence of voice on school change.

2 Educative Research practices and assumptions

Our attempt to develop an alternative method that would alter relations between the research participants, such that those traditionally silenced are given a voice in educational decisions and policy, has been anything but a straightforward process. Instead, the practices have evolved as we have struggled to understand this alternative method and its influence on research participants. In this chapter we look briefly at these evolving practices to give an overview of the project as well as provide a basis for analyzing the underlying assumptions. Because Educative Research belongs to a genre of inquiry methods that have overlapping assumptions, this theorizing of practice will illuminate the ways this approach builds on others and differs from both traditional and alternative methodological approaches.

In describing the events that helped to shape the evolution of the program, we found that the most authentic way to retell this story was to do so in the form of two voices: Andrew's (the university professor) and the teachers'. Each was a shared, yet different experience. To combine our perceptions and reactions into one voice, that of the researcher, would be to create a form that runs counter to our intention of fostering voice among those who are disenfranchized. Over time, the collective began to take shape and gain strength in purpose. To reflect this change, we describe the later practices of the ERP under the banner of 'the collective.'

EDUCATIVE RESEARCH PRACTICE

In the Cooperative Master's program at the University of Utah, twenty-two elementary and secondary teachers from a particular school district go through the coursework as a group. Classes meet in the schools and teachers have a say in determining the direction and content of the program. The length of the program varies, but usually lasts two years and results in a Master's of Education degree for participants.

Because this type of program has a history of collaboration between teachers and university faculty, Andrew felt that it could be very relevant to have the group focus on Educative Research. He introduced the idea to the twenty-two teachers present at the initial meeting. Of those twenty-two, seventeen decided to pursue the proposed program, and committed themselves to the cooperative. Over the next two years, the collective developed and continued to evolve. The following overview of the first two years of the project reflects the perceptions of seven teachers from the original collective: Beth, Karen, Kathy, Mari, Pat, Robyn, and Valerie, and the university professor, Andrew. To create this overview, several group discussions were held during which each of us reflected upon our past experiences. We then combined and condensed the dialogue from the seven teachers into one voice, but in doing so, tried to represent as many differing views as possible.

Andrew

In the initial meeting in September of 1988, I laid out my sense of the dominant relationship between researchers and practitioners, why this relation was problematic, and a possible avenue to confront this relation, namely Educative Research. Because no objections were raised, I assumed a mutual sense of enthusiasm on the part of the teachers and felt enough support to develop a program based on the assumptions of Educative Research. In retrospect, it is clear that the teachers really didn't have a choice, that some were less than excited about the direction and that I was acting in the role of expert who knew what the teachers needed.

Teachers

It is true that in our first meeting together none of us spoke up to voice concerns or hesitations about the direction of our master's program. While Andrew may not have fitted many of the stereotypical notions of a university professor, we still viewed him as the authority. Although he seemed to be suggesting otherwise, we doubted that we really could have a significant say in the program. For the most part, we were resigned to the fact that research, for us, would be somewhat of a necessary evil, something that we would have to do in order to get our degrees. At that point, very few of us imagined that it would have any connection to our teaching practice.

Andrew

Based on the appearance of an agreement to center the coursework on

Educative Research, I suggested that we begin by writing a school history. For the school in which they worked, I asked the teachers to identify common school structures such as curriculum programs or staffing patterns, and to interview teachers, parents, and administrators to get a sense of the evolving culture of the school. I also encouraged teachers to collect information on any other relevant areas that might be of interest. They used this data to compare current school conditions with the recent history of the school and with changes found in the United States system of public education.

Teachers

Many of us found an immediate interest in the writing of the school history. It gave us the opportunity to examine the significant events that had shaped the cultures of our individual schools. In writing our school histories, we began to distinguish 'real' constraints from the commonly made assumptions about what is possible. For those of us working at the same school, the gathering of data for these histories helped to foster camaraderie. On the other hand, for those who worked alone, the writing of a school history increased our sense of isolation from other members of the ERP.

Andrew

At the same time that teachers were collecting the information for their school histories, I also asked them to read articles and manuscripts that in some way focused on the questions being addressed by the school histories. Included in these readings were Eisner's (1979) *The Educational Imagination*, Sarason's (1971) *The Culture of the School and the Problem of Change*, Apple's (1979) *Ideology and Curriculum* and Kliebard's (1987) *The Struggle for the American Curriculum*. Once the data had been collected, I hoped teachers could use these readings to further their analysis of the school history.

Teachers

Some of us were put off by the readings because they did not address ways to solve immediate problems. In some instances, we did not have an overall picture of how a particular reading fitted into our school life. For the most part, however, the readings confirmed much of what we felt. They helped to put labels on concepts and philosophies that we had intuitively understood, provided a sense that certain exposed problems were more shared than individual, and helped broaden our perceptions of not just school and/or district issues, but historical and nation-wide concerns.

Andrew

When the school histories were close to completion I asked the teachers to switch from a focus on the structure and culture of schooling to an exploration of self by writing personal histories. I also wrote such a history. The teachers could pose any question they wanted, but I did suggest that they consider the following questions:

- Why did I choose teaching as a career?
- What shaped me as a teacher?
- What is my philosophy about teaching?
- What, if any, changes have I seen in my teaching philosophy and practices?

I chose these questions because they had the potential to illuminate the politics of schooling by exposing the influence of long-held beliefs, cultural norms, and general patterns of socialization. As was true of the school history, readings such as Apple's (1986) *Teachers and Text*, Leach's (1988) 'Teacher education and reform', and Spencer's (1984) 'The home and school lives of women teachers' were suggested to further the analysis of these histories.

Teachers

Most of us were threatened by the writing, and certainly by the sharing of our personal histories. We wondered out loud who would read these personal texts and why anyone would be interested. As we began to take the process seriously, looking over the development of our lives as teachers became a powerful, but often difficult experience. Recounting the events that had helped to shape us as teachers and as people was illuminating, but knowing where and when we were being completely honest with ourselves made the process very challenging. Some areas of our lives we avoided writing about because they were too personal, too revealing, or perhaps too painful. Nevertheless, when we had finished the writing of our personal histories, each of us had a document that chronicled our individual lives. A variety of experiences, emotions, and insights were brought to light. Whether or not we had chosen to write about all of them, we were certainly affected by the process of thinking candidly about significant events in our lives. We also felt a sense of liberation because the telling of these stories in many ways placed a value on who we were as persons and more specifically as teachers. This process has continued as we remember and explore the meaning our history has on our current situations.

Andrew

To this point, the research was still primarily individualist. If a more community-based approach to research was to occur, I felt we had to find ways to share, compare and analyze what was common and different about the school and personal histories. Towards this end, I decided to introduce the teachers to a set of procedures which would further discussion on these texts as well as other future concerns. I told the teachers that they could use any dialogical model they wanted, but suggested they start with Horizontal Evaluation (Gitlin and Goldstein, 1987). Horizontal Evaluation is an approach based on the work of Gadamer (1975) and Habermas (1976) that focuses participants' attention on the relation between intention and practice and examines this relation by encouraging participants to raise questions about history, language, and alternative practices. As was true of the initial decision to center the Cooperative Master's program around Educative Research, it is now clear that the teachers really didn't have a choice. Instead, I used my privileged position to structure the experience, and, in so doing, lost an opportunity to challenge the dominant relationship between researcher and practitioner.

Teachers

With regard to the area of choice, we were unfamiliar with any other models, so in that sense there were no other choices. Coupled with the fact that most of us still assumed that it was not really appropriate to propose alternative approaches, we all began with Horizontal Evaluation. While the idea of entering each others' classrooms for the purpose of observing and being observed was initially threatening, it was more relevant than the typical observations by principals that we had long been forced to endure. Although we were fearful about our lack of experience in this type of communication and were unsure what the process was about, we were soon to discover that it would be a way to confront our deep sense of isolation.

Andrew

To acquaint teachers with the model, they read several articles that I had written on Horizontal Evaluation, tried the process with a colleague from the class, and then received feedback from the group about their experience. Using this process where possible, teachers were asked to get together in groups and look across school and personal concerns. These collective histories were then shared with all involved in the project and put in a written form. Unfortunately, these collective histories were never really given a chance to make a difference, and were not as effective as I had hoped. As our group later reflected, we all felt that there had not been enough time allowed for this type of complex group interaction and the teachers were rushed too quickly from an individual to a group perspective.

To further our dialogue, and, in particular, to illustrate some political aspects of schooling, I chose a series of articles for the teachers to read that would raise questions that went beyond the typical 'how to' questions that dominate school discourse. These readings included Grant and Sleeter's (1988) 'Race, class, gender and abandoned dreams', Weis's (1988) 'High school girls in a de-industrializing economy', and Perry's (1988) 'A black student's reflection on public and private schools.' I hoped that these readings would show how issues of race, class, and gender influenced the problems we pose and what is taken for granted in the classroom.

Teachers

At this time the ERP was perplexing for most of us. Perhaps it was the uncertainty of where we were going or the purpose and function of the personal and school histories. We sensed that we were being encouraged to make a leap in our understanding, but for some of us the readings were not helpful and raised fundamental questions about why we were taking this journey. However, for a few of us, the readings did lend support to our feminist leanings.

Andrew

Using Horizontal Evaluation, I asked the teachers to observe each other and capture any recurring concerns or problems found in their teaching practice. Because these concerns or problems were articulated in writing (through transcripts of taped post conferences), they became texts that could be related to school and personal histories as well as the collective histories. Two factors were important in making the Horizontal Evaluation experience more helpful for the teachers: first, the teacher who was observing had a paid substitute, and second, the audio-taped discourse that followed the observation was transcribed and given back to the teacher. The funds for these activities were diverted from those normally allotted to me by the university for research.

Next, I asked the teachers to utilize their personal and school histories in combination with the understandings gleaned from their Horizontal Evaluation experiences to pose a research question. This question or concern could be tentative in nature, but it had to be defined in enough specificity to enable them to go to the library and search for relevant literature. As opposed to asking individuals to do this on their own, teachers with related interests worked together to find literature that would inform their study. When the teachers felt they had explored the issue in some depth they were asked to restate their problem and put together a plan that would give them additional insights and some experience with collecting and analyzing data.

As these plans were completed, teachers shared with other members of the project what they considered important articles, as well as their results and questions. At the end of these presentations, the teachers were asked to write a *First Look* paper which reported their findings. When the school year ended, we started on an intensive period of writing which captured the first year's journey.

Teachers

The activities of that first year helped to break down the walls of isolation that so often surround teachers and brought us closer together as a group. The histories we wrote and the observations and dialogues we engaged in were personally revealing and professionally challenging. We had examined and shared our philosophies, intentions, and values. We had discovered contradictions in our practices and beliefs and had risked revealing them to others. We had posed challenges to each other and had raised many questions. Through these processes, bonds began to form and we began to feel understood in ways that had not been possible before. For many of us, our questions, our goals, our experience, and our knowledge were taken seriously for the first time, thus strengthening our confidence and our resolve to make the changes we needed.

Along with this newly found sense of connection and confidence came a sense of dissatisfaction for some teachers. There was an important occurrence at the end of the first year that helped shape the ERP. After a particularly confusing class session, teachers began to talk with each other and complain loudly about not really having a voice within the ERP. The complaint was that Andrew claimed we could make our own choices, but then would redirect us in what appeared to be his avenue of interest. A virtual explosion occurred, and as a result, some of us decided to voice our complaints. We did, and changes were made. It is significant that our first attempt to approach a traditional authority was made within our university program, directed at the very person encouraging such a shift in decision making. Its success had ramifications throughout our lives, and made a significant difference in our relationships with each other.

The collective

At this point in the ERP, the group developed a stronger sense of 'we'. Andrew was no longer solely determining the readings or even leading the class discussions. Instead, the agenda for the class became much more of a joint undertaking. While traditional roles did not disappear, they were at least blurred and for the first time. There was less concern with grades or pleasing the teacher and more with continuing to explore our research questions, and to make a difference in schools. In particular, this second year of the project was an opportunity to take what was learned in the first year and utilize this understanding to rethink our questions, develop them further, or pose complementary concerns. In addition to revisiting continuously developing concerns, we started to share our understandings with others outside the collective. This sharing took two forms: one, a meeting with district administrators and the other, the presentation of papers at two academic conferences. This reaching out had a dramatic effect on the group, not only by confronting the notion that no one would be interested in what teachers have to say, but also in providing a glimpse of our collective identity.

While subsequent chapters will describe the practices of the ERP (personal and school histories, Horizontal Evaluation) in greater detail, it is important to stress that the methods seen as appropriate cannot be imposed on a group of individuals without regard for differences in culture and context. In implementing Educative Research, what is essential is to allow the participants to reshape the methods. When this occurs, individuals are able to build on what they know, and to use their personal knowledge while limiting the possibility that they will become subject to a new, but still dominating method.

ASSUMPTIONS

While this description explains what we did, it does not clarify the evolving assumptions which developed from our experiences. These assumptions expose the politics of the process and allow Educative Research to be seen in relation to other methodological developments. To illuminate these assumptions, what follows will be divided into three areas: the researcher/subject relationship, political aims, and the place of history in research. The concluding section will consider how the underlying assumptions inform issues of validity and reliability.

RESEARCHER/SUBJECT RELATIONSHIP

Traditional forms of research place the researcher and those studied in a hierarchical relationship. In experimental research, for example, by setting up a laboratory-type situation from which generalizations can be made to determine a wide range of rules and laws, researchers make sense of the classroom while subjects are not only excluded from the process, but turned into objects of study, reinforcing the assumption that researchers are the producers of knowledge. Traditional forms of qualitative research also set up much the same sort of relationship. While the researcher has a more personal relationship with the subject in that questions are asked and observations of practice made, because the researcher is urged to influence the research context as little as possible, there are few, if any, opportunities for the subject to play a role in the research process (Agar, 1980). Instead, the researcher forms the questions, and analyzes the data without considering the subjects' impressions, beliefs, and under-standings. The researcher is still the expert, still the producer of knowl-edge and the subject is still silenced.

In both these types of traditional research methodology, the researcher determines the nature of the research, designs and executes the study, and evaluates the results which are then published in a journal to be read by other researchers. Essentially, the production of knowledge is seen as the privilege of the university researcher. At the same time, the subjects are silenced and placed in an alienating situation where their choice of action is primarily limited to either accepting what the researcher says, which at best fosters a dependent relationship, or rejecting the research altogether. This alienating situation becomes even more troubling given that men have had far more opportunity than women to enter into institutions of higher education and to do research (Clifford, 1986).

In addition to producing an alienating situation for those studied and furthering patriarchal relations, the hierarchical relationship between the researcher and subject also is troubling when efficiency is the aim. At the most basic pragmatic level it simply doesn't make sense to exclude those who work day in and day out in our schools from the process of posing research questions. Surely even the most derogatory view of teachers would not suggest that they have nothing to offer in terms of the questions that need to be addressed by research. Furthermore, even if one could justify teachers' exclusion from the research process, the hierarchical relationship between researcher and subject works against research influencing practice because research studies rarely reach teachers, and in fact, are not written for them (Gitlin, Siegel and Born, 1989).

Because Educative Research tries to establish a less alienating relationship between researcher and 'subject' as well as one that is likely to foster school change, those who are normally silenced and removed from knowledge production, namely teachers, parents, and students, are invited to participate in the research process. These participants are viewed as legitimate and equal partners in the creation of new knowledge. One way Educative Research attempts to restructure the relationship between researcher and 'subject' is to alter research from a one-way process where researchers extract data from 'subjects' to a dialogical process where participants negotiate meanings at the level of question posing, data collection and analysis. This dialogical relation, which is endorsed in some forms of feminist research, allows both participants to become the 'changer and the changed' (Lather, 1975). It also encourages participants to work together on an equal basis, to reach a mutual understanding. Neither stands apart in an aloof or judgmental manner; neither is silenced (Bernstein, 1983). Instead, both participants are united by the quest to examine the topic at hand as well as reveal contradictions and constraints within the educative process itself. The intent of this dialogue is not to discover absolutes, or the truth, but to scrutinize normative 'truths' that are embedded in a particular historical and cultural context. In this way, taken for granted notions can be challenged as educators work to understand schooling better.

Robyn's research project provides an example of how dialogue can alter the nature of research problems. Robyn's research question focused on what types of actions can be taken that will enable teachers to express what they believe and participate in a process of school change. Toward this end, Robyn decided to hold a series of teacher dialogue meetings. Instead of just collecting observation and interview data on these meetings, as is typical of most approaches to research, Robyn engaged in dialogue with a member of the teacher support group (her Horizontal Evaluation partner), and used these insights to analyze the meetings. This dialogue produced some dramatic and stunning findings, not the least of which was that Robyn's role in the meetings may have contradicted her intention to develop teacher voice.

> I continue to question my level of direct intervention. Teachers complained of attending meetings where the agenda is determined and manipulated by the administration. How different can it be if the agenda is determined and manipulated by me? Probably a minimal difference. The intention of the project is to give teachers a forum to develop their

voices, in whatever direction that might be. How can that happen if they cannot have a voice in how the meetings are organized? If I perceive my position as one who is more knowledgeable because I have experienced or read more, am I again any different than the administration? No.

(Robyn, *First Look*)

This insight produced quite a bit of frustration on Robyn's part. It did, however, encourage her to rethink her relationship with those studied and to look for ways to establish a different role in the teacher dialogue meetings.

While promising in altering hierarchical relationships, dialogue is not a panacea. There will be situations where one participant takes a dominating stance toward the other. Clearly, long-established roles are not simply going to fade away by involving participants in a process where the intent is to have both participants come to a mutual understanding. However, as Robyn's case indicates, dialogue can provide a beginning for a new type of researcher/'subject' relationship and has the added advantage of being self-corrective; where one participant dominates, this situation can and should be examined as part of the dialogical process.

Besides the importance of dialogue, Educative Research insists that part of altering the relationship between researcher and subject is the need to restructure the nature of teachers' work. Because Educative Research is based on the assumption that the teacher role is a complex one that operates both at a conceptual level and at practice simultaneously, teachers need to have opportunities to see the linkage between conceptual work and practice and to examine both ends of this connected spectrum. Part of this examination requires time away from students, time to reflect, to reconsider, to write, and to dialogue with others. Due to the nature and intensity of their work, teachers normally do not have time to engage in such activities. Furthermore, such activities are often not seen as legitimate or necessary endeavors for teachers, not only by researchers, but also by school administrators, and the public in general. For example, when a member of the ERP asked if a number of teachers in her school could get together during school hours, the principal's response was, 'No, teachers need to be in the classroom.' Teachers' work must be reconstructed in a way that not only allows time for, but legitimizes the need to conceptualize and reflect on teaching.

POLITICAL AIMS

Educative Research is not a value-free methodology aimed at determining universal truths, but rather is an explicitly political method. However, as opposed to some methodologies that have an articulated political agenda aimed at correcting societal problems, such as contesting women's role in society (Weiler, 1988), the politics of Educative Research challenge traditional research itself. These challenges include: contesting narrow notions of legitimate knowledge, developing voice for disenfranchised groups, and fostering school change through the linkage of understanding and practice.

Legitimate knowledge

In many ways, the growing importance of research within the educational community is an attempt to discredit, or at the very least, to cast a critical eye on the notion that personal experience represents a legitimate form of knowledge. From the gaze of those who speak for traditional research methods, personal knowledge is limited not only because of its subjective nature, but also because it is unsystematic and reflects self interest. Research, on the other hand, is thought to provide a more objective, less politicized form of knowledge that would lead the educational community forward. The importance of research in the educational community has strengthened the view that legitimate knowledge is clearly different from knowledge gained through personal experience.

This social construction of what is legitimate knowledge has a number of political consequences. First, it excludes and devalues teachers' rich source of personal experience thereby constraining their ability to claim to be an expert or authority. Instead, it is the researchers, with their complex statistical background and methodological sophistication who are seen as the real experts. Second, it obscures the way all research serves certain interests. Traditional methods serve the interests of those who are removed from the world of practice and have the opportunity to engage in such forms of inquiry. In contrast, Educative Research tries to alter this politic, by valuing personal experience and integrating this form of knowledge within the research process. By doing so, participants are able to 'draw upon their own cultural resources as a basis for encouraging the development of new skills and interrogating existing knowledge claims' (Simon and Dippo, 1986, p. 375). As is true of other alternative methods such as critical ethnography, Educative Research challenges traditional forms of legitimate knowledge, allows disenfranchised groups and those working at the lower ends of the hierarchy to make claims of expertise, and questions the legitimacy of the hierarchy itself.

Clearly, concern about what is legitimate knowledge is not sufficient to alter the role of disenfranchised groups within the educational community, for not only must their experience be valued, but opportunities must be developed where they can engage in sustained indepth inquiry. Put differently, two cautions must accompany the important place of personal knowledge within Educative Research. First, a broadening of what is considered legitimate knowledge must go hand in hand with changes in the work structures that influence the type of knowledge that an individual or group is likely to produce. Second, valuing personal experience is different from accepting it as *the* form of legitimate knowledge. Personal experience, as is true of knowledge produced from traditional research methods, must be examined, questioned, and seen in relation to other forms of knowing. The intent of Educative Research is not to privilege personal knowledge over other forms of knowing or devalue it, but rather to take a more reflective critical stance to knowledge production that examines a variety of forms of knowing.

Voice

By expanding notions of legitimate knowledge Educative Research provides the opportunity for teachers to develop their voice. The opportunity to speak, to question and explore issues is an important aspect of this process. Those who have been excluded have the right to tell their stories and the telling of these stories allows these groups to enter into policy debates, and to challenge the authority of others – such as university researchers, business people, and district and state policy makers – to tell the educational story. But, the notion of voice can go far beyond the exploration of issues and the opportunity to speak; it can be about protest. Understood in this way, voice is inherently political; its aim is to question what is taken for granted, to act on what is seen to be unjust in an attempt to shape and guide future educational directions. While injustice or oppression cannot be defined outside of a historical context, members of the educational community are encouraged to scrutinize relations where one group has power over another. Included in this analysis should be the structures that unnecessarily elevate particular groups and stereotype and constrain others. Voice as a form of protest is directed both outward at the social construction of meaning-making and the structures that reinforce those meanings, and inward at the way the individual takes part in the production of certain constrained beliefs, roles, and practices.

Kathy's story exemplifies what we mean by voice as a form of protest. In the writing of her school history, it became apparent that many of the current school structures remained unchanged not so much because of thoughtful consideration, but rather because of tradition. As Kathy writes, 'Through the school history I came to realize what structures had been imposed on the staff and students purely because that's the way we've always done it.' By seeing that these structures were in place more because of what others didn't say than because of arguments for their existence, Kathy was able to question their legitimacy. When she did so, she realized that the longevity of these structures resulted in part from teachers' inability to articulate alternatives and, therefore, their willingness to accept the status quo.

> I was better able to deal with these structures knowing which ones were in place because of tradition, with no educational basis, others because alternatives had not been investigated and still others because teachers were either satisfied with the status quo or feared the process of conflict and change.
>
> (Kathy, *First Look*)

For the grade level at which Kathy taught, one structure that appeared to be in place because of tradition was ability grouping. Although she had volunteered to teach the low-achieving group, it became apparent that this structure not only left her with a class of fifteen students who were 'hostile toward school, and physically attacked each other,' but also encouraged her to take on a somewhat oppressive role through which she tried to command their attention and force them to learn.

As Kathy examined this authoritarian teaching role within the context of her personal history, the contradiction between her philosophy and practice was clearly illuminated. This experience in the ERP helped Kathy to explore an alternative way to teach.

> The possible alternative was born out of my own experience in writing and examining my personal and school history and through the process of exploring my intentions in the Horizontal Evaluation post-conference. I posed this problem and challenge for myself: can the use of student personal histories promote further understanding of self and others, build trust and develop a sense of community in the elementary classroom?
>
> (Kathy, *First Look*)

Now that Kathy has researched this alternative, she has not only told her story, but has also attempted to rewrite it, albeit with a new ending. As her voice became stronger, she protested the tendency of teachers to accept the status quo, as well as her own role in reinforcing authoritarian teacher/student relationships.

Understanding and practice

For this type of protest to make a difference, insights must be linked to actions. Building on the tradition of action research, we attempted to make such a connection. One of the conservative aspects of most traditional methods is that their aim is to shed light on or capture the essence of a particular event or intervention. This understanding, it is assumed, will then trickle down to the level of practice and inform practitioners on what to do and what not to do. Unfortunately, this result has rarely occurred. For both qualitative and quantitative studies one fundamental problem is that the research is not made accessible to practitioners, they are not rewarded for keeping up with the literature and, importantly, the manuscripts are written in a language that is 'closed' to others who are not steeped in an academic culture. Another difficulty is that teachers and others working at the level of practice are simply resistant to research. It would be easy to blame practitioners for their recalcitrance, but instead it is also possible to see this resistance as a form of 'good sense' (Apple, 1982) which reflects the fact that whatever the potential of the research, the process excludes teachers' voice and therefore reinforces a one-way hierarchy from the all-knowing research sages to the needy practitioners who are assumed to have little to offer. Quantitative studies, in particular, have limitations not the least of which is their relentless pursuit of generalizations which obscure the realities of a particular context. Teachers may be impressed with the results, and persuaded to change practice accordingly after reading such a study, but often can't do so because they don't have the background knowledge, or the opportunities to make the suggested change. For qualitative studies the problem isn't context, for most studies are based on the importance of contextual factors. Instead, traditional qualitative studies separate understanding and practice by having the researcher extract the results, rather than utilizing them to enhance discussion with practitioners. These results are then compiled in an article which is read primarily by other researchers. This approach is evident in this ethnography on the formation of knowledge in a social studies lesson.

> Since I was an observing researcher and not in a supervisory or collaborative relationship with [the teacher], I didn't think that discussing my questions with her was appropriate. But, my vague sense of being troubled about this lesson has pursued me, ultimately compelling me to write this article.
>
> (White, 1989, p. 315)

In sum, when looked at from the perspective of what difference research can have on the level of practice, the politics of traditional quantitative as well as qualitative research is clearly conservative in that it supports the status quo.

Educative Research attempts to reverse this trend by shifting the primary responsibility of doing research from the university faculty member to the practitioner. While the university member still has a role, the focus on the practitioner allows those who are acting at the level of practice also to gain understanding through the inquiry process. There is no need for the understanding to 'trickle down' because the institutional separation between those who do conceptual work and those who practice teaching at the very least becomes more fluid.

Enabling practitioners to be involved in the research process goes a long way toward linking understanding and practice; however there are still several significant threats to this linkage. One such threat is the traditional view of research as a product. When understood in this way, even if conducted by a person acting at the level of practice, understanding is still separated from practice within a temporal frame such that understanding occurs and then is applied to practice. This temporal separation ignores the shifting nature of the educational context. A research study that occurs over a year, for example, has to be applied to a teaching situation in a new class where teachers, students, parents, administrators, etc., are remaking a new classroom history. While much that has been learned may still apply to this group, the classroom culture at the time of the research is unaffected. Furthermore, separating understanding and practice in this way makes it difficult for the research to act back on the research question. Researchers often bracket off all understanding as they go through the research process because to alter the question in mid-stream is to dilute or invalidate the findings. There can be little doubt that altering the question as one goes through the research process is at the very least a messy undertaking; however, staying the course obscures the rich possibilities of connecting research analysis to question posing.

To confront this threat to the linkage of understanding and practice Educative Research is viewed primarily as a process with turning points that redirect inquiry, rather than as a product. This allows the research process to alter the questions asked and influence practice as particular insights are gained.

HISTORY AND RESEARCH

Most educational research leaves the author out of the text; the researcher's judgments, biases, and evolving views are not included as part of the report. This omission is not the result of forgetfulness, but rather reflects the assumption that to present data that will be convincing and deemed legitimate, attempts must be made to bracket out the subjective. While it is true that the illusion created by this bracketing can be very convincing, the author is part of the research not only because the questions posed reflect a focus on one set of concerns rather than another, but also because the constructs developed (i.e. the organization of the data) and even the form and style of the communication are all linked to the perspective and orientation that the author brings to the research project. For research to be authentic, the relationship between what is said and the person(s) doing the talking must be made apparent. One way to do so is through the use of what we refer to as personal and school histories.

These histories suggest that the data presented does not simply emerge on its own, but is connected in strong ways to established traditions, experiences, and structures. In one sense, what these histories allow the author to do is suggest how the story told relates to much that came before. The inclusion of personal histories has the potential to show how past socialization, beliefs, and normative assumptions help shape what we see as important questions, how we frame those questions and the types of procedures we use to address those questions.

The inclusion of these histories not only celebrates the struggle and evolution that takes place as one begins to undertake any sort of rigorous inquiry, but is an important part of voice. For if voice is to be a form of protest, the protest has to be directed inward and outward. If directed inward there needs to be some opportunity to examine the questions one is posing, and the analysis made. Personal histories encourage this sort of examination by encouraging participants to see the relation between past beliefs and socialization and current perspectives and questions. School histories complement this type of relational analysis by enabling participants to see the long-established school structures as well as cultural norms that are an important site for struggle and protest.

VALIDITY AND RELIABILITY

Validity and reliability represent the standards on which research is judged. However, because Educative Research attempts to reconceptualize what is research and its purposes, traditional definitions of reliability and validity must be altered. The validity or 'truthfulness' of the data can be understood no longer as something extracted by an individual armed with a set of research procedures, but rather as a mutual process pursued by researcher and those studied, that recognizes the value of practical knowledge, theoretical inquiry, and systematic examinations. The researchers' knowledge is not assumed to be more legitimate than the 'subjects',' nor is their role one of helping the needy other. Rather, the researcher and subject attempt to come to a mutual understanding based on their own strongly articulated positions.

Questions of validity, however, must go beyond the truthfulness of the data. The influence of the research process on who produces knowledge, who is seen as expert, and the resulting changes at the level of school practice are also part of an expanded, political view of validity. For example, one criterion of validity would be the degree to which the research process enables disenfranchised groups to participate fully in the decision making process, examine their beliefs and actions within the school context, and make changes based on this understanding. The role of research in establishing authoritarian relationships that silence particular groups and limits reflectively would all be threats to validity as we have defined it.

When the central aim of the research process is to develop voice, traditional notions of reliability are also altered. Within traditional methods, reliability represents the ability of independent researchers to come to the same conclusions when the same procedures are used. In contrast, when the aim is the development of voice, it is undesirable and not expected that independent researcher–subject teams would come to the same conclusions. It is also undesirable for the procedures to remain unchanged from context to context. Procedures should be allowed not only to evolve within a particular research study, but also to change given the needs and priorities of a particular population. Reliability, therefore, cannot be based on duplicating procedures, but rather must center on attempts to satisfy the underlying principle of voice and its relation to a particular type of school change.

The practices and assumptions that are part of Educative Research suggest some significant changes in the way we think about and conduct research. Included in these changes is a shift to a more process approach to research, where questions, analysis, and action become moments in a continuous endeavor. This give and take between questions, analysis, and action differs from traditional methods by taking an activist stance toward research and giving more weight to the process of question posing. For it is not only the results which count, but the relation between results, analysis, action, and questions that is of concern. To facilitate this process of question posing, Educative Research encourages those participating to create texts (personal and school histories) which expose aspects of self, context, and wider cultural norms. Horizontal Evaluation is then used to see the relationship between these texts and to enable all research participants to have a say in the questions addressed and the analysis of those questions. When successful, this sort of dialogical process makes it possible for those traditionally silenced to have a voice in educational matters. It can also encourage protests about one's actions and the school context.

3　Personal and school histories

A central aim of Educative Research is the development of voice as a form of protest. This protest is directed inward at the teachers' behaviours and beliefs, and outward at both the contextual structures and wider ideologies that narrow what it means to be educated. To facilitate this sort of protest, Educative Research begins with the creation of two texts, a personal history and a school history.

Personal histories, as one might imagine, focus on the individual, revealing how past experiences, circumstances, and significant events may be related to the perspectives teachers bring to the classroom, the way they act in particular situations, and what they see as problems or questions to be asked about their work and the function of schooling. School histories, on the other hand, center more directly on context, illuminating both the structures and norms of a local school as well as widely held beliefs about schooling. These texts are related to the development of voice in several ways. First, because they are produced by those that have been traditionally disenfranchised, they provide a forum for teachers and others to speak out, to tell what they know. Second, because the focus of these texts is both personal and context specific, their creation signals a challenge to the dominant research position that excludes these forms of knowing from what is considered legitimate knowledge. Finally, because the texts bring to the fore events connected to the self and the school context, they also provide a forum for the participants to 're-search' these events and examine the ways they may foster overly narrow and constrained notions of education.

To think through more fully the relation between Educative Research, the development of voice, and the creation of school and personal histories, we will describe how these histories are created, explore the assumptions that underlie these processes, and finally use an abbreviated school and personal history to give a sense of what these texts look like in practice as well as their import for the aims of educative research.

CREATING SCHOOL AND PERSONAL HISTORY TEXTS

Most of the specifics of how we approached school and personal histories have been previously covered. However, it may be helpful to provide an overview of these methods. The intent of the first draft, for both school and personal histories, was to describe, as opposed to analyze, aspects of self and context. Although all descriptions embody the roots of analysis because they reflect a particular slant on the events told, this form of analysis was not emphasized in the beginning. While largely open-ended, these descriptions were focused around particular themes in teaching and schooling. These themes directed participants to ask educational questions, reflect on their behavior in the classroom, and examine the ethos of the school.

Once these descriptions of self and context were drafted, participants engaged in a reflective process where the intent was to rework the descriptions by considering what was left out as well as to clarify the events and circumstances explained in the text. To facilitate such reflectivity, texts were shared with other members of the project. When the participants thought it was appropriate, they ended this phase of the process and switched their focus from description to analysis. To do so, they looked for recurring themes or categories that seemed to capture their story.

To further the analysis, texts written by others outside the ERP were brought into the process. In part, the purpose was to make it possible for participants to look at the relation between their own understanding of teaching and schooling and others', while centering their specific histories more broadly within the history of schooling. It would be deceptive, however, to suggest that the sole purpose of utilizing texts written by others was to compare one point of view with another. Instead, these texts were also seen as a way to expose the political. While it would be antithetical to our position to argue that *all* personal and school histories must use a particular set of 'political' readings, if voice as a form of protest is the aim of the research process, one criterion for selecting reading material should be its potential to clarify and disclose oppressive formations.

With readings of this type in mind, the analysis proceeded in a free-flowing way with participants using the three sets of texts – personal history, school history, and those written by others – to create a 'plot' that imposed meaning on a set of events. In some cases the analysis of context helped participants rethink their personal histories. For others, the outside readings helped them rethink their understanding of context and vice versa. In either case, the outside readings did not have a privileged status;

it was not assumed that this form of knowing was more valuable, worthwhile or legitimate than the knowledge produced in the personal and school histories. Instead, we tried to value different ways of knowing that were likely to illuminate angles and shades of the question or issue not initially considered.

Once these analyses reached a point where the participants felt satisfied about their authenticity and power, the final stage of the process was to look across school and personal histories to identify common themes and differences. This comparative process enhanced the possibility of identifying constraints and limitations held in common, and raised questions about what was still taken for granted or deemed impossible to change at the school level.[1]

Assumptions

Our method of creating personal and school history texts is quite open. This openness has the advantage of flexibility. It can, however, lead to confusion and misuse. To minimize this type of result it is necessary to sort out what we see as the assumptions that frame our conception and use of personal and school histories. To do so, we turn to the traditions which have used self and local context as a form of research. In this way, we hope to show how our view of these processes builds on and differs from others who have paved the way for such inquiry.

Self

The focus on the individual as a form of research became quite prominent in the field of sociology in the early twentieth century (Goodson, 1988). Under the banner of life histories these personal studies were thought to provide a 'voice from a culture and situation not known to intellectuals generally and to sociologists in particular' (p.7), as well as a corrective to cultural studies that 'experience the person as a fragment of a (deprived) cultural pattern, as a marionette dancing on the strings of (reified) cultural forms,' (p.73). Harold Becker, one of the advocates of this approach, describes the process of life histories this way:

> The sociologist who gathers a life history takes steps to ensure that it covers everything we want to know, that no important fact or event is slighted, that what purports to be factual squares with other available evidence and that the subject's interpretations are honestly given. The sociologist keeps the subject oriented to the questions sociology is interested in, asks him about events that require amplification, tries to

make the story told jibe with matters of official record and with material furnished by others familiar with the person, event, or place being described. He keeps the game honest for us.

(Becker, 1970, p. 64)

One purpose of such an approach, according to Becker, is that it can be used to provide confirming and opposing cases to purported theories. By showing how people subjectively experience institutional processes, for example, life histories can expose assumptions about the way these institutions work as well as counter cases that suggest a new direction for future research. At the same time, these subjective experiences also help researchers 'become aware of the deep biases about such people that ordinarily permeate our thinking and shape the kind of problems we investigate' (p.71). Life histories also focus on a process orientation to research because they describe a continuous evolution where 'people make tentative moves and then adjust and reorient their activity in light of the responses (real and imagined) others make to those moves' (p. 69). Put simply, describing the constant moves and adjustments that are an inherent part of life histories requires that the researcher center on the process of change.

We share many of the assumptions of this approach to life history. First and foremost, by challenging the notion that those studied do not simply act according to larger patterns of influence, life histories move away from a position that simply treats those studied as objects acting out according to a greater master plan. In much the same way, Educative Research also attempts to view those studied as active critical beings, instead of objects of study. Second, the emphasis on a fluid set of events fits very well with our aim to transform research from a product to a process that links question posing, analysis, and action. And finally, the ability of life histories to make researchers aware of the deep biases they bring to the research process and the questions they ask is also congruent with our intent to foster a more authentic approach to research which acknowledges that questions do not come out of the air and researchers certainly have interests even when taking the stance of the disinterested observer.

In other ways, life histories differ dramatically from our use of personal histories as part of Educative Research. Most centrally the difference is that life histories are seen as a way to provide more accurate theories for researchers. As a consequence, these histories do not necessarily enable disenfranchised groups to speak out, or even protest their behaviors and the context in which they work, but rather enable researchers to use the voice of others to enhance their theories and correspondingly their status. It is primarily the researcher who benefits from the life history, not the person telling the story. In most cases, the intent is neither change nor empower-ment of some sort, but rather validation of the researcher's quest for truth. Life histories, therefore, do nothing to alter the relationship between the researcher and those studied nor do they link understanding to change. It is still the researcher giving meaning to events, developing the categories for analysis, and telling the story about the other. While the other's voice is included it is not really heard.

Ironically, these limitations of life histories had little to do with their eventual decline. Instead, the criticism was nearly the opposite: life histories did not elevate sociology to a professional status because of their emphasis on practical knowledge. What was thought to be desirable, in contrast, was the development of abstract theory. As Goodson states, 'sociologists came to pursue data formulated in the abstract categories of their own theories rather than in the categories that seemed most relevant to the people they studied' (Goodson, 1988, 76). The cost of professionalism, therefore, was the abandonment of methods such as life histories. While sociology did move beyond this 'scientific' stage, life histories have never regained a prominent place in the field of sociology (p. 78).

Life histories, however, did not totally disappear from social science research. Instead, they reappeared in the field of education in a different form and under a variety of alternative titles, including personal history and autobiography. Most influential in their resurgence was a group of scholars in the 1960s and 70s that began to reconceptualize dominant assumptions in the field of curriculum. One prominent reconceptualist, William Pinar, attempted to look at curriculum in new ways by laying out a method he called 'currere.' Pinar argued that central to this method was the 'investigation of the nature of the individual experience of the public: of artifacts, actors, operations, of the educational journey or pilgrimage' (Pinar, 1975, 400). To foster this type of investigation students of currere must become 'students of ourselves, before we truthfully can say we understand teaching in [a particular] sense' (p.412). This emphasis on understanding ourselves encouraged others in the field of education to explore more fully the possibilities of using personal history or autobiography as a research method.

One educational researcher who has outlined in detail a method of personal history is Florence Krall. A brief overview of her method is important because it provides a context in which to understand better the relation between our use of personal history and the early use of these histories in the field of education.

Krall identifies five 'movements' to the personal history method: venturing, remembering, comprehending, embodying, and restoring (Krall, 1988, p. 468). The venturing movement revolves around a clarifying and question posing process. 'The point in this approach is to clarify or to discover central questions or issues. The question, when it is present at the start should change, become clearer or present other questions as the inquiry proceeds' (p.469). Remembering is a process where the individual may select 'instances in their past that stand out, that shine like a light in their memory, and release them to view' (p. 470). This process, as Krall notes, is antithetical to most school experiences. To facilitate this process she writes comments on the personal histories of her students to encourage 'confidence, competence and motivation. Over time the students become more self critical and revision of the text becomes an integral part of the process' (pp. 470–1).

After the text is near completion, those doing personal history research begin to move toward more analysis on their own. A major part of this comprehending movement is the development of themes. She describes this thematic process as one where: 'students make a list of one-sentence statements that set forth the major propositions their essays address [and] by grouping the statements under headings or categories, they identify the recurrent themes' (p.471). The embodying movement involves a distancing from the experience through the reading of other works while simply providing time away from the personal text. Restoring is the movement toward the final draft. The aim is to achieve a balance between the 'personal history, analysis, and comparison informed by relevant literature' (p.473).

Clearly, our use of personal history is influenced by Krall's method. The process is similar in that texts are created, and then analyzed by the determination of themes and comparisons with other texts. Personal knowledge is not only seen as legitimate, but is a mark of good research. However, as was true of the use of life histories, there are some notable differences which again help clarify our method.

One important difference is the place of personal history in the research process. In Krall's method the personal is the center piece of the research project. In Educative Research, the personal is part of a larger process that involves consideration of local contexts, empirical work and action. This difference is significant in several regards. First, while we value personal experience, we try not to privilege this form of knowing over other ways. Empirical findings, for example, not only have a place in the research process, but are used to inform personal histories, as, in turn, these histories inform the empirical work. Second, Krall states that 'what is studied [the self] cannot be isolated from social, historical, economic, political and gender factors' (p.475), thereby suggesting the importance of context. We also see context as important. However, by including the creation of both personal and school histories, Educative Research enables participants not only to examine context and self, but to decide for themselves how these factors influence the questions posed, the insights gained, and the actions pursued. The method does not privilege the self over context or vice versa. Finally, while personal histories as used by Krall emphasize reflection, Educative Research tries to strike a balance between reflection and action. Because personal histories are part of a larger process that attempts to alter schooling, action and reflection can be used to examine each other.[2]

Local context

The use of local context as a focus for research has a long tradition in both sociology and anthropology. In sociology, the notion of 'nearby history' became popular in the 1950s. By focusing on the surroundings and the actors with whom one is already familiar, nearby history is argued to be the most natural and logical way for us to understand the broader historical currents of our society and our world. Studying this local context according to the proponents of nearby history will also make the process of reaching decisions more reflective and intelligent (Kyvig and Marty, 1986, p. 103).

In the field of anthropology the use of ethnography made context an important part of the research process. While ethnographers did not traditionally study their own context, they did focus on how patterns of interaction, institutional structures, and artifacts influenced the traditions and rituals of a particular culture. In the early 1970s educational researchers began to use this approach to study aspects of the school culture. In doing so, they took a position somewhat between that espoused by sociologists using nearby history and anthropologists studying culture. On the one hand, the focus of study was not the researcher's local context as much as *a* local context, namely the school culture. On the other hand, the school culture was more familiar to the researcher than were the cultures studied by traditional anthropologists.[3]

School histories build on both these anthropological and sociological traditions. They build on the sociological tradition by encouraging participants to examine their own local context and utilize these studies to become more reflective about how choices are influenced by contextual norms, school structures, and wider ideologies. They also build on the ethnographic tradition by focusing on the culture of the school. With this said, school histories differ from these traditions in some important ways.

As was true of the personal histories, it is not the procedures used to create school histories but their place within the larger Educative Research process that differentiates our use of school histories from other research methods that focus on context. In particular, the activist nature of Educative Research suggests that the purpose of school histories is not only reflection, or a better understanding of how the school works, but also the alteration of practices and norms that lead to oppressive formations. To facilitate this linkage between understanding and action, those researching the school are also the participants in the school. This role for research participants differs from traditional ethnography where the researcher is an outsider and from nearby histories where the *researcher* clarifies for the community the nature and implications of their decisions.

Even the notion of reflection is understood differently as part of the process of creating school histories. It is not simply a matter of becoming better informed or understanding cultural patterns that is the intent of these histories, but rather the development of voice as a form of protest. As such, reflection becomes a political process aimed at identifying and ultimately challenging oppressive formations. The fact that the state, for example, may impose core curricula, is important not only because participants may know more about how the curriculum is developed in their school, but also because this structure narrowly shapes the teacher role and his/her place in the educational hierarchy.

School histories are part of disciplinary traditions in sociology and anthropology that value the local context. In particular, the procedures for doing school histories follow quite closely the ethnographic and nearby 'history' methods. Where these inquiries differ is in who is doing the research, the emphasis on oppressive formations, and the linkage of reflection and action.

THEORIZING PRACTICE

To explore more fully school and personal histories, and consider their implications for Educative Research, this section will be broken into two parts. The first part, based on Beth's work in the ERP, illustrates the descriptive aspect of these histories. The second part will show how these texts furthered the process of developing voice as a form of protest and laid the foundation for the determination of a research question.

Beth's personal history

Fear accompanied me to school for most of my early years. In the classroom I rarely spoke and was always afraid to raise my hand. I was a child that was easy to 'school', though, because I was quiet and compliant. I learned quickly to follow rules and to avoid drawing attention to myself. Follow the rules, don't take any risks, don't express opinions, better yet, don't even form them. These themes seemed to repeat themselves throughout my elementary years. Neither school, nor home were places where I ever felt free to express myself.

Throughout high school [early 70s] I maintained the 'good girl' image – never skipped class, always did assignments, obeyed curfews, etc. Because of high grades, I was in a few advanced placement classes which I found stimulating and rewarding. I was still very insecure about speaking up, however, and felt intimidated by my classmates and teachers who could express themselves and defend their ideas. The fact that I had never been encouraged to participate in discussions at home, and felt that my ideas were wrong or incomplete on the rare occasions when I did try, kept me from developing an external voice. There was an inner voice, but rarely could I bring it forth.

When it came time to leave the student role and choose a career, teaching seemed a suitable choice given my family socialization. Of the women in my immediate family, five were teachers and one was a nurse. Although I wanted to see myself in a less traditional role, the extent to which I internalized these familial and societal expectations is quite revealing in retrospect.

My role as a teacher began to be shaped during my first student teaching experience in 1976. The cooperating teacher was very authoritarian with her students and filled the day with workbook practice. Every night she took home mounds of workbooks to correct and as her student teacher, I did the same. As I look back, I feel that she cared about her students mostly in terms of what they could produce. She insisted that they work hard, but the nature of the work had very little personal relevance, and I do not recall any emphasis on cognitive development.

By the conclusion of my student teaching experience, my assumptions about the teacher role had been solidified. These assumptions revolved around the appropriateness of teachers being in control. What had been modeled for me was a teacher-centered instructional approach with just a glimmer of student involvement. I left student teaching feeling that teaching was definitely not for me. I was overwhelmed by the tremendous amount of paper work, and the stress of managing the behavior of 35 children. I did not want to assume power over students in the way it had been modeled, but my reluctance was based on more than just what I had observed in this classroom. It came from a pervasive feeling that I sensed about schools in general: they were places where little bodies came to be filled with knowledge that someone else had determined would be good for them. It was this assumption that, while not wanting to claim as my own, I was willing to condone as normal and let go unchallenged.

After student teaching, I completed a music therapy internship at a psycho-educational center for severely emotionally disturbed children. My approach to discipline had additional roots in the training I received during this internship. I was taught to be consistent, follow through, and to portray a sense of control and calm in the face of any disruption. Group decision making and group formulation of rules and consequences were important skills for these children to acquire. In this respect, the orientation was much more student-centered than was my student teaching experience. However, I found it difficult to implement this student-centered approach because the students I was working with were extremely volatile, hostile, and both physically and verbally aggressive. To try to support them as they learned how to take control of their lives was frightening. I was quite intimidated by their behavior, but felt that I had to hide and overcome my feelings at all cost.

These fears, although I tried to downplay them, later followed me into my first few years of teaching in the public schools. They added fuel to my sense that it was just too difficult for me to avoid a teacher controlled classroom. I believed in a student-centered approach, but I had not seen it work. I had not seen students successfully manage their behavior, their time or their choices. Instead, I had observed disruption and chaos. Although it was contrary to the atmosphere for which I yearned and wanted to establish, it was safer and quicker for me to assume control.

I have always struggled with the issue of control. At this point in my career, the struggle revolved around three aspects. First, I wanted something that I didn't know how to achieve – a student-centered classroom. Second, I felt safer taking charge in order to avoid chaos. Third, assuming that the controlling I had observed during student teaching was part of a 'normal' teaching role, then the way I was structuring my teaching was appropriate. Following the common sense notion that the teacher should be in charge, I adopted the role, but I still knew that I was ill-prepared for the realities of teaching. I took a job as an aide in a resource room, planning to observe, ask questions, and essentially fill in the gaps created by my student teaching experience.

My 'apprenticeship' was short lived. In October of 1980 I was offered a full-time position in a fifth grade classroom. I was apprehensive, especially when I learned that this particular group of students had already been taught by three contract teachers, and two long-term substitutes. There were various reasons given for their resignations, but the last teacher clearly stated that the class was quite out of control.

I assumed this position with determination and a lot of energy. How bad could it be? I had worked with disturbed children with behavioral problems, I knew how to set limits, I knew how to take control. I tried to apply what I had learned from the internship. I was consistent, firm, and calm. It didn't work. I had inherited a group of students that, even now, after seven additional years of teaching, I would find exhaustive and challenging. One group of students in the class had high academic capabilities, and another very low academic skills. Both groups were unmotivated, unruly, and used to doing whatever they wanted. Somehow, we all survived, and actually ended the year on a fairly positive note. Even though I fell into many traps of teacher control, I still managed to communicate to my students a genuine respect for them, and for what went on in our classroom. I believe they knew I cared about them as people. I'd like to think that my *desire* to teach in a way that encouraged student empowerment came through in subtle ways of spirit, if not in fact.

This tentative reach toward student empowerment was contested by the introduction of a research study to reinforce appropriate on-task behavior in my class. The idea promoted by these researchers was that in order to get students to work, it was appropriate to use reinforcers such as points and tokens. After the study ended, I continued to use reinforcers, not exclusively, but fairly substantially, in order to survive. Although I had mixed feelings about their appropriateness, 'experts' had set up the program, and it was effective. The stress of teaching was significant, and I was certainly open to suggestions. I therefore put aside my hesitancies in favor of something that seemed to work.

My colleagues at the school were of little or no help. Many had been teaching in the same grade and the same building for many years and were simply waiting to retire. Teaching took place behind closed doors and was marked by a climate of conservatism. The 'old guard' at the school had tremendous power. These teachers did not want to take any risks toward change and fought hard to maintain the status quo. As a beginning teacher, these educators were instrumental in my socialization. I did not intentionally pattern my own teaching style after their stagnant methods, but I had little encouragement and virtually no models upon which to develop a more innovative or progressive way of teaching.

My first three years of teaching were characterized by unresolved tensions. From my internship experience, I carried with me a great fear of what can happen when students are out of control. Because of this fear, I felt it was necessary to be in control, and to be seen as the authority figure in the classroom at all times. However, this role actually contradicted the basic nature of my personality. With each year of teaching, I felt a longing to nurture my students' ability to take control, and assume responsibility for their learning. Even so, I continued to use teacher-centered methods. Feeling the pressure to adhere to a time schedule, and to bring all of the students to a certain level of academic success, I was not confident that I knew how to make a student-centered approach work.

At this point, I was worn-out and dissatisfied. I felt stifled and did not see this school as an intellectual community in which I could look forward to growth and change. I decided to transfer to a new school in hopes of renewing my enthusiasm and aligning myself with more enlightened colleagues. At this second school, I did find a more innovative and supportive staff, but also a greater teaching challenge. One third of my class was functioning considerably below grade level and another third had limited or no English speaking ability.

The pressure to bring all students up to grade level was ever strong. I had no idea how to deal with so many students who were so far below this standard, let alone how to help those without a knowledge of English. I went home daily feeling pulled in every possible direction, trying to meet everyone else's needs, with no time for my own. I felt like I was giving all I had and still it was never enough. It was the situation of giving without getting which Sarason so aptly describes.

> Inherent in teaching is giving, that is, the teacher is required to give of himself intellectually and emotionally. . . . Constant giving in the context of constant vigilance required by the presence of many children is a demanding, draining, taxing affair that cannot be easily sustained. . . . To sustain the giving at a high level requires that the teacher experience getting. The sources for getting are surprisingly infrequent and indirect.
>
> (Sarason, 1971, p. 167)

After two more years, I decided I'd had enough of teaching. I knew that I had given a lot of myself to my students. I knew that students, parents, and colleagues considered me to be an excellent teacher, but I could only think about getting out. I felt my life was completely ruled by school bells and children. I was tired of feeling like I was on stage from 7:30 a.m. to 4:00 p.m. and I wanted to spend more of my day involved with adults. I was tired of giving all I had and still needing to give more. I didn't know how to make my job easier, less stressful, and still be effective. In fact, I seriously doubted that this was possible.

I took a leave of absence for a year and worked as an associate librarian for the city library system. During this year, I realized, for perhaps the first time, some of the positive aspects of teaching. When my library duties became tedious, I realized that rarely while teaching did I watch the clock. I had often been exhausted teaching, and yet, it was also stimulating. As I shelved the children's books, I missed being able to share them with my students. I missed the creative energy that went into planning a teaching unit that truly excited and interested me. I realized that there are many other jobs which are more routinized than teaching and lack the spontaneity and unpredictability that teaching does offer. These factors drew me back into teaching and when the school year began, I accepted a position in a different school.

After two years, I again felt disillusioned. At this point, I was aware of a pattern in my love/hate relationship with teaching. At each of the schools where I had taught, I had been respected by colleagues, and well liked by students and parents. Nevertheless, I could maintain a tolerance level for the constraints of teaching for only two or three years at a time. After the first three years I had tried a new school and new grade. Two years later I had tried a new profession, only to return to teaching. Now, after two more years, I was again searching for more satisfaction. The constraints of teaching under a mandated curriculum, with large numbers of very diverse students, made me feel that my own philosophy of teaching was continually getting lost and failing to solidify. I still wanted to shift the focus of my classroom from being teacher-centered to student-centered, and to assume a more cognitive approach to curriculum. In hopes of expanding my theoretical knowledge and finding a more effective and personally satisfying way of working with my students, I decided to take another leave of absence, this time to pursue a Master's degree.

Beth's school history

The students

Richmond Elementary (fictitious name) serves a population of about 680 students, the majority of whom are considered to be 'at risk.' Seventy per cent of the student-body come from low-income families and many of these are single-parent homes. Forty percent of the students are minorities, primarily Hispanic and Pacific Islanders. The students are typically achieving from one to two years below grade level. Over the past ten years, our academic achievement scores on national tests have dropped from the 60th percentile and now range between the 20th and 30th percentile. They are currently the lowest in the district. Our mobility rate is 48 percent and our attendance figures again place the school at the bottom of the district.

Our students have considerable difficulty with time-on-task and with exhibiting appropriate behavior. Playground difficulties and fighting have been continual problems. Students have, however, learned to be very accepting and supportive of the handicapped population at our school. Many classes adopt the special education classes and involve them in their activities. Older students often volunteer to be tutors and aides in the handicapped classes.

The teachers

Our faculty is dedicated and hard working. Teachers come early and stay

late. Cars begin arriving between 6:30–7:00 a.m. and the parking lot is
rarely empty before 6:00 p.m. Teachers demonstrate initiative and those
that hold leadership positions devote even more time and energy. Although
we are diverse in our educational philosophies, most teachers tend to utilize
an effectiveness orientation to curriculum making. Nevertheless, from its
very beginnings, the school has attracted teachers who also favor a
cognitive approach that stresses personal relevance.

The principal reports that in terms of instruction and educational aims,
we have been fragmented and without a central focus. This problem has
been compounded by the number and variety of programs where students
are pulled out of the classroom for remedial instruction. Many students
have participated in one and often two programs of this kind. This has led
to considerable inconsistency with regard to educational goals and
accountability. At times, a certain amount of resentment and intolerance for
the variety of curriculum orientations can be observed among teachers in
our school. Many of the students in the school are such low achievers that
the tendency is to shift the blame for school failure.

In terms of support for new teachers and for those who want to examine
their teaching methods, several teachers formed a literacy support group
and have met, on their own time, for the past two years. The purpose of the
group has been for teachers to raise educational concerns, ask for help,
clarify aims, and share ideas.

Principal/staff relations

Our present principal has provided direction and consistency for the school.
She is a highly visible person in the building. Her level of interaction lets
both students and teachers know she is available and aware of day-to-day
problems. Teachers are becoming more open in discussing problems with
the principal. She observes, gives suggestions, and lends support. At the
same time, she is not intrusive and allows teachers the freedom to teach
their classes in the manner in which they are most comfortable. She deals
with our diverse faculty with sensitivity and open-mindedness. She listens
to teachers and incorporates their ideas into the vision that she has for the
school.

Recent history

When our school began to receive funding for students who were below
grade level, there was a new emphasis placed upon the basic skills, almost
to the exclusion of everything else. In addition, there seemed to be an influx
of 'at risk' students. Burn-out began to strike everyone, tension was high

and morale was low. Behavior problems began to escalate, and the community was extremely unhappy. Several suspensions occurred daily and there was essentially little positive reinforcement for students or teachers.

A major staff change occurred during the summer of 1986. Nine teachers transferred and the principal left to assume a new position. I was one of ten new teachers placed at the school. Our new principal had the task of pulling together the newly hired faculty with an established faculty that was basically discouraged and worn out.

One of her first major decisions in this regard was to implement a discipline policy based on Canter's (1976) Assertive Discipline model. We received training and were encouraged, but not required, to follow the constructs of Assertive Discipline, which included putting teachers in charge, and using positive reinforcement techniques. Rules were posted throughout the building and both rewards and consequences were specifically stated. There was a replacement of home suspension with in-school suspension and detention. Our primary focus in using the Assertive Discipline plan, however, was to emphasize the positive. There were monthly behavior reward activities, 'Good Note Home' rewards, lunchroom behavior rewards, and 'Citizen of the Month' honors. In general, the plan was well accepted and the school climate began to change for the better.

At the end of her first year, the principal then introduced a three-year plan to improve the school. The challenge was stated as follows:

> To mobilize students, staff, and parents around a school in which students are expected to achieve. We will set and enforce standards to make the school environment orderly, safe, and academically demanding.

Even though there were fewer suspensions and fights under the reward system, the student body as a whole continued to have difficulty with three major areas: following directions, staying on task, and accepting correction from an authority. The reward system seemed to be effective in motivating the average students with minor behavior problems, but there were many students with severe behavior problems who were not significantly influenced by this discipline policy. The principal concluded that we were spending a lot of time focusing on positive and negative consequences, but little time teaching these identified types of behavior. As a way of enhancing our existing disciplinary techniques, we began to use the Administrative Intervention Program. 'Administrative Intervention' is a term used to identify a set of procedures developed from the Teaching Family Model (a group home and residential treatment program for troubled children and for youth who experience behavior deficits) that has been adapted to educational settings.

Administrative Intervention operates on the philosophy that when students misbehave, they must be re-taught in much the same way they would be re-taught had they made a mistake on a math problem. Given the fact that there is not enough time in the day for teachers to teach the core curriculum, let alone social skills, a major strength of the program is that the intervention is done by the administrator. Initially, teachers are responsible for teaching the 'social skills,' such as staying on task, to their entire class. When a disruptive event occurs, however, the principal steps in to provide the necessary re-teaching and intervention strategy. The re-teaching strategy combines empathetic response, positive and negative consequences, and detailed record-keeping with the re-teaching of specific behaviors. During the first year of implementation, our principal spent 90 percent of her day involved in interventions. It was clear that our students truly did not know how to perform many of the behaviors that are termed social skills. As the program's effectiveness became apparent, even those teachers who had not participated began to become involved. In the second year of use, the principal reported that the percentage of her day devoted to interventions had decreased from 90 percent to 50 percent.

Following the Administrative Intervention Program, the focus switched to the development of school-wide teaming and ability grouping in reading and math. Within this approach, teachers are encouraged to group across grade levels, but most choose to group within their own grade. Each grade contains four groupings from severely low to high abilities. There is now a school-wide block scheduling, consisting of a two hour block for reading, followed by a one hour block for math. At the conclusion of the math block, the students return to their heterogeneously grouped home rooms for science, social studies, health, music, and art. Team meetings, held weekly, allow for discussion about individual students and the sharing of instructional strategies. Each team has a person who acts as a liaison between the team and the principal.

Another part of the reform was the creation of a time-on-task room and the hiring of a supervisory aide. Students who are unable to stay on task are sent by the teacher to T.O.T. for instruction on the identified social skills and the completion of their work in isolation.

Revisiting the histories

After these descriptive parts of the personal and school histories were completed, Beth returned to the texts at a later time, to strengthen the analysis. To illustrate this analytic emphasis and its import on the development of voice, we will again use Beth as an example.

In one respect, simply the writing of personal and school histories is a step towards enabling silenced groups to speak out. However, if voice is to be more than a solipsistic endeavor, the story not only has to be heard, but also must be seen as valuable. Ironically, even those groups who have been silenced often do not value their experiential or practical knowledge. This is not surprising given their lack of power and the dominant view about what counts as legitimate knowledge. An important part of developing voice, therefore, is seeing stories of the self as valuable. For Beth, this process occurred during the sharing of personal histories.

> I continuously learned by listening to other teachers' personal histories, and by having my own history listened to and valued. It gave me the incentive to keep searching for a way to fulfill my dreams of the teacher I wanted to be. And yet, as I wrote, I sometimes had the uneasy feeling, 'But this is just my story.' I found myself wondering at times, 'Is this real academic work, does it count?' When my paper was returned I was still awed by the fact that my story had been read, heard, and responded to seriously. Myself as text; it was such an incredibly empowering experience for me. I had never developed a sense of voice. On the contrary, I had grown up in classrooms that deposited information in the heads of students just like the one to which, as a teacher, I sadly realized I had succumbed.

Speaking out, especially when one has been historically silenced, is an essential part of altering power relations. Just the fact that a particular group no longer has the exclusive privilege to speak alters to a degree the decision making process of a culture, community or even a society. However, if voice is to be more than speaking out, if it is to be a form of protest that enables groups to contest structures and their own part in fostering narrow and limiting forms of schooling, then part of the process involves valuing difference, while contesting conformity. In Beth's description of her history it became clear that her past was one of following rules and not taking risks. With the writing of her personal and school history, however, the old patterns of compliance became obvious and Beth began not only to speak out, but to pose questions about the school district's policies while challenging her acceptance of those policies.

> I had deliberately built into my curriculum times of choice, times where there were no right answers, no put downs, times when students were free to express any and all opinions. These were some of the most sacred moments to me in teaching, the times I was most fulfilled. There was a

sense of being able to give to kids what I had been denied. Yet, these experiences could not be easily measured or standardized. They did not fit the mold of the district's basic skill requirements. Therefore, I had let them slip away, and let the skills I was required to teach take precedence. There was a glaring contradiction between what I wanted to accomplish and what I felt compelled to accomplish and teach.

By identifying tensions between policy and practice, Beth also gained confidence that she could raise questions instead of depending on others to pose these queries. She was more willing to take a critical stance toward her own history and the knowledge presented by others.

My ability to formulate ideas and to raise questions began to expand while my self-doubt began to diminish. I began to listen less and less to my self imposed censor, and to risk sharing my perceptions with others. I noticed that I was able to think critically not only about my own ideas, but also about the knowledge that others communicated. The writing of these texts also gave me the opportunity to think critically about my own history and how it might interact with the history of my students.

Once Beth was willing to confront her history and look critically at the arguments posed by others, she had the foundation to direct her protest both inward at self and outward at context. These came together in her analysis of the Administrative Intervention Program being implemented in her school. Her first concerns were directed at the policy itself.

As Apple (1979) points out, schools tend to devalue conflict in favor of compliance. They also develop student roles that will contribute to the maintenance of society. The specific content of social skills taught through Administrative Intervention supports this idea that schools prepare students to become good workers who will uphold the work ethic of their society. While the social skills teach children to be respectful and to work hard these same skills also encourage passivity and place considerable value on order and routine. Consider the components of the rules 'follow directions' and 'stay on task'.

Follow Directions	*Stay on Task*
1 Eye contact	1 Self start
2 Say O.K.	2 Work steadily for required time
3 Do task immediately	3 Do not make distractions
4 No arguing	4 Ignore others' distractions

These behaviors are the very ones that are seen as desirable in industry. They are the behaviors a supervisor looks for in factory workers, but are they the ones we should be emphasizing in schools? How much do they contribute to the intellectual growth of the student?

While Beth has not come to any conclusions, she has raised a number of questions which enable her to examine how the implementation of policy acts to serve particular interests, those of producing good workers, while fostering overly narrow forms of education. Her protest, however, is not limited to the context in which she works, she also looks inward at her role as teacher.

At times, I lose my balance. Working with 'at risk' students, it is easy to fall into the trap of an over-reliance on teacher authority, but this is not the answer. To find the answer we need to go beyond our classroom walls. We need to look at the cultural values that such students bring with them to school in order to determine how to help them succeed. For example, in the descriptive part of this history I made the statement that our students 'truly did not know how to follow directions, stay on task etc.' Why do they not know how? Is it that the values we teach in school are not those that are applicable to them at home? Is it possible that their parents do not have the same white, middle class values that the school espouses? What do our parents value and hope for, in terms of their children's education? Are students able to use the strategies we teach to help them solve problems at home? Do they agree with these strategies and with these values? Is it that our students do not know how to implement the expected behaviors of the school or do they just not care? If they do not care, might it also be due to a long history of irrelevant curriculum and rigid teaching practices that do not allow them to be involved in their own education?

As Beth continued to pose a number of questions about self and context, an outline for the research question started to emerge. While this outline did not take the form of a question, it clearly laid out what Beth wanted to achieve in the classroom and therefore provided the basis for raising potential concerns about the gap between these aims and her practices. Not surprisingly, her insights about her past silence held the key to what she wanted for students.

In the ERP each of us had been guided and supported in finding, developing, and expressing our voice. But how had 'voice' been protected and nurtured? The answer lay not with finding a student-centered approach, but with achieving a sense of mutuality and reciprocity between teacher and student. Freire has said that education begins 'with the resolution of the teacher/student contradiction, by reconciling the poles of the contradiction so that both are simultaneously teacher and student' (Freire, 1970, p.59). The environment that I now envisioned for my class, was one based on a truly reciprocal community where all involved would be considered teacher–learners. No longer was I willing to deposit the information into the heads of my students, thereby setting up a subject–object dualism. Essentially, I wanted to provide them with the same sense of empowerment that I gained from learning to produce, rather than simply receive knowledge.

While the link between the production of texts, voice, and question posing is important to Educative Research, the process does not stop at question posing. Instead, as mentioned previously, where possible, attempts are made to act on and contest the type of schooling offered students. For the most part, these action plans were determined when teachers used dialogue to look at their intentions and practices as part of the Horizontal Evaluation approach. However, the first attempts to think through what one might do in the classroom were typically formulated during the analysis part of the school and personal histories. In Beth's analysis the beginnings of an action plan revolved around an examination of the words instruct and educate.

How was I to begin to make these changes I now envisioned? Turning to the etymology of the words instruct and educate I found both clues and contradictions. The word instruct comes from the Latin, in + 'stuere' meaning to build. In my classroom rarely had students and I been able to concentrate on building or creating. Instead, we had been required to follow the practices common to instrumental rationality which encouraged us to reproduce rather than to build. I had deposited information; they had reproduced and memorized facts, knowledge from others, which more often than not, had little connection to their own lives. To confront this type of education I had to find a way to introduce a process of building and creating.

When I then studied the word 'educate', I found that it comes from the Latin derivative 'educare', meaning to rear. These etymologies seemed to confirm for me a notion that I had felt for a long time, while illuminating what had been so frustrating and limiting to me as a teacher: There is a fundamental connection between educating and rearing children, however, it is a denied and devalued connection that is gender-related. When we are educating, we are rearing, but women are expected to educate in ways that may contradict often what we know about living and being with children. The rearing of children involves intimacy and nurturance. Home is a place of exploration, a place where the development of initiative and curiosity is carried out in the daily activities that women do with children. It is a place of continuous and evolving relationships that if they are to succeed, are built on caring, cooperation, and the listening to and valuing of difference. School, on the other hand, is a place of control and compliance. It is a place where children, while being observed, measured, and evaluated, must master tasks that are broken down and compartmentalized. Rather than fostering intimacy and nurturance, relationships in schools center around theories of expertise and authority leading to a sense of detachment and isolation.

Although the majority of teachers are women, the culture of schooling is based on concepts that are a denial of womens' experiences. Grumet views schooling as a passage from the domestic world to the public world, and consequently, also to patriarchal institutions.

> We have required women to draw children out of the intimacy and knowledge of the family into the categorical and public world. We have burdened the teaching profession with contradictions and betrayals that have alienated teachers from our experiences, from our bodies, our memories, our dreams, from each other, from children and from the sisters who are mothers to those children.
>
> (Grumet, 1988, p. 57)

As I looked back on my personal and school history, I began to see the part that I was playing, and being forced to play, in perpetuating this passage. I understood how the agentic school structures and my own personal history had worked together to try to separate me from a nurturing, communal approach to education. Often they had been successful. When this separation occurred, I would look for something to change – grade, school, occupation – and when it became unbearable I left teaching, twice. Yet each time something drew me back. Now I knew what it was – the need to use and value maternal knowledge. It was the desire to connect the private and public spheres which not only schooling, but also society, has forced apart.

As Beth looked for ways to make this connection, she wanted to change the metaphor of her teaching from 'factory' to 'family.' Assertive Discipline may have gotten her through the day, but the price of using these techniques was that she was forced to use behaviors that would lead her away from intimate relationships. As the authority figure and controller, Beth had put aside the very behaviors that would nurture her students and sustain her in teaching. With these thoughts in mind, she developed the following general goals for the next year:

1 To build a community of teacher/learners based on care, concern and connection.
2 To develop a sense of voice in my students by helping them recognize

the importance of their experience. And to use this knowledge to build and create new knowledge and further their understandings of themselves and the world.

3 To bridge the gap between school and home.

One of the first steps in the realization of these goals was to establish more reciprocal relationships. Beth began to look for opportunities where her role as *the teacher* could be eliminated. Rather than relying on the procedures of assertive discipline and her pre-constructed rules, the management of the classroom could be a shared responsibility. Regularly scheduled, student-run classroom meetings in which Beth would facilitate group problem solving would replace the teacher-controlled approach to management.

Theory into Practice: Beth's reflection

I have stated that the maternal influence in teaching is energetic, resilient, resourceful, and persevering. In day to day work with children, however, these qualities are continually tested. My quest for developing a community of teacher-learners has not been, and seems will not be, a smooth or easy one. Although I anticipated it to some degree, I was nevertheless discouraged to see the resistance of students to my new curriculum. Despite the preliminary changes in the curriculum, the acting-out behavior has limited my initial attempts to form a community. At age seven, their lived experience has already taught them not to trust. These students are so used to fighting, ridiculing, and complaining that even personally relevant curriculum has so far had little impact. They have learned to be tough and rebellious and to think of care or concern as a sign of weakness. To cooperate or connect with others is to somehow lose face.

Although they rebel against authority, when given opportunities to make rules and decisions for themselves, many are at a loss. They look to 'teacher,' and consider me, as an adult figure in the room, to be either the creator of their problems – in which case they rebel – or the solver of their problems – in which case they become dependent. Initially they did not respond to my efforts to establish care, concern, and connection. What they responded to were the M&Ms – those extrinsic rewards that I found myself using once again. I have been angry, frustrated, and fearful that they were going to force me back into that position of the authority and controller that I had worked so hard to escape. They have not done so, but this experience has shown me the incredible difficulty of finding the balance between giving up and holding on to my previous role.

We do not yet have a community of teacher-learners. What we have is a group of individuals struggling to discover where our voices begin and end in relation to each other. In order to be able to get to the point where we can begin to work on the development of our voices, I have done considerable talking and modeling of what it means to be a teacher-learner. As a class, we have talked about the qualities of teacher-learners and we have looked at the many people in our lives that serve as 'teachers' – parents, siblings, peers, ourselves. We have examined the other environments in which we can and do learn besides our classroom.

The path to reconciliation of the contradiction between teacher and student is indeed an arduous one, but one I shall continue to follow and to invite my students to join me. Our next task, the recording and sharing of our personal histories, will be a big risk for them. But I believe that as they read and respond to their own histories, they will gradually gain the sense of empowerment that can come from using their own voice.

At this point, they must practice learning to listen to and value each others' voices, and we may yet go through more bags of M&Ms. Nevertheless, I am committed to making this change in my teaching and am encouraged by recent promising moments. Last Friday, when I asked my students, 'Who is the teacher in this room'?, a few fingers instantly pointed to me. But then I saw several heads shake and heard Melissa's voice indignantly retort, 'Huh-uh. We *all* are.'

As Beth's personal and school histories point out, these texts can play an important role in facilitating the aims of Educative Research. They give teachers an opportunity to tell their stories and, importantly, can release them from a cycle of compliance. When this occurs, they often see value in what they do and know and then can use this new confidence to take risks, to look critically at themselves and their world, and to protest what is narrow and constraining about schooling. This development of voice, in turn, allows them to take some initial steps in posing questions about schools and teaching as well as to consider what actions they might take to remake the education offered students.

4   Horizontal Evaluation

Educative Research attempts to alter the relationship between researcher and 'subject' by changing the inquiry process from a one-way endeavour aimed at extracting data to a mutual process of question posing and analysis. To facilitate this mutual process, members of the ERP engaged in Horizontal Evaluation. Horizontal Evaluation is an evaluation process that attempts to foster school change by enabling teachers to base practice on a critical accounting of the moral, political, and ethical consequences of schooling. It does so by utilizing a dialogical approach that transforms the evaluator from a fault finder, to one who works with the other participant to understand schooling in ways which enable them to escape habit and challenge taken-for-granted views. To understand better Horizontal Evaluation and its relation to the ERP this chapter will: 1) describe the Horizontal Evaluation method, 2) analyze its underlying assumptions, 3) clarify the role it plays in Educative Research, and 4) draw on transcripts of those who used the model to give a concrete sense of what can occur when participants engage in dialogue as part of a larger process of question posing and data analysis.

THE HORIZONTAL EVALUATION METHOD

Horizontal Evaluation is a process in which teachers collaboratively analyze the relationship between their teaching intentions and their practices in ways that point to 'living contradictions' (Whitehead and Lomax, 1987). This is another way of saying that they are searching for the gap between what they desire to do in their teaching, and what they actually end up doing. Where there is not this mismatch between intention and practice, teachers think through why they want to achieve the particular ends they have identified, as opposed to unquestioningly accepting them. Intentions can be stated in advance or can emerge from discussion. When stated in advance, they become a text for analysis. A teacher, for example, might hold the intention of having all students obey the rule, 'raise your hands before speaking.' Instead of simply observing the extent to which her/his practice reflects this intent, it is important that participants discuss why the rule is important, and under what conditions and when it might be most appropriate, or inappropriate. Once issues like these are clarified, their desirability can be examined and debated in relation to a normative framework.

To become clearer about the relationship between educational means and ends, Horizontal Evaluation draws primarily on the work of Gadamer (1975) and Habermas (1976). In particular, their arguments have helped shape three methods, 'communication analysis,' 'historical perspective,' and 'challenge statements' which can be utilized to enhance and deepen the dialogue between the teacher and observer.

Communication analysis

Communication analysis makes it possible for participants to understand how the prejudgments they hold about teaching frame and shape behaviour. For example, if a teacher regards chaotic student behavior as being caused by the 'low' abilities of the students, the question, 'What do you mean by 'low facilities'?' could be posed. Implicit values that lie behind statements and practices like this can, therefore, be made explicit and thus reconsidered by the participants. Reconsideration of these values can amount to a transformation in the way teachers make and remake school reality on a daily basis. For example, if teachers realize that some, if not most, of the labeling they use is inappropriate because it is based on an undisclosed view of the socio-economic status of the students, then classroom structures and pedagogy can be reorganized to reflect a more egalitarian view of the ways students should be treated.

Historical perspective

Adopting a historical perspective with respect to particular teaching strategies allows apparently common sense notions and actions to be seen not as natural and immutable, but rather as choices which are part of a historical tradition that serves particular interests while denying others. For instance, if a teacher regards teaching as a process of depositing information in the heads of students, adopting a historical perspective can encourage discussion about what factors have encouraged this kind of pedagogy in the past, including teachers' experiences as students. The interests embedded within such a view can then be more fully analyzed.

Also, where applicable, this understanding can be incorporated into a research program.

Challenge statements

Where discussion between teacher and colleague about in-class activity has become stilted, stalled, or bogged down and cannot go beyond clarifying values and prejudgments, then either of the parties can initiate a challenge statement designed to get discussion moving again. For example if a teacher holds to the view that students should obey her classroom rules in all circumstances, questions can be raised about students' and teachers' rights, and about the role and purpose of adult authority. The resulting conversation might seek to investigate the legitimacy of adult authority and the implications this holds for the education of students in a democracy.

Alternatives

In addition to these methods, Horizontal Evaluation asks participants to link the insights gained through dialogue to the realization of alternative teaching practices. The alternative is not an end point, an unalterable part of the teachers' repertoire, but rather a turning point for further discourse on the relation of intentions to practice. In other words, while the dialogue may end with a suggested alternative, this alternative then becomes part of a new set of practices which are examined by the participants. Alternatives are an important part of the dialogical process because the intent is not only just reflection and understanding, but action.

UNDERLYING ASSUMPTIONS

Horizontal Evaluation differs from traditional approaches both in its insistence that the focus be an understanding of teaching by both parties, not solely the participant being observed, and by fostering a broader notion of teaching that includes the beliefs and practices of the participants. In particular, Horizontal Evaluation is based on the following assumptions: 1) understanding, not control, should be the central purpose of evaluation, 2) understanding requires a consideration of history, 3) evaluation should be a dialogical process not a monologue given by the evaluator, and can provide a beginning point to confront the individualism of most evaluation schemes.

Control and understanding

Teacher evaluation as commonly practiced reflects several taken-for-granted assumptions about teachers, teaching, and the purpose of evaluation. One such assumption is that teachers are not experts. This assumption is reflected in the fact that administrators, not teachers, are for the most part seen as the individuals most qualified to evaluate teaching. While it is true that peer evaluation is becoming more common, it is often a senior teacher, coach or mentor who is evaluating the 'regular' teacher. And even in these situations the peer evaluation approach is typically something added onto the existing evaluation structure. In the final analysis it is the common hierarchical forms of evaluation which really count. Another assumption is that good teaching is related to a set of identifiable behaviors. Evaluation schemes consistently focus on teaching behaviors to the exclusion of other aspects of teaching, including the beliefs and aims of the teacher and those of the students (Gitlin and Smyth, 1989). Finally, it is assumed that the main purpose of evaluation is to weed out poor teachers or to inform competent teachers of their strengths and weaknesses. In total, these assumptions suggest that evaluation, as commonly practiced, is a hierarchical process that primarily aims to change what teachers do, without considering how they think about teaching.

Horizontal Evaluation rejects this emphasis on control on both political and efficiency criteria. In terms of politics, the emphasis on control treats participants as objects, thereby creating an alienating condition that rejects the expertise of women and others who have historically been linked to the practice of teaching. In an ironic twist, this emphasis on control also is very ineffective in altering behavior or creating change in any sense. Because participants often understand an event like traditional evaluation as being alienating, they respond to the process in self-protective ways. Two strategies dominate teachers' approach to evaluation: give the evaluator what s/he wants and then go back to typical routines or contest the process and the recommendations on the grounds that what was seen was not typical or representative of their teaching. Given that teacher evaluation rarely occurs more than twice in an academic year, it is difficult for this process to capture what is typical. On the other hand, if the observed teacher gives the evaluator what s/he wants then all appears to be well and everything goes on without an examination of classroom practices and teaching. While these strategies are quite appropriate given the way teacher evaluation is practiced, they make it unlikely that evaluation will result in a significant long-lasting change at the classroom level.

As opposed to control, Horizontal Evaluation places understanding at the center of the evaluation process. The emphasis on understanding suggests that teaching is more than a set of techniques that one masters. Teaching is, within this view, a political, moral, and ethical activity. This turn toward a political notion of teaching not only allows for a wider range of questions to be asked, but also makes it possible for evaluation to address non-technical concerns that typically reside outside the evaluative process. Finally, centering the process of evaluation on understanding, especially a mutual process of understanding, suggests that the primary purpose of evaluation is teacher growth and improvement. In essence, Horizontal Evaluation assumes that the central role of evaluation is not to weed out teachers or to inform them of strengths and weaknesses, but to find ways to enable practitioners to work together to examine what they do, consider why they do it and, based on these insights, propose ways to alter their practices.

When successful, this process has advantages over traditional forms. On political grounds, the evaluation process is less likely to be hierarchical and alienating. Teachers observed are not treated as objects, and because teachers are evaluating other peers there is less of a sense that the expert evaluator is coming in to help the needy practitioner. As evaluation moves away from an alienating endeavor, possibilities open up for evaluation to be taken seriously, to be seen as something that is part of the teaching process, not something imposed. The preliminary studies of Horizontal Evaluation suggest that as opposed to putting on a show, observed teachers wanted the other participant to see what typically happens in the classroom and, in some cases, actually requested that the observer focus on a 'problem' class (Gitlin, 1990). What this suggests is that teachers are not opposed to evaluation *per se*, but rather to the types of hierarchical, alienating forms that dominate school practice.

History

Traditional approaches to evaluation are ahistorical in a number of regards. At the most simplistic level they are ahistorical because one evaluation session is not linked to another. In other words, the evaluation process has a history which is obscured such that the visit occurring is rarely related to what happened before. And even when one visit is related to another, the linkage is only in terms of following up on the concerns raised in the first meeting. This stance toward evaluation ignores what issues were addressed, what sort of relationship was developing between the evaluator and the observed teacher, and an assessment of the 'helplessness' of the evaluation process.

Commonly practiced forms of evaluation are also ahistorical in that they sever teaching from its context. When an evaluator comes into a classroom, at best s/he can obtain a snapshot of what is occurring. This snapshot is always distorted because it highlights certain aspects of classroom practice while obscuring others. In addition, the snapshot is usually presented as if it doesn't reflect an ongoing classroom history. What the evaluator sees does not simply emerge. Instead it is a point on a continuum, a continuum that started long before the evaluator entered the room and continues long after s/he is gone. By presenting the snapshot as if it were a free-standing picture, the roots, origins, and developments that in some ways have influenced the snapshot become muddled and, importantly for our discussion, are seen to reside outside the boundaries of the evaluation process.

Traditional evaluation schemes also present the snapshot as if the picture of the teacher tells the whole story. Whatever the evaluator may see the teacher doing, no matter how deficient it may seem, understanding these actions is difficult, if not impossible, without some consideration of their history. What a teacher does and even what s/he believes is in part related to a series of events, discussions, and relationships in the person's past. Without an examination of these historical factors the assessment of the snapshot is likely to focus on what is apparent, simplistic, and technical, ignoring some of the more complex, deep structures that may be at the root of the observed behaviors.

A teacher's history, of course, is not one of isolation, it is a history of an individual embedded in a cultural context. One such context common to all teachers, therefore, is their professional culture or what might be referred to as the culture of teaching. While a professional culture is not as fundamental to one's being as, for example, the Navajo culture is to a Navajo, it is clear that one's work culture includes a set of norms and structures which shape to a certain degree the way participants view schooling and act in the classroom. And yet the culture of teaching is not a monolithic entity. Instead, it is a contextual construct which is made and remade on an everyday basis. Unfortunately, this active process of the making and remaking of culture resides outside the boundaries of traditional evaluation schemes. These schemes cannot account for how that history impinges on the snapshot they describe. Specifically, most types of evaluation do not consider how wider school and societal structures as well as taken-for-granted norms affect what is observed. This form of ahistorical knowing, therefore, is not only limited, but ignores issues which place schools within a societal context.

In sum, the view of knowing embedded in traditional forms of evaluation limits the process and, importantly, distorts the types of explanations and analyses offered. To confront these limits Horizontal Evaluation places history at the center of the assessment process by utilizing both personal and school histories as two of the texts that participants bring to this dialogical process. These texts enable participants to include in their dialogue consideration of an evolving self, the changing nature of their school context, and the wider professional culture that, taken together, influence so much of what happens in the classroom and how we understand it.

Dialogue and individualism

Because Educative Research attempts to transform research such that the 'subject' does not become a mere object of study, it is essential that the key aspects of this process, of which Horizontal Evaluation is a part, also reflect this priority. Horizontal Evaluation is based on establishing 'relationships of communication' where one participant doesn't dominate the question posing process or the analysis. To help foster these types of relationships, Horizontal Evaluation relies fundamentally on the process of dialogue. What we mean by dialogue has already been discussed, but it may be most helpful to talk through the potential implications of dialogue within an evaluative context.

There can be little doubt that most evaluation schemes involve a one-way communication from the evaluator to the teacher. While in many types of teacher evaluation the observed teacher could respond to the evaluator's assessment, it is rare that the teacher can set the agenda for the evaluation conference or determine the categories on which they are judged. The observed teacher is in an adversarial relationship with the evaluator. This type of relationship makes it likely that evaluation will become a game, where winning means finding ways to please the evaluator. Lost in this game is the potential for evaluation to become a process that breaks the isolation and individualism of teachers and enables them to alter in significant ways the nature of education offered in schools.

Individualism is strengthened by traditional forms of evaluation if for no other reason than that teachers are put in a kind of competition with each other. Given that informal benefits and small resources often result from a positive evaluation, it is in the teachers' interest to not only 'look good', but also to look better than other teachers. Common interests, and the potential for cooperative action, are therefore constrained by traditional forms of evaluation.

Current forms of evaluation also give teachers little opportunity to develop an understanding of the nature of education or alternative visions because the categories of assessment are predetermined and interpreted only by the evaluator (Bullough and Gitlin, 1987). What is a good education and what is good teaching lie outside the bounds of the assessment. Instead, the purpose is to see how well the teacher's behavior matches the predetermined categories.

Horizontal Evaluation attempts to confront these limits by centering evaluation around a dialogical approach. This emphasis on dialogue ensures nothing, but creates a set of possibilities that go far beyond those of traditional schemes. Specifically, the emphasis on dialogue brings teachers together in a common quest: the understanding of teaching. Not only is competition minimized, but opportunities are likely to arise where common interests, points of view, and a sense of needed action can be articulated. Further, because the categories for assessment are not predetermined, it is the responsibility of the observed teacher as well as the observer to help determine them. This joint responsibility brings with it questions about what categories should be included and why. And it is this set of questions which links the evaluative process to the consideration of what is good education and good teaching. If teachers are to pose research questions about their work, while protesting and transforming areas that are seen as weak, it is essential that a continuing dialogue take place on taken-for-granted assumptions about education and teaching.

PRACTICING HORIZONTAL EVALUATION

At the point that Horizontal Evaluation was introduced as part of the ERP, several aspects of a research question had already been developed. First, a start had been made in understanding how the questions we asked are related to a series of beliefs and events embedded in our personal histories. Second, the way the questions we asked are related to the school culture and context also became apparent. One aspect of the question posing process that was still missing, however, was the way questions arise from our understanding of the limits and tensions embedded in our everyday practices and between our practices and aims. Horizontal Evaluation was used, in part, to encourage this type of reflection and in certain cases to enable research participants to work together to pose questions and examine data.[4]

The transcripts of those using Horizontal Evaluation provide a vivid account of the part this process played in Educative Research. To illustrate the relations between Horizontal Evaluation and Educative Research, we will take one or two transcripts that focus on a particular topic and trace the path the participants traveled as part of a process of understanding teaching. Using this segment as a text, we will revisit the dialogue to consider its import. Emphasis will be placed on one of the participants to show more clearly the relationship between the evaluation process and Educative Research. The various segments will be organized along a continuum beginning with those related to the development of a research question, followed by those that helped refine that question, and ending with several examples that enabled participants to reflect on the types of interventions initiated as part of the ERP.

Posing a question

In this example, we again return to Beth's story. At this point in the project, Beth has struggled unsuccessfully to come up with a particular research question. What follows, describes an early stage of question posing where the focus was on an examination of the limits and difficulties in trying to be a 'good teacher.' In time these concerns played a part in the identification of a research question.

As is typical of Horizontal Evaluation conferences, Leslie, the observer, asks Beth how the lesson went. Beth responds with a barrage of frustrations:

> I wasn't together. I wasn't up for it. I felt I was talking too much. I wasn't getting from them [students] what I wanted. I was kind of telling them the answer. They were sort of confused. They were like saying, 'Why are we doing this?'

After venting these frustrations, Beth tries to make sense of these feelings. She focuses on the school-wide management scheme, Assertiveness Discipline, that asks teachers to simply put a check by a name on the board for negative behavior and praise positive behavior.

> This whole business about Assertive Discipline, I am so confused about it. I'm so frustrated because I'm trying to pull away from it and I'm thinking that is the reason I'm having these frustrations. I'm not so sure the underlying philosophy is what I want to be doing. But you have got to have a management technique. My theory is to try to talk to them and try to get in touch with how I'm feeling. But I feel like that doesn't come through to the kids because I try to hide it and gloss over it and maintain a calm, collectiveness and keep it all together. But inside I'm so pissed off.
>
> You're trapped once you start to use it. Am I not a strong enough personality to deal with them by talking? I've come to think that was part of the problem because I didn't talk enough to students. I just put them on leashes.

Leslie then asks what happened when Beth did talk to her students. Beth's response reflects some personal doubts about her ability and the resulting need to rely on teacher-centered approaches.

I'm not a real assertive person. It's been these outside control things – assertive discipline – that I have relied upon. Which is why I always end up resorting back to teacher-centered things; but I don't believe in them; I want to be more student-centered.

Beth feels stuck. She disagrees with the teacher-centered approach, and yet feels that a student-centered approach, while good for students, wears her down and leaves her frustrated.

We have spent a lot of time talking about how teaching is real close to mothering and nurturing in the sense of taking care of students. You give and you give and you give. But just like with Katie [a student] you feel like you're doing all these things for them and then they step on you.

Her dislike of the external controls and the teacher-centered approach encourages her to look for a compromise. In the next Horizontal Evaluation session, her intention for the lesson is to 'maintain on task behavior without Assertive Discipline.' The examination of this intention encourages Leslie and Beth to look more closely at what on task behavior means. Beth starts this process by saying:

How am I defining on task behavior? Immediately I thought I don't want kids talking when someone else is talking. I'll define it as I want you to look at the person and not talk. Then I thought why did I define it that way. Why didn't I define it as being emotionally involved in the lesson? . . . In the back of my mind what I'm thinking is that what I really want here, is for kids to be emotionally involved. But in order to get that I don't say to them, 'I want you guys to be on task and that means emotionally involved!' Instead, I say, 'I want you to be looking at the person who is talking.' Then I get trapped into saying 'Stephanie is talking.' Are the kids at this table looking at her?

This tension between Beth's implicit theories of teaching and her practice leads her to consider what a significant alternative would be like. She would like a community of learners where the school was responsive to the needs of students, while parents and others would become involved in the classroom.

In the ideal at the beginning of the school year I would call parents, kids and teachers to decide what the curriculum should be like. This is what the kids are interested in learning, this is what we are going to work on this year.

What this dialogue suggests more than anything is a frustration on Beth's part. She is angry with her students for not staying on task and not giving back what she gives to them. She's angry with herself for not having the strength to teach in ways that she believes are 'right' and beneficial for students. These tensions encourage Beth to consider other ways for students and teachers to meet in a classroom setting. Not surprisingly, when Beth finally settles on a question it concerns a fundamental part of the teaching process: the relationship between student and teacher. She put it this way:

> There is an inequality in my classroom, a contradiction in the sense of balance between student and teacher. The lack of true reciprocity has contributed to my students' emotional disconnection from their learning, and to my own frustration and unhappiness as a teacher. When my students are not emotionally involved in the classroom their behavior problems increase. I then take on the role of the controller who maintains their behavior as well as the authoritarian who 'deposits' the information they are supposed to know (Beth, *First Look*).

By exposing a living contradiction, the dialogue resulting from the Horizontal Evaluation conference produced a mirror that allowed Beth to look at herself. This self-reflection, in turn, formed the basis of a research question: 'How can I reshape the teacher/student relationship in a way that will meet my needs and those of the students?' Within this question were the seeds for an alternative relationship that is based on the needs of both student and teacher. Reciprocity became a theme of sorts that would guide Beth's desire to restructure teaching. This issue exposed a number of gender concerns. When these issues and concerns were taken together, Beth had this to say about teacher/student relationships and education in general:

> An integration of Freire's concepts of dialogue and community begins the process toward transformation. There is greater power in the communal mode, in the feminist approach to the education of children. There is nothing submissive, feeble, or timorous to be found here. The maternal influence is robust, energetic, resilient, resourceful and persevering. Should not the true purpose of education be to rear children who can build a better, more humane and just world? (Beth, *First Look*)

Rethinking and refining questions

For others in the ERP, Horizontal Evaluation played a role in helping them rethink and refine their questions. Karen, an elementary special educational teacher, is a case in point. In this example she is talking with Eeva, an elementary school teacher from another school. The demands of teaching special education students have left Karen tired and with a great deal of confusion about the aims and purposes of schooling. She has, at this point in the ERP, identified the question 'What is success' as the focus for her study. Because this question is so broad in nature, however, Karen and Eeva use Horizontal Evaluation to both refine and rethink what is success in the classroom. The dialogue that follows describes the participants' attempts to think through and examine the identified concern. Instead of starting with an examination of the notion of success itself, they begin by looking at classroom practice. After Eeva asks how the lesson went, Karen raises some concerns about the observed spelling lesson:

> I'm going to jump into the fire here and say that I am really uncomfortable in doing the kinds of activities I'm doing with students right now. I have been asked to try to improve students' spelling scores. So, the activities that I have been doing have been directed toward the scores, to improve the outcome on Friday's spelling test.

After coming to a quick agreement that there is more to spelling success than improving scores, Eeva asks Karen what should be the purpose of teaching spelling. Karen's response indicates that while she disagrees with a notion of success that is linked to test scores, she also acknowledges that it has certain advantages in validating the 'success' teachers are having with students.

> With a lot of the kids that I work with, I want them to have greater academic success. But in my mind, improving their spelling tests wouldn't be the highest priority in addressing academic success because it doesn't have anything to do with their ability to think through why those words are important . . . Sometimes it ends up happening that in order for me to feel successful as a teacher I'm going to those 'regular' teachers and finding out what the outcome of the kids' spelling tests were as though it were the outcome of my teaching.

This tension between the role that tests play in validating teachers' success and the role they play in denying a certain type of student success that values their opinions, encourages Karen to alter her approach to teaching and become a better listener.

> I have this sense that I have been talking less and listening more. Like when my students talk I hear them out a little longer, I'm a little less likely to jump in and tell them what they mean. I think that is a change for me . . . I guess I'm having a major personal awareness that maybe I haven't ever really listened to them [students]. You only listen with one ear and don't hear everything. I was always much too quick to jump in and finish the sentence, or assume what they wanted.

By holding back and relinquishing some control, Karen is able to let the students play a larger role in the meaning making process, especially as it concerns success. However, Karen also finds that, as was true of test scores, giving up the role of authority figure is especially difficult when one's self-worth is tied up with having 'the answers.'

> I have generated many more questions than I had when I started. I guess I don't want to portray myself as someone who is burdened down by too many problems and too many questions, because somehow I get the idea that part of being a professional is knowing that you can teach kids and knowing that you can accomplish certain things . . . You know it is sort of a double bind. I find that sometimes I have to put on the hat of expert, but that doesn't feel comfortable. Then there have been other times that if I say, 'Gee that is a hard problem. I hear you, I understand. What do you think you are going to do about it?' They don't want you to be that way. So I think I have this identity crisis right now in terms of my job description.

Clearly, this Horizontal Evaluation dialogue has not provided an answer to Karen's question of what is success. It has, however, helped expose a number of the dimensions of the issue that might be lost if the examination was not grounded in practice. Specifically, Karen has shown her own part in reinforcing particular notions of success. She has also exposed the tensions between role expectations that encourage an expert stance and her evolving view that success involves a process of listening more carefully to what students say. Where previously Karen's research question was almost unmanageable, this refinement of the question has pointed to specific aspects of the complex issue of success that can be analyzed as Karen continues to participate in Educative Research.

Reflections on school change

Once the participants in the ERP posed questions, many tried interventions in their classrooms. Kathy and Robyn, two elementary teachers in the same school, for example, used Horizontal Evaluation to examine their interventions. Kathy's intervention involved the use of personal histories with her students. She started the dialogue on personal histories by describing several questions she had about their use in the classroom.

> I want to talk about the validity of using personal histories with elementary children to make them participants in their learning rather than trying to take a program and inserting it into them. Is this really valid knowledge? What are my expectations, what are my intentions?

And how can I combine this program with other expectations for what is to be learned in school? There are certain standards supposedly that we have to meet, and the accountability is usually in a testing kind of situation. How can I combine these two [personal histories and the need for accountability] to make a viable program that is relevant to all the participants?

In this opening statement Kathy has raised a number of issues that will facilitate the dialogue on personal histories including what is legitimate knowledge, what is the teacher role in the process, and what is the relation between the use of personal histories and other structures such as testing that are likely to legitimate a different sort of knowledge. To begin to address these concerns Robyn suggests that they explore the question of how kids learn before they come to school. Kathy responds by saying:

. . . by observation. They learn not by having people tell them. Everything they learn when they are young is experienced. Learning to ride a bike, learning to walk, learning to talk. No one tells someone how to walk when they are little. You can talk to a person and tell them how to ride a bike, but the person cannot ride the bike unless they go out and try it. Motivation also plays a role. They have to have a reason to do it. They want to learn how to ride a bike. They desperately want to learn how to walk. Watching a child learn to walk is an excruciating experience, but they learn. And talking, they go through all those stages, but it is because they want to.

This emphasis on experience and motivation, according to Kathy, directly contrasts with the structure of learning found in schools.

[In schools] it is not appropriate for you to learn because the experiences do not match the required curriculum. This is what you are supposed to learn about plants when you are five. This is what you are supposed to learn when you are six and this is what you are going to learn when you are seven . . . so we have a number of constraints on their motivation to learn.

Robyn builds on the contrast between home and school learning by asking, 'Why are we forcing them [students] to learn? Kathy responds with the following statement:

I think maybe part of the problem is that as teachers we walk in the door and treat them as a group and we say, 'You are the class and I am the teacher. This is what I am going to put into your head. You have no choice as to what comes in.' We also don't know anything about prior learning . . . We assume that they are coming from certain kinds of homes. Sometimes we look at them and make assumptions. Sometimes we gather little things from what their parents have said and we are making assumptions that often times is not what has really gone on. So it is important that we find out what their prior knowledge is, what their prior learning is, how they learn, what they want to learn, what is their motivation for learning, why they should learn about certain things. In doing personal histories they have come up with all these things.

Robyn pushes the analysis of personal histories further by suggesting that an understanding of their import for students may be gained by looking at what Kathy learned from writing a personal history.

What I learned from [personal histories] is why I do the things I do, what I know, where my knowledge comes from and what I still have to learn. It has helped me to work with that, to evaluate that on my own ... What I am saying is if kids look at the history of their life, they could not only realize how they learned the things they know, what they know, what they still don't know, but it could help them make decisions as to why that learning might be important.

This statement suggests that one important part of personal histories is their ability to further reciprocal relationships. Kathy picks up on this point by stating, 'Okay then, it is important also that before we as teachers have a student examine their personal history, the teacher should examine their own.'

At this point in the dialogue, Kathy feels that schools can and should foster the type of learning that occurs quite naturally and successfully outside school. She also feels that learning is a two-way process requiring teachers as well as students to take a careful look at what they know and why they know it and what the gaps are in their knowledge. This notion of a two-way participatory type of learning that builds in what they know also suggests fundamental changes in the way Kathy treats her students.

I thought it was important to treat them the same, and now I'm finding that the opposite is true. That nobody can be treated the same. I don't want to be treated the same as everyone else. I want to be treated as a human being and I think I need to do that with my students too. I just want to make sure that it is valuable to them and that it can be relevant to them because if it is not, there is no point.

Unfortunately, treating students in this way is difficult given standard school structures such as the core curriculum which predetermines a set of objectives that need to be covered in a specified time for all students. The tension, according to Kathy, centers on both a lack of trust in teachers and the need for accountability measures.

The intent of the core curriculum is to make sure teachers are doing something or held accountable . . . It is all accountability to make sure that the students know these facts. But I want to do it in a different way than pouring it in. I want to base it on their prior knowledge and their interests and their feelings and their humanity so to speak. I want them to feel a part of what they are doing . . . And yet in the core curriculum they assume that all children are learning at the same rate, 'By the end of second grade you will know this'. It doesn't happen and nobody talks about it. They just say the child failed. Did the child fail or is the system not geared to the child?

This dialogue about the use of personal histories has produced a number of insights which assess and further the process of school change. In particular, for these teachers personal histories are part of a return to a type of learning that begins before formal schooling and takes as its primary assumption the need to link learning occurring outside school and that which occurs inside the school corridors. This view of learning requires not only changes in curriculum making, but, importantly, changes in the teachers' role. Part of this change is fostering a two-way approach to learning that reveals both the students' and teachers' point of view while also respecting differences among students.

Where Kathy began by trying to determine the effect of personal histories for her students, after her dialogue with Robyn she has not only a clearer sense of the rationale for such a process, but also an understanding of some of the barriers, such as core curriculum, that are likely to constrain this type of curriculum making. Dialogue, therefore, played a role in illuminating the implications as well as furthering the process of change.

Horizontal Evaluation is not a cure all. To undertake such a process participants must develop enough trust to really examine and challenge their understanding of teaching. However, a process of this sort, when successful, can be an important part of an educative approach to research. It provides a forum in which the insights participants have gained through their personal and school histories, as well as their readings, can be linked to the questions they raise, and the types of change they want to implement in their classrooms.

5   The research context

To this point in the discussion of Educative Research, we have focused primarily on the assumptions and practices that guide this alternative approach. Our claim has been that this method has the potential to foster more reciprocal relationships between researchers and those studied. Our experience in practicing this alternative method, however, has helped us see that method alone will not alter relationships. Instead, changes in method must go hand in hand with changes in the research context. One event that helped center our attention on the research context was a conference attended by many of the members of the ERP.

A four-part symposium in which we gave a series of papers that talked about our struggles as part of the ERP was given at the Curriculum Theorizing Conference in 1990. The context for the teachers' talks represented a clear separation of groups: teachers were giving papers and academics were in the audience. The situation ran counter to tradition in that the academics were doing the listening and teachers the talking. After the presentations, one comment from the audience had a familiar ring: the questions the teachers posed lacked talk about structure and didn't readily address wider concerns about the economy and the importance of history.

On one level this query seemed quite appropriate, these concerns had not been addressed. Yet, something about the question was troubling. In time we realized that our problem with the question was not its content but rather the privileged position of the academic that allowed him to ask it. Wider concerns such as these can easily be raised when one is not immersed in practice and has time to reflect. But, when one is teaching six or seven classes daily that require literally thousands of decisions, there is a pull to stay at least relatively close to concerns of practice. It seemed possible, therefore, that the questions we ask are related to the material conditions of our work. If this is true, then the question of Educative Research could not be limited to refiguring method, but must also include a restructuring of the research context, that is the material realities and commonly held beliefs that shape relationships between the research participants and the questions they ask.

Because question posing and analysis are in a fluid relation within Educative Research, this rethinking of the research question was not a cause for concern. Instead, it was a motivation to inquire further about the focus of our research question. When we looked more carefully at the boundaries of our question, we could see that a consideration of the institutional history of universities and their relation to schools was ignored. By not considering this institutional history, we had failed to raise questions about the material conditions of teachers and researchers, and their influence on the types of relationships we currently see between these groups. To confront this gap in our understanding, we decided to develop a historical sketch that would suggest what else besides method would need to be altered if new relations were to develop between researchers and teachers.

Because a complete institutional history could fill the pages of many books, we decided to look at the development of institutions of teacher education as they evolved from the normal school to the teachers college and eventually to schools of education within universities. In tracing these institutions, we focused specifically on the question of professionalism. An analysis of professionalism was important for our newly developed research question because it would give us information on who was seen as expert and why, how particular forms of knowledge gained legitimacy, and what role teachers and others played in this struggle. Put simply, it would show how the research context helps shape the typical relationships between teachers and researchers that we find today in our educational communities.

The analysis of professionalism also had an unexpected result: it showed that our emphasis on how method informs relationships had obscured questions of gender. It is not only researchers and teachers who are brought together through the doing of research, but also men and women. In an attempt to make gender concerns more central to our project, this historical sketch includes an examination of what we refer to as 'the woman question.'

THE QUEST FOR PROFESSIONALISM

Competing conceptions

It was commonly assumed in the late nineteenth century that teaching could not become a profession without the establishment of institutions of higher education. Wright notes, for example, that the purpose of the normal school (the first teacher training institution) was to 'transform teaching into a profession' (Wright, 1965, p.29). Steere, commenting on teacher colleges, suggests much the same function for these institutions by arguing that, 'We can never hope to raise teaching to a profession until we establish professional schools to prepare teachers for such work' (Steere, 1931, p.192). And Larson notes that the role of the university is to 'provide the ideological legitimation for both old and new professions as well as provide models, sponsorship, equipment, and resources' (Larson, 1977, p.245). While there was widespread agreement about the need for these institutions of higher education, the struggle to professionalize teaching represented a number of competing positions.

In the early 1900s, at least three different notions of professionalism were competing for legitimacy. One notion originally espoused by people such as Horacé Mann, an early proponent of the normal school, was that professionalism was fostered by instilling a sense of dedication into those who would work in public schools.

> [Professionalism] involved first a deep sense of being 'called' to serve . . . a sense so strong that one would persist in service regardless of the difficulties entailed or the temptations of other activities . . . The desire to produce teachers who possessed these characteristics is the central motive of the normal school.
>
> (Borrowman, 1965, p.24)

Another view of professionalism was tied to the importance of practice and the methods of teaching. In particular, to be a professional teacher was to receive training that specifically focused on the process of instruction and learning.

> If our teacher-training institutions are to produce professionally trained teachers who really know how to do the work expected of them, should not those responsible for the development of such schools be thinking in terms of copying the specific methods of professional schools [processes of instruction] rather than in terms of the more general methods of liberal arts colleges?
>
> (Steere, 1931, p.193)

The special attention given practice did not suggest that other more 'theoretical' activities, such as scholarship, played no part in the quest for professionalism. Rather, the type of proposed scholarship differed from the writing encouraged in other professional perspectives in that it was neither research-based nor intended primarily for other academics. Woodring captures this view of professionalism when he states that individuals should 'write articles for the magazines that reach millions of readers even though this means that our professional associates may look down their noses at our efforts to "popularize" our ideas' (Woodring, 1958, p.14).

A third view was the one that was reinforced by the long-standing legitimacy of scientific research. Within this view, to be professional was to do scientific research within a prestigious institution of higher education. The intent was not to popularize ideas, but to produce 'higher forms of scholarship' (Judd, 1929, p.878). Practical experience and haphazard empiricism were problems that must be challenged if education was to become a profession (Powell, 1971, p.406).

In sum, underlying these notions of professionalism was the struggle to determine what counts as legitimate knowledge. If doing scientific research was seen as *the* way of producing legitimate knowledge, then those immersed in the academic culture would be better able to make claims about their expertise. And, if scientific research was combined with the notion that the teacher's role was to serve others, the claims of academics would be less likely to be challenged, and the hierarchy between these groups would be strengthened. Finally, if experiential knowledge was seen as a form of legitimate knowledge, teachers and others working at the level of practice would benefit. What follows suggests that the struggle over professionalism was also a struggle to determine the place of particular groups within the educational community.

HISTORICAL INFLUENCES

Normal schools

As normal schools developed in the mid to late nineteenth century, they adopted a view of professionalism based on the importance of experiential knowledge and the need to develop a 'calling' among teachers. The quest of the normal school was to legitimate teachers' practical experience against the backdrop of the long-established liberal arts/scientific tradition. Many normal schools, for example, used the concerns of practicing teachers to organize a spring conference in which the normal school faculty revised their curriculum based on teacher recommendations (Judd, 1929). This conference structure enabled teachers to have a say in policy matters and, importantly, linked the normal school curriculum to public school practice. Many normal schools also hired teachers on a regular basis to work in their program. The teachers' experience was valued and these practitioners could easily shift back and forth between the normal school and the elementary and secondary classroom. These priorities and structures made it possible for the normal schools to treat teachers as experts and strengthen the view that practice was a legitimate form of knowledge.

Unfortunately, the admission of large numbers of students who did not plan to teach diverted the normal school from an exclusive focus on teacher training (Herbst, 1989). Even though all who entered this institution had to sign a pledge that they would teach, this control mechanism was easily avoided. In certain normal schools only one-fifth of the students were trained to be professional teachers. To accommodate those who did not plan to teach, a business orientation was added to the curriculum at certain institutions while others added courses that would help 'finish' young women (Wassermann, 1979).

The fragmentation of the normal school curriculum made it difficult for those who believed in this institution to assert their view of professionalism to the wider public. By accommodating a variety of students, the single mindedness of effort and focus needed to challenge competing notions of professionalism simply was not forthcoming. This difficulty did not cause advocates of the normal schools to alter their course; instead they held tenaciously to a concept of professionalism based on practice and a 'calling.' Over time, however, the fragmentation of the curriculum and the influential shadow cast by the university strongly challenged the normal school's position and the legitimacy of the normal school itself. It is at this juncture in the first quarter of the twentieth century that the teachers college started to flourish.

Teachers college

In many ways, the teachers college quest for professionalism in the early twentieth century was a compromise between the view based on research and the one embodied in the practices of the normal school. The teachers college did try to maintain an emphasis on practice. One of the clearest indications of this was the continuing presence of laboratory schools on the campuses of teachers colleges. In contrast to the normal school, however, they also attempted to emphasize research.

Unfortunately for those who supported the teachers college, this institution never really established itself as a powerful force in the quest for professionalism. In one sense the reason for this failure was quite simple. The university community had serious doubts about the research produced within the teachers college and, therefore, didn't endorse or support this institution. One reason the research produced in teachers colleges was not thought to compare favorably with that coming out of the university was that the teachers college was less bound by the scientific approach. The research commonly conducted within the teachers college was a combination of practical observation and insights and scientific methodology. Furthermore, although teachers colleges were much more reluctant than normal schools to hire teachers, they did hire a number of practitioners. Because it was assumed by those within the university that practitioners couldn't produce quality research, this factor also played a part in casting doubt on the quality of research produced in the teachers college (Strong, 1950, p.83).

Besides the problems the teachers college encountered with the university community, this institution was also weakened internally by the developing split between male and female teachers. In particular, male teachers endorsed the teachers college as a way to separate themselves from their female counterparts who they viewed as inhibiting any possibility to professionalize teaching.

> How, it could be asked, might teaching ever aspire to the status of a profession when so many practitioners were women, especially the single women on whom teaching relied because of pervasive regulations against employing married women teachers? The apparent answer was that it could not be professionalized.
>
> (Clifford, 1986, p.42)

These men hoped that the teachers college, with its emphasis on standards and higher academic achievement, would act as a filtering device between those who wanted to become educational leaders and those who wanted to remain in the classroom. In practice, what this meant is that normal schools, at least the few left at this time, would train women for teaching and the teachers colleges would train men for leadership.

It should be noted, however, that even the men graduating from these institutions and the faculty teaching at these colleges were not considered of the same quality as those associated with universities. While the teachers college tried to move away from the legacy of the normal school and male teachers tried to separate themselves from female teachers, in the end these changes did not enable men or women teachers to be seen as an expert of one sort or another. Furthermore, this institution also drove a wedge between those working at the level of practice such that support for the teachers college quickly eroded (Bigelow, 1957).

Schools of education

The early to mid twentieth century saw a dramatic decline in the number of teachers colleges. In their place, schools of education, housed within colleges and universities, began to flourish. The popularity of schools of education housed in this setting seems related to two dramatic changes in their orientation to professionalism. First, they shifted toward a research emphasis. Schools of education were on solid ground when they argued that association with the university is essential to the quest for professionalism, since historically 'all the professions which have successfully established claims of expertise and their control over training and access are affiliated or connected with the university' (Larson, 1977, p.200). Second, they clearly separated themselves from the world of practice. One aspect of this movement was that schools of education began to de-emphasize teacher education and offer more graduate programs (Wiles, 1967). The number of courses directly related to teaching was cut, and teachers found it more difficult than ever to be admitted to the newly established graduate programs. Their difficulty stemmed from the fact that most teachers majored in education as opposed to a subject matter emphasis, and therefore did not have the prerequisite courses for graduate study.

Another sign of this shift away from practice was that teaching experience was no longer a prerequisite for hiring at the university level. As Goodlad *et al.* state, 'the appointment of C. Vann Woodward to the professorship at Yale in the mid 1950s sent out a significant signal to the academic world: no teaching required' (Goodlad *et al.*, 1990, p.10). Others argued that practice was actually a hinderance rather than a benefit. Judd, for example, comments that, 'the 10 years of teaching and administrative experience of the average applicant is evidence of a retardation of a career, a handicap rather than an asset.' And Inglis of Harvard observes that, 'an able bodied person would be sick of kids by the time he was 35' (Clifford, 1986, p.433–4). These views seemed to carry the day because in a short period of time universities primarily hired persons who were researchers and scholars and, after these positions were filled, hired those with practical experience. By the 1980s this trend made it likely that, 'professors of education in these schools [that emphasize research], if involved with future teachers at all, were more likely to be studying them than to be preparing them to teach' (Goodlad *et al.*, 1990, p.10). The movement away from practice created some tensions between schools of education and the educational community at large. More and more the interests of the professors were split from the interests of those working in the classroom. Specifically, academics were interested in achieving legitimacy and status within the university, which meant doing basic research and publishing in high-status journals, while teachers and others in the community were interested in improving schooling, understanding classroom life, and addressing the complex and messy business of trying to teach. Clearly, research can, and has, played a role in addressing some of these concerns. More often than not, however, research didn't find its way to the school level, wasn't related to the problems teachers and others were trying to address, was written exclusively for other academics, making it largely inaccessible, and blamed the teacher for school problems. Even those professors in the 1960s who linked politics and education saw teacher interests and those of radical professors as oppositional. As Clifford and Guthrie state, 'Teacher bashing was de rigueur among the new cadre of recruits to schools of education at Berkeley, Madison, or Cambridge' (Clifford and Guthrie, 1988, p.3).

While the tensions between research institutions and the educational community continue today, this break with practice and the emphasis on research has not enabled teaching to achieve the prestige, status, and material rewards associated with professionalism.[5] Instead, as Clifford points out, 'school administration and educational research were being made self conscious professions; teaching was not' (Clifford, 1986, p.434).

The designation of the university scholar as expert had a direct effect on teachers and the relation between schools of education and public schools. For if expertise was linked to the doing of research and an explicit separation from practice, then teachers who were intimately involved with practice, with little or no time to do research, surely were not expert. In this way, schools of education within universities were distinctly separated from public schools and the hierarchy between the two groups was strengthened. This hierarchy separated experts from non-experts and helped define role boundaries. Specifically, the emphasis on research in higher education helped establish a division of labor between those who did conceptual work and those who executed the ideas established by others. While teachers still find ways to do conceptual work, these actions often come at the expense of adding to their already busy day (Bullough *et al.*, 1984).

The hierarchy between schools of education and public schools also had material consequences for those groups working within these institutions. Academics, because they were considered expert, were able to gain privileges in terms of the intensity of their work. It was common in the normal school for instructors to teach up to twenty courses per week. Schools of education that firmly established themselves as research institutions, in contrast, often required professors to teach only two courses per week (Judd, 1929). This decrease in the teacher load only exaggerated the difference between schools of education and public school teachers whose intensified work structure was largely unchanged by the quest for professionalism.

The quest for professionalism also helped further differences in governance structures between the two institutions. Schools of education that had met the dominant 'standard for professionalism' by moving to a research orientation were able to initiate a system of peer governance. Fundamental questions of tenure, retention, and promotion were decided by colleagues. Teachers, on the other hand, worked in institutions where supervisors, principals, and district officials not only made tenure and retention decisions, but also influenced the curricular aims and practices found in the classroom. As was true of the teaching load, the quest for professionalism left the work structures of teachers largely unchanged, but had a dramatic influence on the work structures of schools of education. This influence, not only differentiated these institutions, but also put those who worked in schools of education in a hierarchical relation with teachers.[6]

In sum, the quest for professionalism has had a constraining influence on teachers. Not only have their intensified work conditions been maintained, but teachers' ability to claim to be expert has been severely limited. The current housing of schools of education in universities in the last half of this century represents a strengthening of opposing sets of interests between public schools and these institutions of higher education. It may not be much of an exaggeration to say that the privileges of academics are related to the need for continuing constraints on teachers in terms of their work conditions and role.

THE WOMEN QUESTION

The quest for professionalism is related to another struggle: the women question. Professionalism didn't simply constrain teachers, it also directly influenced women both in terms of the opportunities they had within the educational community and their ability to make claims of worth and expertise. What this suggests is that the research context serves not only the interests of those housed in the university, but also the interests of men in relation to women. The connection between professionalism and research, therefore, is not only about asserting a particular notion of legitimate knowledge, but also about furthering a set of distorted values about women. If the research context is to be altered in ways which allow for multiple notions of expertise, we must not only confront the institutionalized forms of professionalism that split the educational community, but also challenge the patriarchal values that underlie these notions of professionalism. To consider the link between professional and patriarchal values and relations, we begin at the time of the first normal schools, the mid nineteenth century.

The women question was very much on the minds of those who developed the normal school. As opposed to other institutions of higher education that would not admit women, the normal school let women in and in some cases restricted enrollment to women (Wright, 1965, p.27).[7] Allowing women into normal schools appears to have shaped notions of professionalism and influenced occupational specialization within the field. As mentioned previously, one of the competing notions of professionalism promoted by normal schools was that a professional was one who did his/her job regardless of the difficulties or possible distractions. Professionalism, therefore, was linked to a type of service that in many ways would encourage teachers to accept the constraints and problems associated with their work. Developing this compliant behavior was beneficial not only in terms of producing the needed teachers to fill the rapidly expanding common schools, but also in reinforcing the hierarchical relationship between men, who dominated the leadership positions, and women, who worked exclusively in the classrooms.

The men of the normal school were for the most part quite conscious of their position in relation to women and acted to reinforce their advantageous location in the educational hierarchy. One line of argument was that the normal school should have specialized tracks: a track for the classroom teacher and one for those who desired to hold administrative positions. Given that almost all administrative positions at this time were held by men, this specialization allowed men to distance themselves from women and the lack of respect given to the occupation of teaching.

> The sources of occupational specialization have yet to be fully explained, but a critical factor seems to have been the deeply felt need of careerist male educators to separate themselves as much as possible from classroom teaching. Teaching by and large was viewed as transient, unrewarding, unprofessional, and female. Separate organizations, journals, and university courses were demanded by former teachers seeking a better and more respectable career identity through specialized administrative positions.
>
> (Judd, 1929, p.880)

By fostering occupational specialization, men played a role in dividing the normal school population as well as strengthening their position at the top of the educational hierarchy. Their arguments also augmented a new line of attack for those who were critical of the normal schools' approach to professionalism: the 'problem' was the abilities and psychological make-up that women brought to the occupation. These attitudes persisted into the early twentieth century. Cubberly, the Dean of the School of Education at Stanford, for example, questioned the abilities of women by stating that:

> What teachers need more than anything else is a knowledge of democracies' needs and problems and of the conditions to be met. Our teaching force is composed largely of women and women are seldom interested by nature in this point of view.
>
> (Cubberly, 1909, pp.67–8)

Judd used much the same demeaning argument in laying out the problems of the normal school.

> Many of the graduates of American schools are immature girls who have had no contact with the great industrial machinery of modern life. They are ignorant of government in all except its most formal aspects. They may know there is a president in Washington who has a cabinet, but it is safe to venture the statement that not one-tenth of one percent of them know anything about the Bureau of Standards or about the markets information service of the department of agriculture.
>
> (Judd, 1929, p.880)

The 'inferior' psychological make-up of women was also a concern to those who were frustrated with the quest for professionalism in the early twentieth century. The Harper Commission, set up in 1898 to reform schooling and teacher education in Chicago, for example, introduced a proposal to differentiate salary based on sex, with men receiving the higher salaries. The commission inserted this recommendation because '[It] believed that male teachers were more adequate authority figures than the female teachers, with greater stamina and influence over boys. Obedience not merely sugar coated willfulness, is a needed part of every child's education for citizenship' (Wrigley, 1982, pp.94–6). The argument made to correct these 'deficits' was not to eliminate women from teaching (this was unthinkable given a rapidly increasing demand for teachers) but rather to alter the training of teachers by focusing on research of a scientific kind. Scientific research, therefore, was seen as a corrective to the perceived deficits and limitations that women brought to teaching. 'What we demand then is not rules, but principles not mere tricks or the art of sleight of hand, but science; science which explains and authenticates art; which makes men masters of their work, and not mere imitators and operatives' (Clifford, 1986, p.434).

The struggle for a scientific orientation to teacher education and its links to distorted views of women was not won easily by men and those championing the values of research. Courageous women working against all sorts of difficulties were able to raise questions about this orientation and achieve small victories that acknowledged the values and abilities teachers bring to teaching.

The Harper Commission, for example, with its proposals to differentiate salaries based on gender and utilize scientific research, was challenged by the Chicago Federation of Teachers (CFT), a teacher union founded in 1896. The president of the federation, Catherine Goggine, commented 'caustically on the absence of women members on the Harper Commission' (Wrigley, 1982, p.94). She was also aware, however, of how a scientific orientation was likely to exclude women from policy decisions. There is no clearer example of how scientific research acted to exclude women than the approach the Harper Commission took in seeking opinions on restructuring the normal school. 'While the commission had actively sought the opinions of educational experts from around the country, it had not bothered to solicit the opinions of the largely female teaching staff' (Wrigley, 1982, p.94). Margaret Haley, another leader in the CFT, also was critical of the new efficiency movement and its ties to scientific research. From her point of view, the problem wasn't simply the exclusion of women, but how scientific research would strengthen the hierarchy between the men who would do this type of research and the women working at the level of practice. In a 1904 address to the NEA, she argued that scientific research would:

> Increase the tendency toward factorizing education, making the teacher an automaton, a mere factory hand, whose duty it is to carry out mechanically and unquestionably the ideas and orders of those clothed with the authority of position, and who may or may not know the needs of the children or how to administer to them,
>
> (Haley, 1904, p.148)

The CFT also believed that its suspicions about the all-male Harper Commission had been justified, 'when the commission recommended that teachers be hired or retained on the basis of teaching efficiency, with the principal being the initial arbiter of each teacher's efficiency' (Wrigley, 1982, p.94). Professionalism was linked to patriarchy not only in terms of limiting women's access to decision making and their ability to claim to be expert, but also in terms of giving those in supervisory positions the power of science to bolster their authority.

The efforts of the CFT defeated the Harper Commission's recommendations. In addition, when Ella Flagg Young was appointed superintendent in 1909, the union lent support for teacher councils to assure teacher input in decision making. However, this small victory was short lived as proposals similar to the ones put forth by the Harper Commission came up again in 1917 as part of the Otis Bill. This time, however, an amendment was added to the proposals: the promise of tenure for teachers after three years. Given that sixty-eight teachers had just been fired for participating in union activities, teachers for the most part supported the new bill. Security came at the cost of limiting the decision making of teachers, as well as reinforcing their place on the lower rungs of the hierarchy (Wrigley, 1982, p.156).

Even Haley realized that a total separation from the new efficiency movement would limit teachers' ability to move up the education ladder and achieve better working conditions. As a consequence, she fashioned a strategy where the federation accepted the value of science, but insisted that the working conditions of teachers be altered so they could do this type of research and that teachers could decide when 'scientific teaching is possible and when and in what respects it is lacking' (Haley, 1904, p.150). Unfortunately, over time this strategy failed. Scientific research continued, as it does today, to gain legitimacy while the working conditions and authority of teachers remained largely unchanged.

Challenges to the normal school were based on both their practice emphasis and the inclusion of women in these institutions. To achieve professional status required not only a move away from practice toward scientific research, but also a move to differentiate the work of teachers, commonly seen as women's work, from the educational leadership positions held mostly by men.

The transition to schools of education within universities in many ways continued the patterns initiated in the teachers college: professionalism required a move toward research within established institutions and the need to contain women on the lower rungs of the educational hierarchy. Stanford, for example, established quotas for women undergraduates, Harvard limited women's involvement to elementary education, and the University of Chicago refused to admit graduates from teachers colleges (Clifford, 1986). In all these cases, the actions taken limited the access of women to prestigious institutions of higher education. While over time women did enter institutions of higher education in increasing numbers, there is some indication that this change did not so much signal a lessening of patriarchal relations, but rather the fact that universities had been overbuilt and women accounted for two-thirds of the high school graduates (Graham, 1978). Not surprisingly, therefore, increased access seemed to do little to change women's relation to men within the university setting. Women continued to be clustered in the intensified parts of occupations linked to practice, such as education and home economics, at the same time that the quest for professionalism was pushing for a closer linkage between expertise and research.

The establishment of Teachers College in 1887 at Columbia illuminates the connection between this quest for professionalism and patriarchal values. Those who helped develop this institution were interested in distinguishing this college from the normal school and building an institution worthy of university status (Whittemore, 1965). To do so they required either graduation from the normal school or competence in typical school subject areas as criteria for admissions (Whittemore, 1965, p.510). Teachers College would also stress educational theory and research. These emphases encouraged some to remark that, 'the College was emerging as an institution comparable in almost every respect with the existing professional schools of Columbia University' (Whittemore, 1965, p.511).

The stress on theory, research, and a differentiation from the normal school traditions indicates that Teachers College followed the assumptions of the dominant orientation to professionalism. The women question, however, created a dilemma for the founders of the institution. On one hand, association with Columbia brought status, on the other, there was considerable sentiment among the central administration at Columbia that women should not be allowed into the university. The opposition to women at this 'elite' institution was initially so strong that when the proposal to establish Teachers College was received by the Columbia Board of Trustees in 1886, they rejected it primarily on the grounds that women would be roaming the halls of Columbia.

[T]he trustees, suspicious of all new schemes, were doubly suspicious of a plan that promised to cost money and that would inevitably be co-educational. The specter of women in Columbia's celibate halls proved so unsettling that the board even rejected Butler's modest proposal for a regular course in the principles of education.

(Whittemore, 1965, p.509)

Professionalism, in terms of emulating university life, went hand in hand with deeply held patriarchal values about the proper place for women within educational institutions. To resolve this dilemma the founders of Teachers College put together a proposal where women would be separated from men when taking liberal education courses.

This separation between men and women continues today in several ways. First, women were (and still are) the ones primarily working in the school classrooms, while men dominated the positions in teacher training institutions; and second, women were by and large confined to the lower-status institutions, the normal schools, and teachers colleges. As these lower-status institutions started to disappear and women gained access to the university, the separation has not only continued between higher education and public institutions, but has also persisted within schools of education. For example, in a western university that has over the last decade made an explicit attempt to move into a research orientation, the foundations division, with closest ties to the liberal arts orientation, has seven men and two women. The secondary division, that maintains some contact with other departments, has three men and three women. The elementary division, which is for the most part self-contained, given that students can major in this area, has thirteen women and four men, and the clinical faculty, who have increased coursework and more field responsibilities than any of the other groups, are all women. While far from conclusive, this distribution of men and women suggests that as the ties to practice become greater and the connections to research lessen, women appear in ever greater numbers. The problem with this separation is that in a patriarchal society, the association of practical knowledge and women has led to women's subordination within the educational community. Schools of education have clearly gained status, authority, and resources with a move to a research orientation, but women's relation to men within these schools and between the university and the world of classroom practice has remained largely unchanged. Women, in increasing numbers, have moved up the educational hierarchy. As a group, however, their roles have been constrained in ways which run counter to the direction fostered by the dominant approach to professionalism.

The shift to schools of education within universities more or less continued this trend of dealing with the women question and the quest for professionalism; education schools moved to research, and a theoretical orientation. Women were formally and informally separated from men. Furthermore, their role in educational decision making was also limited (Clifford, 1986).

This is not to say that women have passively accepted these separations and constraints on their role. In addition to the types of challenges posed by the CFT in the early twentieth century, there have been more recent attempts within a university setting to contest the link between the women question and professionalism. One of the most powerful actors in this regard is Corrine Seeds, an educator at University of California at Los Angeles and a strong proponent of the lab school.

As was true of many schools of education within universities that were trying to gain status, the move to a strong research orientation was far from easy. One difficulty that many of these schools faced was that there were visible signs on campus that tied the school of education not only to the world of practice, but also to the traditions of the less prestigious teachers college and normal school. The lab school was for many such a 'problem.' The University of California at Los Angeles, for example, had a prominent lab school, the University Elementary School (UES), which was established on the campus in 1945. Even though this school had a good reputation in terms of the education offered young people, there was a move by UCLA administrators to close the school. On one level, those trying to close the school saw the UES as taking resources away from the research orientation encouraged by the university administration (Clifford and Guthrie, 1988). On another level, however, there was also concern about the women question. Because 'women had been losing their places in school administration since the second or third decade of the [twentieth century]' the UES represented a place where women held not only positions on a university campus, but also administrative positions within the school. Having women in these positions forced men in the schools of education to interact with these women, and more than a few were thought to be 'uncomfortable in dealing with women' (Clifford and Guthrie, 1988, p.266).

The UES, therefore, brought together the quest for professionalism and the women question. The connections between professionalism and patriarchy were apparent to Seeds. She argued strongly that the practical was a legitimate form of knowledge and that researchers would do well to pay closer attention to the wisdom of the UES teachers. When the conference on 'Education for the Post-War' sent none of the participants to the UES, Seeds declared that the 'UES had much to offer to the vitality and reality of the discussion' (Clifford and Guthrie, 1988, p.274). She also was aware of potential limits on the teacher role if research was colonized at the university level. To challenge these potential limits she suggested that work structures be changed to enable teachers to 'engage in action research and living experimentation' (Clifford and Guthrie, 1988, p.275). While Seeds and others successfully fought for the survival of the school, the university was able to impose a research orientation that would reinforce the school's dependence on the university and women's dependence on researchers who were mostly men. 'They [academics] proposed that the [UES] staff conduct objective evaluation of various forms of curriculum and method using control groups and systematic evaluation in place of the exploration and innovation by creative master teachers' (Clifford and Guthrie, 1988, p.275). Along with these measures, student teaching was limited to one day a week, a core curriculum was imposed on the school, and UES teachers were required to work on advanced degrees (Clifford and Guthrie, 1988). In all these instances a move away from practice, part of the quest for professionalism, reinforced women's position on the lower rungs of the educational hierarchy.

Ironically the continued existence of the UES worked in the favor of UCLA. They could claim, as the president of the university did in 1930, that 'research gives a university its real reason for existence' (Clifford and Guthrie, 1988, p.272) while also maintaining that they cared about practice. At the same time, they continued to assert the superiority of research over practice and keep the almost exclusive women staff of the UES under the guidance of an established core curriculum and the objective findings of their scientific evaluation schemes.

While women challenged the move to a research orientation, the quest for professionalism reinforced patriarchal relations by limiting women's access to institutions of higher education, separating them from men within these institutions when they gained access, and clustering them close to the world of practice. Because research was an integral part of the quest for professionalism, part of the foundation for this process was built on a debunking of practical knowledge. The institutions of higher education that moved to a research orientation and their relation to public schools therefore were structured not only by the quest for professionalism, but also by the quest to differentiate men from women such that men could effectively make claims about their authority and expertise in relation to women.

This historical sketch suggests that power struggles over the quest for professionalism and the women question have helped establish the current relationship between schools of education and public schools. By moving in the direction of research, academics housed in institutions of higher education have been able to gain privileges in terms of working conditions, claims of expertise, and educational decision making. Those working in schools, on the other hand, have limited access to decision making, are less able to make claims about expertise, and continue to work within intensified work structures. These institutional relations also reflect patriarchal values in at least two ways. First, women are grouped primarily at the school level or in a hierarchical relation within a school of education and, second, notions of expertise are narrowly construed ignoring such important foundations of knowledge as practical experience.

The question of Educative Research, therefore, cannot be adequately addressed simply by giving teachers an opportunity to do research or by entering into collaborative relations. Both proposals ignore differences in working conditions for teachers and academics, and the narrow view of expertise that research represents. While it is important for teachers to do research and for university researchers to collaborate with practitioners, these efforts must go hand in hand with structural changes that alter the work conditions of teachers and expand views of legitimate knowledge. If the central aim of Educative Research is to foster voice as a form of protest, then this cannot be done while institutional structures and taken-for-granted beliefs separate those who work within these institutions in hierarchical ways.

The question of Educative Research also cannot be focused totally on the contestation of oppressive formations. Simply directing the research process in this way ignores the limiting features built into the dominant research context. Even if research moves away from quantitative methods and is openly ideological in its orientation, for example, it is still the case that research acts to deny women legitimate claims of expertise and strengthens hierarchical divisions between men and women. Not only must the aims of research become more political, but the research process must be made problematic to allow competing notions of expertise to gain a fair hearing.

It is time to challenge the ever widening schism between schools of education and public schools that not only tears at our educational community, but also constrains and oppresses teachers, and women in particular. To do so, working conditions must be altered such that academics and practitioners can both spend time in classrooms and do research. Along with systematic research processes, ways must also be found to value the practical so that the knowledge teachers and others have gained through experience is seen as valuable. Within this altered context, it is possible to see how alternative methods could produce knowledge that challenges constrained and narrow features of schooling without recreating an oppressive situation among the research participants.

Part II

Case studies in Educative Research

6 Out of the silence: developing teacher voice

The struggle between silence and voice has been lifelong for me. The ramifications of swinging back and forth between the act of speaking out and reticence are markers along a path that defines who I am. Society told me to be seen and not heard, like some naughty child, while an inside whisper begged for a listening ear. It was within this state of fluctuation that I began a journey into further study of the educational system. This chapter is about my chosen project of developing teacher voice, but more than this, it is about my own travels in this previously uncharted terrain; to speak and to be heard.

When asked to write my personal history, as part of the ERP, I could not imagine any obvious benefit, never mind any connection to my life as a teacher. I wrote mostly of my educational history, unconsciously dismissing the importance of my personal beliefs and experiences. Reflecting on this omission, I began to realize that one's voice is silenced by self-regulation, as much as when no one will listen. Throughout my life I have learned to be silent. As the oldest child in my family, I had the good fortune of being listened to more than my siblings. Nevertheless, I was taught by my family and teachers that there were times I must not talk. As I accepted what my family expected of me, the learning process toward self-censorship had begun.

In many ways, the men with which I have had contact furthered this process of self-censorship. On occasion, a man has asked what I thought about something, but I soon discovered that it was often used as an introduction to his own expression and not out of real interest in mine. This confirmed observations I had of my parents' conversations when their friends visited. When men and women were together, they carried on separate conversations, or the topic was dominated by male opinion. While dating, I modeled what I witnessed as my mother's behavior, feigning interest in sports and avoiding the development of opinion. When my frustration with this pretense became intolerable, I began talking and watching for an authentic listener. I found none among the men I currently knew, and gave up dating in bitterness. Soon, I resigned myself to the seeming inevitability of my role in society, returning to what appeared to be a normal social life, while holding onto my secret cache of silent rage.

When I entered teaching, little did I realize how suited to silence was my occupational choice. My mother promoted it as the 'ideal woman's profession.' It wasn't until much later that I discovered that teachers have historically held a passive voice in the whirlwind of educational research and theory. This passivity, in my case, was often coupled with strategies to falsify my behavior to please others. As I note in my personal history:

> My 'falsifying' or 'cheating' took on three main behaviors, recognizable even in my personal relationships. These are described by Jackson as common to most schools' implicit curriculum. ' ... (1) to behave in such a way as to enhance the likelihood of praise and reduce the likelihood of punishment . . . (2) publicize positive evaluations and conceal negative ones . . . (3) behave in ways that disguise the failure to comply.
>
> (Jackson, 1968, p.26)

These lessons were so well learned, that I didn't realize I was participating in them until the moment I stopped. I am still living the imprint of these lessons as I cope with the balancing act of being as others wish me to be and gaining an acceptance of self.

Professionally, I face this quandary each time my principal enters my classroom to do a teaching evaluation. The dilemma is one of accepting the common sense notion that a good classroom is a quiet one versus my belief in the importance of voice. This conflict is reflected in the following example from my personal history:

> My classroom is noisy. I can't seem to keep it quiet. Perhaps I don't care enough for the value of silence to really work on it. I also haven't found a method to reinforce quiet behavior that isn't offensive to me. I don't want my class to refrain from interacting. I am embarrassed, though, and would feel more comfortable if I could have a quieter class, if only to please the principal and the parents who volunteer in my room. Some people have a hard time seeing that I am a good teacher and my students, good students, because of the noise.

Through direct and indirect ways I have been dealing with the issue of voice and silence in myself and others for many years.

The writing of my school history furthered my understanding of voice and silence by pointing to the way school structures silence teachers. Within the first paragraph of my analysis, for example, I noted how decisions about the architecture of the classroom had silenced my beliefs about education.

> I am assigned to a small, inner room on the second floor. I have two large windows that look out into the hallway, and four frosted skylights. I have plants at the windows that have some access to sunlight from an outside window in the hallway. I recently learned that the district intends to replace my windows with bulletin boards, thus completely cutting me off from any outside view. This will be accomplished without consideration for my wishes and, in fact, will be done in the face of my strong feelings against it. The rationale for this is the windows are against the fire code. Having no windows is against the humanity code as far as I'm concerned.

I also found that the mandated curriculum used at the school played a role in silencing my educational beliefs and aims.

> These curriculum structures allow for efficient and measurable evaluation, but they treat teaching as a science, while promoting one method of teaching and only one orientation. Teaching is an art. As in other artistic fields, the human factor is all important. What is the classroom atmosphere like? How can you measure a teacher's interest in and relationship with the students? If this standard of evaluation were applied to determining great art, it would proclaim all paintings as priceless if they include the colors red, yellow and blue, and have everything the right size and shape. Where would Picasso fit in this evaluation?

Finally, my analysis of a teacher survey, conducted as part of my school history, suggested that required texts also act to silence teachers.

> There is so much already determined by the state core and the district, that many of us limit our involvement to how and in what order the material will be presented. Some don't even do that. This causes one to suspect that teachers have almost completely withdrawn from the professional aspects of curriculum planning and development. But not without hard feelings.

Much of my growing awareness about educational voice and silence was also enhanced when I explored a vast array of literature as part of the ERP. These readings, including the works of Sarason (1971) and Jackson (1968), released me from the guilt of what I could not change, and gave me permission to change all I could. I gained confidence in my teaching. I began to speak out and not hide behind my 'closed classroom door.' This signified a major shift in my relation to the system. I had learned to conceal what I was doing to survive in teaching. Now, I recognized how my own hidden curriculum was perpetuating a profession of silent subversion: a political act that continued the hierarchy and status quo. I realized that I had been a guard in a prison of my own making.

This growing awareness and my newly found confidence encouraged me to speak out on educational issues. I began to lose my fear and shame about my inadequacies as a teacher. I could now face and admit the almost universal difficulty teachers face, as outlined by Sarason:

> The professional [dilemma] . . . stems from the knowledge that the teacher is unable to do justice to each child in the classroom. . . . The personal dilemma, which stems in part from the professional one, consists of the need to adjust in some non-disabling or disorganizing way to the personal consequences of the professional dilemma and, in addition, to cope with the equally upsetting realization that part of the problem resides in the teacher's inadequacies in knowledge, understanding, and technique.
>
> (Sarason, 1971, p.155)

I also realized that my fears, inadequacies, and lack of voice as a teacher were shared and understood not only by the teachers in my school, but by a wider audience than I would have ever guessed.

Horizontal Evaluation furthered my desire to understand the issue of voice and silence by providing the first glimpse of what could be done to confront my silence and the silence of teachers generally. I found that when I used this dialogical process, I was increasingly willing to examine and change my old teaching patterns. I also found that others would listen to what I had to say. The benefits of this form of evaluation were numerous, as I note in one of my Horizontal Evaluation conferences.

> The benefits are spreading as I develop a stronger voice about my values with regard to school issues. Newly found confidence in my teaching and its underlying values enables me to express my views to colleagues, parents, administrators, and the school board. I have found I have more to say at our faculty meetings. I'm more willing to risk exposing my opinions about our school structures and issues. This benefit has come directly from Horizontal Evaluation as I reflect on my values and express them in the clearest terms to Kathy, my partner-teacher.

It was for these reasons that I decided to reach out to my peers, through dialogue, to share in this adventure of the development of teacher voice.

THE INITIAL DEVELOPMENT OF A QUESTION

As I participated in each of these aspects of the ERP, a common theme began to emerge: teachers, in general, do not have a voice in educational reform. Further investigation led to the realization that school structures, such as teacher isolation, job intensification, and the schedule of the teaching day, as well as the historical feminization of teaching contributed to this result.

The simple act of talking about these issues began to change my professional life. I was beginning to gain a sense of empowerment that coincided with Gore's view as she examined what the over-used and popular term could mean:

> [A] major shortcoming of construction of empowerment in critical and feminist pedagogy discourses is that they conceive of power as property . . . [and] to em-power suggests that power can be given, provided, controlled, held, conferred, taken away . . . . Rather than conceiving of power as a possession or a commodity, a thing to be held or exchanged, Foucault (1980) argued instead that power is 'exercised, and . . . only exists in action.'
>
> (Gore, 1989, p.5)

The empowerment for which I so longed in my profession and my life was within me. That is not to say there were and are no structural barriers, but as I addressed the self-imposed restrictions, the other barriers were more clearly defined and understood.

These changes in my perception of the teacher role caused me to look at how others could also benefit from dialogue. A recurrent question began to appear in my thoughts and writing. How might our school, or even our profession, change if discussion and reflection were made available and encouraged in a wider audience of teachers? As this possibility was discussed at length with Kathy, my Horizontal Evaluation partner, I began to look for a way to answer that question.

One direction that held some promise in this regard was the establishing of a consistent block of time for dialogue with peers about the educational issues with which they were concerned. If such time was made available, thought, research, and further exploration by teachers could expand into a willingness to express ideas in a wider forum. Thus, a breaking down of the traditional barriers of silence could ensue. My own willingness to speak grew as my trust of Kathy was strengthened. If more teachers gathered to discuss educational concerns, couldn't trust develop among them and confidence be gained, thereby leading to an articulation and examination of values and beliefs previously suppressed? Somehow, I felt that the development of teacher voice was a key to membership in the historically exclusive club of educational decision making. Without a firm concept of what exactly I wanted teachers to express, change or become empowered to do, I leaped into my research. All I knew with any certainty was that I wanted us to start talking to each other.

With this rather vague framework in mind, I looked for a way to have other teachers at my school begin a dialogue. I was warned by several people that this could become an exercise in futility, with teachers merely using the dialogue forum as a gripe session. While I wasn't sure that allowing teachers to gripe was all bad (as a peer pointed out, some might call this 'problem-posing' if mentioned in reference to, say, businessmen), I did hope for a more substantive interaction and began to search for a method of reflection that might serve that purpose. Although I read of many formats for reflective dialogue, I had a great deal of trouble focusing on one and implementing it in the dialogue sessions. I finally centered on the basic tenets used in Horizontal Evaluation simply because they were most familiar to me, and I had found personal growth in their use.

There is no doubt that I entered this project with a great deal of conviction about the importance of teacher voice – my own and that of others. I saw it as one possible avenue toward the restructuring of the educational hierarchy, of making some impact on the invisibility and silence that Thorne (1984) argues is an inherent part of a gendered profession. As a previous member of this silent majority, having seen the adverse effects of continuing voicelessness, I yearned for new ways of making myself visible and heard, while bringing with me a chorus of other teachers.

THE STUDY

Toward this end, I decided to: 1) determine teachers' attitudes about professional dialogue, defined as 'a discussion among two or more colleagues about issues related to the profession'[8] (see Appendix A), 2) organize a method for the development of teacher voice through dialogue, and 3) evaluate and analyze the dialogue sessions to better understand their import. Results of the teacher attitude survey were analyzed in combination with the themes and patterns found consistently within the teacher dialogue sessions.

Participation in the teacher dialogue sessions was voluntary to anyone on the faculty. Of the fourteen that came most regularly, ten were in self-contained, 'regular' classrooms, three in special education, and one in a gifted and talented classroom. Although three men were on the faculty, none attended regularly, but each did attend at least one session. Eventually, during the second phase of this study (the 1989–90 school year), a 'core group' of seven teachers developed from this cluster, all regular classroom teachers, and all women.

During the week following each of the first four teacher discussion sessions, and twice during the 1989–90 school year, Kathy and I met to review and compare notes. This comprised a second area of data collection. Horizontal Evaluation was used to compare the intentions of the meetings with the realities of what actually transpired. My assumptions about the meetings were explored, as were possibilities for the next meeting. Transcripts of my dialogue with Kathy provided an additional text to determine how the process was influencing each dialogue session.

As I describe my two-year study, I start with the question of professional dialogue and consider how this concern changed over time. I then discuss the recurrent themes found in the survey (teacher interest, perceived administrative support, and constraints on dialogue). Reflection on the meetings, possibilities for change among the participants, and future directions will follow.

Revisiting the question

When I began this project, I assumed everyone knew what I meant by dialogue. As a consequence, within the survey I defined it simply as 'a discussion among two or more colleagues about issues of, related to, or suitable to the profession', as found in *Webster's Dictionary*. Although I had started to rethink the notion of dialogue in a more specific, formalized way with regard to educational practice and theory, it was still relatively undeveloped. However, I felt this definition would be specific enough for the survey. As a teacher, I had not participated in any but the most informal discussions about educational issues, mostly revolving around my own classroom and school complaints. Rarely can I remember discussing educational aims, or the values underlying any choice of curriculum or methodology before my involvement in the ERP. Nias (1989) categorized typical teacher discussion as:

> So, in these staffrooms, educational theory, long-term plans, discussions about basic purposes and underlying assumptions are virtually absent features of teacher talk. Sharing is confined instead to stories, tips and news – to things that will not intrude upon or challenge the autonomous judgment of the classroom-isolated teacher.
>
> (cited in Hargreaves, 1990, pp.7–8)

While I tend to agree with Hargreaves and Nias, I feel that the inability of teachers to influence larger educational decisions also contributes to their tendency to focus on topics of immediate concern.

At this point in time, I did look upon a more formal dialogue about broader educational issues as preferable to the common presentist talk of teachers. I have, however, since rediscovered the value inherent in informal conversations among teachers. Between dialogue sessions, teachers were *informally* talking to each other about our *formal* discussions. I, also, was carrying on conversations that influenced future sessions, faculty meetings and teacher relationships. These encounters helped me accept and respect teachers' more typical talk, in both their informalized nature and topics. These informal discussions were a foundation for teachers to break through their isolation and build confidence. It was only where trust and openness were encouraged that a more formal sense of dialogue took place. Since the more common, informal talk of teachers provides a starting point for more formal dialogue, any combination of the two was acceptable for the purposes of the survey. With this developing sense of dialogue in mind, I turned my attention to the question of why, as a group, teachers' voice is not heard.

In search of an audience

The most important things are the hardest things to say. . . . [Y]ou may make revelations that cost you dearly only to have people look at you in a funny way, not understanding what you've said at all, or why you thought it was so important that you almost cried while you were saying it. That's the worst, I think. When the secret stays locked within not for want of a teller, but for want of an understanding ear.

(King, 1982, p.289)

It appears that silence and its seeming flip side of talking has a lot to do with the question of audience. At times, silence can be more a lack of acceptable voice, than an absence of voice. Teachers do discuss educational issues, but these issues tend to be skewed toward classroom concerns (what to do about Suzy's behavior, how to deal with yet another district mandate, etc.). Teachers' tendency to focus on these sorts of issues has much to do with the expectation that no one of importance will listen or consider their views. They have grown to anticipate the continuance of school structures and mandates, instigated without their input and often in the face of their objections. The challenge for teachers, as well as other silenced groups such as black women, is not to 'emerge from silence to speech, but to change the nature and direction of our speech. To make a speech that compels listeners, one that is heard,' (Hooks, as quoted in Ellsworth, 1989, p.313). There is much that people traditionally silenced share and the shift of voice to 'one that is heard' is exactly what teachers must do if we hope to have an impact on current educational structures, theories, and aims.

One way to move the dialogue from futile griping to one that 'compels listeners' might be to incorporate research as a way to cultivate ourselves and validate our views. I found a growing audience as I learned to cite research to support expressions. Surprisingly, I discovered a maturing acceptance of my expertise as a practitioner through reading the works of those considered educational experts.

Teachers typically have very little awareness or access to current research which could contribute to teacher dialogue. While recognizing the value of practical knowledge, my own as well as others', I have grown to accept and respect the place research can hold in informing practice. If research is to be made more available to classroom teachers, the assumptions of the process need to be examined. Research cannot be accepted as 'truth,' but rather as a focus for discussion and comparison to the practical concerns of teachers. Although I have been hesitant to read journals that continuously blame the classroom teacher for our educational ills while promoting strategies that are out of touch with the realities of class size, minimal pay, and intensified scheduling, I have also seen how this absence of outside input has limited the expression of my educational views, thus contributing to my frustration and aura of silence. As I wrote in my *First Look* paper:

> Our professional hegemony currently promotes the image that teachers are uninformed and unable to make knowledgeable decisions about their own classrooms. In many ways, we are unaware of current research. When the district asks us for input, we moan about the extra time needed to respond to their request, and then give our feelings about the topic. Without the benefit of research to back us up, we then accept whatever the district is pushing knowing that when we close our doors, we still have the final say in what we teach.

This lack of research-informed dialogue that has contributed to the inhibition of teacher decision making. Teachers perceive themselves as having little of import to say, subconsciously believing in their subordinate role to those considered expert. Practicing dialogue with the inclusion of research could be a beginning step toward voices that will be heard. As research literacy has proven to be so important to the growth I have experienced over the past two years, it seems crucial that this gap between researchers and teachers be bridged. These barriers must be addressed by people on both sides of this chasm. Perhaps one path that holds some promise is in the growing trend, of which the ERP is a part, for teachers to do their own research.

A vital connection in this access to research is time to share this material among peers, whether such discussion entails their own or others' research. An important aspect of my own development was the opportunity to discuss research and educational theory with others as I discovered how it applied to my classroom and teaching. This was effective in bridging barriers of resentment or questions of relevancy that I carried about researchers and my perception of their distance from reality and me, a practitioner. Again, dialogue proved to be an important link between research and the reality of my classroom. With these developing assumptions regarding the cultivation of an audience shaping my perspective, I turned to the analysis of the results of my survey and the recurrent themes that I found.

The survey's findings

The survey addressed three major areas of concern in relation to dialogue: teacher interest, administrative support as seen from the teachers' point of view, and constraints on teacher dialogue. Each area has been expanded and informed by an examination of the dialogue sessions themselves.

Interest in professional dialogue

Teachers indicated in the survey that they sought out dialogue at least once a week. However, many (fourteen out of twenty-one) indicated the need for more time. For example, one teacher expressed, 'Stolen moments leave a lot of discussions without closure.' The six teachers that stated they did not feel more time was needed for professional dialogue commented on ways they fill the need themselves, often on their own time, further verifying a desire for discussion.

If dialogue was organized outside of the regular, salaried schedule, a majority of teachers (fourteen) indicated they would be interested in attending such meetings. The view of these teachers was clearly summarized by one who stated, 'It's important enough to me. I need the professional stimulation.' Six teachers said they would not attend, and many had comments about why, most of which involved adding another time commitment to their teaching. One particularly revealing comment was, 'I am not compensated for my work as a professional at this time and don't expect to be in the near future. It is difficult for me to justify working extra time when I am not adequately paid for the time I am working.'

When asked if they would attend a scheduled time for dialogue within the regular school hours, twenty teachers said they would. Of the comments given on this question, four observed that having that time would tend to make them feel like they were being treated as professionals. One expressed the stipulation that teachers 'are deciding and running it.' The single teacher that said she would not attend expressed this reasoning, 'I basically do what I want with or without discussion.'

These results seemed to confirm what I had believed from the inception of my project: that the teachers' level of involvement in the discussion of educational issues would deepen if they were given the opportunity, and that the basic reasons they discussed only immediate, technical concerns are a lack of time and encouragement. I soon came to realize, through further experience and research, that there is more to this inhibition of dialogue than time.

The range of benefits cited as gained through dialogue included sharing ideas, expansion of knowledge base, and easing teacher isolation. One teacher added, 'to incorporate thoughtfulness into rote academia.' Another stated, 'in an effort to better serve students and grow as professionals, dialogue time is not only needed, it is vital to our role as professionals.' Finally, a teacher summarized:

> A more holistic approach to teacher awareness and reflection should be pursued. We, as educators, get caught in the web of trivial issues and are sometimes unable to make our way into the integration of academia and student education. Perhaps professional dialogue – when it isn't a vehicle for complaints about salary and work-overload, is the answer.

In the determination of how productive current professional dialogue is, on a scale from very productive to not very productive, only four felt it very productive. From this, it would seem that most teachers felt their discussions could be improved. Certainly being participants in discussions whose results are questionable or less than satisfying, as in the case of the usual faculty meetings or those stolen moments at recess, could affect the interest in and amount of dialogue pursued. I held out the hope that perhaps the introduction of a more formalized forum could help focus and deepen discussions leading to greater satisfaction. It was my belief that this could help 'incorporate thoughtfulness into rote academia,' as one teacher wished. I thought I had the answer to the needs identified by these teachers. In many ways, I was developing an answer to questions that other teachers had yet to ask. With this eager attitude, I was falling nicely into the traditional role of researcher: I had answers to my own questions. I only needed teachers to verify them for me. Fortunately, the format of dialogue helped me recognize my place in this traditional trap and rethink my role in time for the teachers involved to formulate their own questions and answers.

From the survey's twenty-one responses, it can be generalized that most teachers at this school have sought out, participated in and would like more dialogue, even though time and lack of result were listed as large concerns. Dialogue was perceived to be productive and beneficial. All but one teacher stated they would attend meetings designed to promote dialogue if scheduled within the regular school day, which could begin to address the professional needs that teacher isolation breeds or ignores. These positive results gave me the encouragement I needed to proceed with my project. I was ready to joust with windmills in the face of structural barriers, questions of power, and conflicting teacher priorities. With the armor of teacher interest securely in place, I turned to the issue of administrative support, as viewed by teachers.

Administrative support

The majority of teachers (fifteen) responded negatively to questions regarding administrative support, listing examples that gave credence to their perceptions. Comments addressed a range of topics from the fact that salaried time was not allotted to teachers for collegial exchange, to the observation that when time was provided, the discussion had to be on the administration's own terms. The discussion usually allowed, found in faculty meetings and specified areas of teacher training, was defined as 'controlled' by one teacher, who summarized the process as, 'outcome before dialogue.' Another teacher went so far as to say the district was not supportive of dialogue because lack of support is a way to 'divide and conquer.' Six teachers felt the administration to be supportive of dialogue.

The responses to the survey indicate an awareness that whether or not the administration supports dialogue, there is little or no time provided for it during the regular school schedule. Faculty meetings are not seen as a good time for dialogue where the agenda is determined solely by and for the administration. When dialogue is allowed during other salaried time, say during career ladder days (scheduled, optional time for teachers to work at school while students are not there), it is again 'controlled' in content, and one teacher felt the outcome was pre-determined. If teachers are to gather for dialogue, in which the content is determined and controlled by teachers, it has to be on their own time, and in addition to meetings administratively scheduled.

Before time will be allowed within the current school system for teachers to gather for dialogue, administrators will need to be awakened to the values inherent in this type of forum. At present, it seems the creation of methods to arrange schedules or manipulate the current system is dependent on that awareness.

Constraints on dialogue

The ramifications of this lack of administrative support compounds the structural constraints to dialogue inherent in the educational system. One predominant concern of the surveyed teachers was that of time. Many expressed concern about the time constraints under which they had to work. Even those teachers that stated interest in and commitment to attending dialogue sessions outside regular school hours qualified their answers with disclaimers about subject matter and time limitations. Other scheduled responsibilities had to be taken into consideration at the expense of dialogue.

There were several expressions of anger about how much extra time is expected to be donated by classroom teachers. It is becoming a matter of principle to refuse gratis time, especially when considering minimal monetary compensation. If professional dialogue is arranged outside of salaried time, it is perceived as another contribution of time and energy to be given freely for the benefit of teaching. Personal lives suffer when professional concerns overwhelm teachers' available resources. Protection of that time and energy becomes vital. Hence, scheduling for dialogue becomes almost impossible.

As this project developed, I began to see time as my biggest obstacle. No matter when the dialogue sessions were scheduled, conflicts arose. I believed if time could be officially allotted, my problems in establishing dialogue with my peers would be solved. I found much support for this belief in my readings. Traditionally, teachers' work has been defined solely in terms of student contact. Time away from students to plan or discuss educational concerns has been scarce. Hargreaves furthered my understanding of time by arguing that it was directly tied to power relations, (Hargreaves, 1990, p.6). I realized that the younger the students you teach, the more your time is co-opted. High school teachers receive more planning time than elementary school teachers, and university professors, even those in colleges of education, are allocated much more time than those in elementary and secondary schools. Administrators in our district schedule their weekly meetings during school hours and think nothing amiss in their expectations that principals attend. Notions of gender and power relations are implicated in this uneven distribution, since most elementary school teachers are women, while men are most often found in teaching situations in the secondary schools, university levels, and administration. This realization fueled my anger and frustration at the lack of time for my dialogue sessions.

In my continued search for solutions to this time dilemma, I looked to possible structural changes. What I found within the literature confirmed my own experiences that when teachers are given more time, it is taken away through administratively-regulated agendas. This forebodes another consideration that if teachers were given time for dialogue and the development of collegiality, it would most likely be hierarchically mandated in topic and result. In my readings I found this 'growing administrative colonization of teachers' time and space' (Hargreaves, 1989, p.29) to be more wide-spread than just my district. Teachers not only need more non-contact time for dialogue, but they must be allowed to determine how that time is used. They also must be given something substantive to discuss. In the traditional approach to the common time filler, continued specified teacher training, the administration commonly determines the educational needs. All that is left to do is train the teachers in the previously chosen solution. My whole project is based on the belief that teachers have something to say about educational issues on all levels of decision making. I have since come to see that a necessary step in gaining administrative acceptance for the allowance of time for teacher-generated dialogue would involve a campaign to convince those in power that it can be a benefit for education.

As my understanding of the issue of time grew, I began to recognize another factor that complicated the question. In addition to the absence of time for teachers to engage in dialogue, the question of how important this process is in relation to other teaching responsibilities becomes a central concern. When I was first asked by the instructor of the ERP to get together with a peer to discuss educational issues, I was willing to do so because it was required, not because I felt a burning desire to enter into such an arrangement. It wasn't until well into the process that I began to see the import of what we were doing. I naively expected my peers to make a similar leap in the redefinition of their role without the same motivation. The traditional training of teachers includes the perception that their domain of influence is solely concerned with practical issues. The determination of educational aims is left for experts. If that is the case, why waste limited time on dialogue that is outside the range of traditional concerns? Part of the difficulty I faced and continue to address is this constructed role boundary.

Along with this limit, another major obstacle to promoting dialogue is the dichotomy of teacher isolation/autonomy. This double-edged sword is seen as the last refuge of teacher control and there is great reluctance to surrender it for the uncertain results of professional exchange (Goodlad and Klein, 1974; Tye and Tye, 1984; Freedman *et al.*, 1986). As Flinders (1988) notes, isolation is often used as an adaptive strategy, to protect time and energy for the more immediate demands of instruction. As a result, teachers may be reluctant to give up isolation for the potential benefits of dialogue.

This preference must be seen in the context of the pressures and demands of a complex occupation. If some of the other pressures of teaching are not relieved, dialogue will rarely appear at the top of a teacher's list of priorities.

Until these multiple constraints are addressed, along with the lack of administrative support, there will be limits on the quality and quantity of dialogue available and pursued. Given the system as it is, along with teachers' growing protection of their personal time, supporting and sustaining dialogue will be difficult. The current structures of the educational system do not allow for regularly scheduled sessions; therefore, few teachers or administrators are aware of the advantages to be gained from it. Teachers are reluctant to add one more item to a growing list of demands on their time outside contract hours. Faculty meetings are currently reserved for the administration's agenda, excluding this as a place for teacher-generated dialogue. These constraints have had definite effects on the actual sessions promoted through this study.

Reflections on the dialogue sessions

When I discussed the first teacher dialogue session with Kathy, I found my intentions were too numerous and expansive for the one hour time block. The topic was 'Teacher Isolation.' Teachers were eager to talk to each other, but my agenda got in the way. Fortunately, I could read this during the session, and adjusted my agenda accordingly. The meeting was scheduled during a career ladder day and twenty-five teachers attended. Some objected to my request to audio-tape the session, even though I assured them I would be the only person who would hear it, and it would be used only for the purposes of my research. Promises of anonymity were rejected, so we went on to the topic at hand. One teacher expressed the idea that if teachers felt isolated, they should come earlier in the morning and walk the halls talking to other teachers. It seemed necessary to define teacher isolation more clearly at this point. In fact, this took up the majority of the time, since inherent in the definition is the issue of autonomy, as well as other factors that make isolation a problem. Although many people participated, it was hard to give everyone a chance to voice their views, let alone begin to generate solutions. Breaking into smaller groups would have helped facilitate discussion and increase individual participation. Nevertheless, several teachers continued animated conversation after the meeting had ended. One teacher enthusiastically commented during recess duty, 'Congratulations! You've gotten teachers talking to each other!' I was feeling quite pleased and believed this dialogue session idea was going to work. I did feel that perhaps teachers just needed time to talk about whatever was on their minds, so I picked a topic for the next meeting with the intention of letting the discussion flow freely.

The second meeting, entitled 'Classroom Decisions: Who Makes Them and Why?', scheduled Wednesday after school, conflicted with another, previously unscheduled meeting. The session, therefore, got off to a late start, and seven of the twelve people in attendance had to leave early. Approaching this meeting with the intention of allowing teachers to talk about whatever was on their minds gave the session a lack of focus. It became so diffuse that summary was impossible. Feeble attempts at refocusing were dropped and the session flowed on its own indiscernible course. From this, I developed fears that teachers no longer would attend because the session was unproductive, and that they would judge me unqualified and unprepared to facilitate the dialogue adequately.

A common fear that I faced and with which I continue to deal concerns my own abilities and qualifications in conducting these sessions. I had never attended a professional dialogue meeting before I introduced them to my peers. My experience was composed solely of faculty meetings. I knew I did not want to duplicate those, but what type of session would be an appropriate model? When few teachers attended or participated, I was certain it was due to my inability to discern their needs and desires. Surely, another teacher with better skills and knowledge could do justice to this cause, yet who was this person? Where could I go to learn how to do this?

During my conference with Kathy on this second session, my fears, intentions, practice, values, and frustrations were examined and clarified. One conclusion we came to was that the sessions needed narrower topics and more direction. My history of hesitance in taking responsibility for meetings with adults was acknowledged, but the necessity for more direct guidance required that my hesitancy be set aside and direction given precedence.

I prepared for the third session, entitled 'Time Constraints,' by outlining the agenda on the chalkboard. My fears and frustrations were explained to those in attendance as the rationale for a more directed discussion. The results were more focused, covering all of the agenda including the possibility of gathering during school time for the final meeting of the year. Within the forty-five minute session, more was accomplished than at the other meetings as far as a defined, identifiable outcome. However, I continued to question my level of direct intervention.

> Teachers complained of attending meetings where the agenda is determined and manipulated by the administration. How different is it if the agenda is determined and manipulated by me? Probably a minimal difference. The intention of this project is to give teachers a forum to

develop their voices, in whatever direction that might be. How can that happen if they cannot have a voice in how the meeting is organized? If I perceive my position as one who is more knowledgeable because I have experienced or read more, am I any different from those in administration? No.

(First Look paper)

The final teacher discussion session for the 1988–89 school year, on 'Site-Based Decision Making,' was attended by four teachers. The arrangements teachers had tentatively made to free themselves for the session during school time fell through in one case, gained insurmountable complications in three others, and one teacher forgot. This is the reality of teaching. Complications and the necessary adjustments constantly arise, which makes meeting for dialogue very difficult when students are in the building. A teacher's responsibilities are too great to arrange around these unforeseen changes successfully in many cases, especially without support for creative scheduling from the administration. Because so few teachers were present, it is impossible to compare this meeting to the other three. However, it does illustrate what happened when a session was scheduled during school time.

As I reflected over the four dialogue sessions in the 1988–89 school year, I realized I had certain naive expectations about how they would transpire. I thought that given the chance to discuss educational issues with their peers, many teachers of diverse philosophies would attend often. I expected to establish a core group, at the very least. This core group, by the end of the first year, was composed of Kathy, who had attended to enable me to reflect on the session (however, she did indicate an interest and willingness to participate), and of course myself. Somehow, these dialogue sessions seemed not to be meeting teacher needs. Otherwise, attendance would be a priority.

Other structures and issues also affected attendance. The lack of trust among teachers, as well as between the teachers and administration was obvious. The refusal to participate if the first session was audio-taped is one example of this lack of trust. The interference of other scheduled meetings also limited attendance. Our sessions lacked official status, recognition, and power, so obstacles continued to be placed in the path of scheduling. The absence of administrative support, although not altogether unexpected, did surprise me in its intensity. A refusal to allow teachers to gather during school time while classrooms were under the care of substitutes, arranged through alternative funding, was disappointing. Questions about my level of influence in the sessions continued to be raised in my mind. Where was the balance for me in direction and control? How could I conduct these meetings with maximum input from those attending, while still guiding them toward a solution or resolution? Within that realm of guidance, is there the opportunity still to make the meetings relevant and the property of those attending? It was within the storm of these previously unforeseen obstructions, priorities, and questions that the 1989–90 teacher discussion sessions were approached.

Dialogue sessions continued

My desire for this new year was to turn over the content and process of the meetings to those attending. After questioning my level of direction within the group in the previous year, I worked toward returning the agenda to my fellow teachers. We selected a name for our meetings, Professional Dialogue Sessions (PDS), developed a schedule of meeting the third Friday of each month for lunch, and generated a list of topics to be discussed during the year. It was also suggested and arranged that the sessions be used as a line of evidence for teacher leadership positions. These changes provided more support and structure for the dialogue research, but did not quiet my questions of control.

At this time, the notion of dialogue was maturing within my mind. At first, I wanted teachers to have the opportunity to gather and talk. I had not really focused on what they would talk about, other than educational issues and classroom practice. As I examined the first four sessions, I knew the process of dialogue had to have structure, but not of the kind the administration provided. I knew that reflection was promoted by many researchers as a necessary step toward possible change (Berlak and Berlak, 1987; Weiler, 1988; Grumet, 1989). As I struggled with this issue, I felt that if these meetings were set up to encourage and initiate change as teachers reflected on educational issues, then teachers could learn to give thoughtful accountings of what they believed, and why they took the actions they did in the classroom. If teachers explored with each other the values and history behind the choices made, they could then express those values to those in positions of power. I hoped that through this articulation, administrators and teachers might begin a dialogue, achieve some level of agreement, and move forward toward new educational horizons. Unfortunately, this goal was limited by a number of problems.

One problem was the difficulty in developing consistent attendance in a core group of teachers. In addition, the length of time between each session strained cohesive discussion. Hence, while one group of teachers decided on the schedule, another group was held to it. One group picked the topic, another group discussed it. Time constraints continued to be inhibitive to our dialogue. There seemed to be a constant struggle and juggle of schedules. One teacher expressed the fact that she had to do 'other work to survive in the classroom the next week,' and therefore could not attend the meetings. 'Other work,' she went on to explain, included planning and preparation, as well as 'p.r. stuff like calling parents.' In addition to these constraints generated by the intensified nature of teaching, the brief time that we had to meet continued to be seen not as a priority by the administration. District and school meetings were scheduled without prior warning, requiring the attendance of those teachers that had previously planned on attending the PDS.

The question of trying to make the meetings belong to those in attendance kept surfacing. The sessions were still referred to as 'Robyn's meetings.' This increased my feelings of being solely responsible for their success or failure, and decreased the chance of ownership by others. I hoped, however, that if others could come to feel some sense of ownership for the sessions, perhaps my sense of inadequacy would lessen. That was not to be the case through most of this school year. One teacher summed up her inconsistent involvement in the sessions as 'supporting (me) in (my) little deal.' How could I make it her 'little deal' too? Questions I started asking myself included:

– Why would I, as a teacher, get involved in the group? – How can I get the teachers past the stage of thinking this is what they do for me and toward doing it for themselves? They picked the schedule and the topics, yet still the meetings are my 'little deal.'

This question of ownership is ingrained in the traditional structures of teaching. So much of education removes the teacher from critical decision making, that it detaches them from responsibility for a particular conditional outcome (Apple, 1986; Gitlin, 1987). This similarity in traditionally detached responses to administrative meetings and structures seemed to point further to the possibility that the professional dialogue sessions were not yet meeting teachers' needs.

During the December meeting, teachers decided they would work on a specific project, the development of a proposal for a computer lab for the school. An earlier request for a computer lab had been refused. This push for what we wanted in the face of the administration's refusal was an aspect of empowerment previously unseen. The organizational power of the group, in contrast to individual effort, had begun to be realized. I was thrilled to see this leap to reach for change. Suggestions for researching benefits and detriments found in other schools with labs was pursued, as well as exploring costs and potential funding. One of our teachers had studied the philosophical implications of computer technology with regard to gender and class, and was asked to present her findings. A visit to a school with a lab allowed us to see how it worked at the levels of practice. We found this particular lab to represent a potential alternative in developing thinking and questioning skills thus addressing many of our concerns about technology raised in the research presented by our informed peer, Tiess (1989). With this topic as a focus, and the possibility of change within the reach of teachers, a core group of seven began to formalize. During this investigation, the state legislature passed funding to put a computer lab in each elementary school, further opening the door to the realization of our goal.

Another surprising turn of events occurred when the district offered the schools the possibility of piloting one of three computer systems. When a computer committee was selected to investigate and choose the one for which we would apply, all four members were, by chance not design, from the core group in the PDS. As has often been the case in our district, there was limited time for the committee to make a recommendation. We were given the weekend to find out what we could by Monday's faculty meeting, when our findings would be presented. There was little contact between the members of the committee before the presentation, due to the obvious time constraints. What each individual reported was that little information was found. Everyone contacted, however, thought it ridiculous to make such a costly decision so quickly and without personally examining the hardware and/or software. Our faculty meeting became a forum for discussing the assumptions behind the administration's practice of giving us choice among limited options, and very little time for making informed, well-investigated decisions. The PDS group that had decided to present a proposal to the faculty for a computer lab recommended the rejection of the option to pilot any of the three systems on the premise that the district's procedure of limiting our choices was not a choice. The faculty enthusiastically approved.

At first glance, this may seem contradictory: to work toward a proposal for a computer lab, and then reject a choice of three options presented. However, it is possible to see this rejection as a reflection of legitimate choice. The administration traditionally allows only pseudo or partial participation as outlined by Pateman (1970) in her definition of democracy. This was a decision that involved full participation, initiated by the teachers on the committee and adopted by the rest of the faculty. These teachers began to address the constitutive rules of their profession, as opposed to accepting 'implicitly held rules of [their] activity,' (Apple, 1986, p.87). Our faculty recognized and examined common parameters to the educational choice usually given teachers, such as choosing between a limited number of alternatives, and found them unacceptable.

The big finish

The developing sense of full participation greatly affected the nature of our next PDS, attended by the district superintendent. He had previously indicated an interest in our meetings and accepted our invitation. We began by discussing the recent turn of events: the rejection of piloting a pre-selected computer system, and our future likelihood in choosing and obtaining the computer lab of our choice for our school. Many questions were directed to our superintendent, and notes were taken on future possibilities generated by both the teachers and superintendent. It appeared, from his suggestions and approval of our ideas, that we would have many options from which to choose, including the technology lab previously investigated by the group. A committee was later organized to continue the investigation for a computer lab that would better fit our needs.

Other topics discussed at this meeting with the superintendent involved the district's recommendation of the use of only *one* kindergarten through sixth grade science program. The superintendent found our questions about this policy to be relevant, well researched and thought-out. We discussed other possibilities such as funding science equipment and materials instead of classroom sets of textbooks that, for many of us, most likely would sit unused on the shelves. Negotiation was pursued and ideas explored as we worked around the previously perceived impenetrable structures and mandates of the administration. Many teachers, myself included, were unaware of this potential flexibility on the part of the administration. This was also a significant shift in the teachers' willingness to discuss issues of concern with those in power. Something had happened to this group and this faculty, now given the chance to gather together and discuss concerns and possibilities with our district's superintendent. The alternatives we explored were taken to the faculty and discussed further. Many intended to follow the alternative path and order equipment, not textbooks. Empowerment through dialogue and our ability to make more substantive choices was beginning to be experienced.

Whispers of change

At the beginning of this journey, I asked a question: how might our school, or even our profession, change if discussion and reflection were made available and encouraged in a wider audience of teachers? Change is an elusive perception, hard to document and prove. Nevertheless, I believe change has occurred for teachers and administrators. While recognizing that changes within me were motivating factors for this project, I, too, have continued to change. The sections that follow look at the changes that were fostered by the dialogue sessions for teachers, administrators, and myself.

Teachers

Teachers discussed some perceived changes during our last PDS of the 1989–90 school year. In general, it was enthusiastically agreed that isolation was decreased and trust was growing between members of the group. Support for each other in faculty meetings was cited as an example of trust transferring beyond the confines of our dialogue. One teacher put it this way, 'If we stick up for you here, you know we'll stick up for you again.' Friendships were developed among teachers. One teacher said she felt 'safe' within this setting, that she could say 'anything she wanted and not be judged.' Another stated that in the past, she felt she was the only person that held a particular view. Upon discussion with the members of the PDS, she found her view was shared. Often the topics we discussed were continued among a wider audience during lunch. Comments about more sharing between grade levels were made. Barriers of isolation were beginning to break down.

Teachers discussed the heightened sense of power a group can hold, as opposed to individual teachers attempting to initiate change. The speed with which those changes can take place, when a group of teachers are supporting them, was also explored. Issues discussed in the PDS provided preparation for these same topics when they came up in faculty meetings. It seems this process has begun to break down traditions that are decades old and hundreds of cultural mores thick (Jackson, 1968; Apple, 1986; Kliebard, 1987). These expressions are of change within lives, teaching, and perceptions of the profession. This growing sense of empowerment to address and change structures through dialogue and a growth in trust is in direct contrast to the traditional isolation and acceptance of the hierarchy. As more and more educational issues are addressed, these teachers are redefining and recreating their own sense of professionalism to include the investigation of the aims, as well as means, of education.

The administration

While changing the administration was not a goal, it was an unforeseen side-benefit that occurred as teachers began speaking of their views and concerns. Administrators began to listen. One change transpired at the beginning of the 1989–90 school year. The principal announced that our faculty meetings would have scheduled time for sharing ideas, and discussion of professional issues generated by the faculty. Only a small portion of time would be taken for business and administrator-generated items. This had not been addressed by our principal before, and she admitted that this was a response to the interest displayed in our dialogue gatherings. However, our principal must have had some of the same struggles I had experienced as far as the issue of control goes. Unfortunately, the reality of our meetings often allowed for an average of three minutes for discussion and sharing, with the bulk of time devoted to business. Only on two occasions were the topics for discussion generated and controlled by a source other than the principal. Some teachers expressed frustration over the fact that one issue for which they requested time for discussion had been given very little time in actuality, even though it appeared on the agenda for weeks. Business kept getting an abundant portion of the meetings, leaving mere minutes to discuss the issue and come to an informed decision. Principals are products of the same system which has discouraged dialogue among teachers. Although they have the authority to help encourage and enable discourse, they might not hold it as a priority in the face of more immediate demands.

Our superintendent, as was mentioned earlier, also seemed to develop a general interest in the potential of the dialogue sessions. He inquired about them from our principal, and has attended one. He has spoken highly of our attempts to generate dialogue among the teachers in our school. In a recent letter, he wrote:

> I enjoyed the discussion . . . and was impressed with the importance of the issues you dealt with and the thoughtfulness with which those issues were discussed. I think that you have launched something very important and worthwhile. I would like to see similar groups develop all over the district. I think if teachers had the opportunity to participate in discussions such as [these] they would find their professional work much more stimulating and growth promoting. Moreover, there would be, over time, an increase in the quality and effectiveness of teaching and learning.

It appears our superintendent is redefining traditional notions of professionalism in favor of the idea that dialogue is conducive to growth. This bodes well for future possibilities for this forum. He has also indicated a willingness to consider creative scheduling of the school day to accommodate such dialogue. This is a pleasant change from the lack of flexibility commonly associated with district policy.

The dialogue between the teachers and our superintendent extends the range of possibilities within this study, our school, and our district. As I wrote in a letter to the superintendent after his visit, 'It is important for me and others at my school to see your interest in what we are doing. I'm sure

I can no longer speak of 'the administration' as a . . . faceless power structure, as I have been known to do in the past.'

Personal changes

As I have discovered over the past two years, this study is about process. It has no final product, no end result. It is the evolution of the researcher and the research. In my initial efforts to write this story, I learned yet another way of denying voice and my experiences by molding them into a more traditional research format, into the voice of the disembodied researcher. Over time, I realized a new level of acceptance of my experience as text. Weiler proposes that within the realm of feminist research, women must begin with themselves (Weiler, 1988, p.58). It has taken me a long time to come to a place where I could accept my views as legitimate and allow my voice to be heard. I began with a personal history that continues to be written in the light of new discoveries and experiences. It is impossible for me to separate my evolution from the evolution of this project. This study will continue as long as there are teachers interested in dialogue, as my respect grows for the process and the people that have so much to say. This is not the end; it is the beginning.

Learning to be silent can entail a lifelong training. To unlearn it, and begin to speak, can also require education. The issue of voice and silence has been representative of more than the mere production of sound; it has ramifications for my sense of being, of becoming a person, that resemble the metaphor repeated in *Women's Ways of Knowing*, 'We found that women repeatedly used the metaphor of voice to depict their intellectual and ethical development; and that the development of a sense of voice, mind, and self were intricately intertwined' (Belenky *et al.*, 1986, p.18)

Through the past year, I have begun to reassess the assumptions with which I began this journey. I had hoped to lead teachers out of the tyranny of their prison of silence. As the dialogue sessions developed, I realized they would lead themselves to the level of articulation for which they were ready. I found I could not force change in a pre-determined way, as our district often tries to do. I could only offer a forum and encouragement, then let teachers choose among a range of self-determined options and proceed from there.

I began with self-doubts about my abilities to establish such a forum for teacher dialogue. Those doubts and feelings of inadequacy continue. As a core group developed, I felt my own level of direction and responsibility ease while others seemed naturally to involve themselves as interest grew. There was a time I feared that would never happen. The outline of changes within me has moved from enthusiasm and wanting to share in a possible process of evolution, to feelings of despair for seeming lack of interest in the sessions back to a revitalized enthusiasm as teachers and administrators began to see the potential of dialogue. That tortuous path, in itself, has held many lessons for me.

Eventually, my historical hesitance to give direction to adults helped me explore a minimal level of intervention. Direction is necessary, but it can be mediated with an abundance of input from others. As I examine my future goals, I want to find ways to encourage those other, silent members of the staff to participate in these sessions. My original interest was in developing teacher voice, and that includes more than those already inclined to speak.

When I analyzed my school history, the established school structures seemed impenetrable and unchanging. Time constraints and district mandates in particular seemed to be the walls within which I had to make myself comfortable. I can now see they have doors, and some are made only of paper. As dialogue continues within our school, we see more structures crumble as we ask questions and seek answers. I am learning to accept less on face value, as I dialogue with my peers in a 'language of possibility' (Aronowitz and Giroux, 1985).

Horizontal Evaluation continues to influence my questions and investigations as this research process develops. It has helped me construct a mindset that examines my own assumptions as I direct others in dialogue. Without it, teachers, myself included, often adapt to the intensification of their teaching day by using survival techniques that have political implications. Hiding behind a closed classroom door, for example, has personal advantages, but also limits possibilities for school change. I have been and continue to be guilty of using such techniques. The awarenesses I have gained, however, make a wider variety of choice available.

The Professional Dialogue Sessions are continuing through the 1990–91 school year. Tentative plans have been developed to incorporate levels of personal history into the sessions, as a recognition of its impact in professional decisions. The first session had a short introduction where teachers shared why they became teachers. Women and, by implication, teachers, need to start with themselves and their context in order to gain understanding about the structures within which they live and work (Weiler, 1988). This understanding can then be subject to critical reflection through dialogue with peers. Incorporating personal histories into our discussions can deepen our understanding of ourselves and each other while giving us a point from which to grow.

The incorporation of a reflective model continues as another goal for the sessions. I discussed my desire to implement such a method on a trial basis with those involved. Those in the PDS were supportive of seeing if this brings a difference to the quality and substance of our discussions. The level of our concerns remains immediate and concrete in most cases, but our vocalizations are increasing and feelings of empowerment are growing.

It seems my best intentions and plans to arbitrarily decide the form and function of these meetings must be put aside to best meet teacher needs and desires. Once again, I found myself struggling with attendance until turning the meetings totally over to those who wish to participate. As I contemplated discontinuing the sessions after November's bleak turn-out and re-writing this whole chapter to include a disheartening end, I decided to give it one more chance. The topic for December's meeting was 'How can these sessions better meet your needs?'. A strong group of seven people came with ideas and a course of action. I am continually learning to trust my peers to know what they want in a discussion format. They are helping me to define my role as the person who sets up the sessions and then sits back and participates in what next transpires. It is essentially what I had originally hoped would occur. My goals are changing and now correspond more with Rorty in his stressing that, 'the conversation should be kept going rather than to find objective truth,' (Rorty, 1980, p.377).

It is important that more dialogue be cultivated between teachers and administrators as the usual questions of method grow to include educational aims and the traditionally unseen parameters of teaching. Hopefully, exploring the deeper political and moral implications of education can help remove the layers of resistance administrators and teachers wear for defense. As educational values and assumptions are explored, the usual threat the hierarchy poses can ease and give way to a more egalitarian community.

There is still much to be addressed and attempted within our dialogue sessions. The option of inviting our superintendent or principal to all of our 1990–91 sessions was discussed at our first meeting. Some teachers felt little or no hesitancy in expressing their views in front of administrators but had concerns that it might discourage others from participating. Although we recognized the need to include the administration in our dialogue at some point, it was agreed that the invitation should be withheld for an undetermined amount of time in the hope that freer dialogue among teachers could ensue.

The personal and professional ramifications of this study expand in all directions for me as I see the broader implications of dialogue and educational empowerment. Parents and students have been even more discouraged from speaking than teachers. Eventually, I must find ways to include their voices as well. My hope is that I can encourage my students' voices while providing them with a receptive audience. This is what I have wished for myself. My personal journey to develop my teacher voice has taken me further down the path to the doors of more partners in silence than I imagined to be possible.

Ultimately, for me and for my profession there is much unfinished work to be done in the area of developing teacher voice. Encouraging and/or ignoring the silence has not produced positive educational results. For, as Adrienne Rich (1978) acknowledges in 'Cartographies of Silence', there is more behind this silence than at first appears:

> It is a presence
> it has a history a form
>
> Do not confuse it
> with any kind of absence
> (Rich, 1978, p.17)

APPENDIX A: A SURVEY OF TEACHER ATTITUDES ON PROFESSIONAL DIALOGUE

Individual responses to this survey will be kept confidential. Participation is voluntary. The data from this survey will be reported to those in the Educative Research Project and will be available to participants upon request. Thank you for your candor and participation in this project.

Present school assignment _____

Number of years teaching _____

Career Ladder Status? _____

Definition of 'professional dialogue' – a discussion among two or more colleagues about issues of, related to, or suitable to the profession.

1 How often is time for professional dialogue provided by the administration?
   a once a week or more _____
   b once a month or more _____
   c once a term or more _____
   d once a year or more _____
   e never _____

2 How often do you seek out professional dialogue, on average?
   a once a week or more _____
   b once a month or more _____
   c once a term or more _____
   d once a year or more _____
   e never _____

3   Please indicate the topics most often addressed during the time, if any, you spend in professional dialogue: (check off one or more)

a complaints _____   d curriculum development _____
b classroom ideas _____   e student issues _____
c educational philosophy _____   f current research _____
other, (please specify): _____

4   How would you characterize the professional dialogue in which you participate most of the time?

a not very productive _____
b somewhat productive _____
c productive _____
d very productive _____

5   Do you feel a need for more time spent in professional dialogue?
Yes _____   No _____
Please explain: _____

6   Do you feel your principal is supportive of professional dialogue?
Yes _____   No _____
Please explain: _____

7   Do you feel the district is supportive of professional dialogue?
Yes _____   No _____
Please explain: _____

8   If a schedule for professional dialogue was arranged at times outside of your regular, salaried time, would you attend?
Yes _____   No _____
Please explain: _____
_____

9   If a schedule for professional dialogue was arranged during regular school hours, would you attend? Yes _____   No _____
Please explain: _____
_____

10 Of the following ideas, which do you believe reflect benefits to be gained from participation in professional dialogue? (Prioritize from #1 most important, #2 next, etc.)

a to ease teacher isolation _____
b to develop a support group _____
c to share ideas _____
d to explore alternatives _____
e to discuss educational issues _____

f to expand my knowledge base   _____
g to learn what others feel and think   _____
h very little or no benefit, that I can see   _____
i other, (please specify): _____

Thank you for your cooperation in this project. Feel free to add comments on the back. Please return your completed survey to Robyn Russell.

7   Out standing in a field: one teacher's search for success

The view of life as a journey is a common metaphor. When one is on a journey, the notion of traveling is implied, but it is often difficult to explain the route, the distance covered, or the lessons learned from the events encountered along the way. Perhaps, not until there is some natural passage of time, and one can reflect back on those events, can a particular meaning be identified. Such is the case for me as I reflect back on my experiences in the ERP. Within this chapter I will document a journey, and disclose the lessons that my students taught me about the process of becoming educated, and the complexities of creating successful student and teacher relationships. My experience represents a collapse as well as a restoration, as my students helped me to see a range of possibilities that I never expected to find.

FINDING MY FEET

In the early summer of 1990, I went for a hike by myself along a trail near Guardsman's Pass, and found myself standing in a field of thistles. The path before me was narrow, and I chuckled as I looked down at my dusty toes poking through my leather sandals. I mused to myself that I was certainly not wearing the proper gear for a hike. Here I was looking down at my feet, trying to maintain a steady balance so as to not prick my toes by focusing on the ground, ignoring the blue sky above and the power of the mountains around me. I declared out loud: 'Education is like a field of thistles!' It also occurred to me that special education had special hybrids that defied any model's concise description. I knew then I would never figure anything out with any real certainty, but I felt I was standing at a very familiar place.

From my earliest childhood memories, I have always been preoccupied with looking at feet. I still wince when I recall the memory of fiercely pedaling my tricycle, looking down at my feet at the blur of the sidewalk below, and running into an old lady and knocking her over. When my parents rushed out to come to her aid, they were utterly dismayed with my behavior. I will never forget my father's face admonishing me to watch where I was going. As an older child I learned to be more careful. I jumped the cracks in the sidewalk with confidence as I looked down at my feet in proper white anklets and patent leather shoes. I felt secure with my place in the world, but my gaze was still on my feet and the narrow path before me.

As I moved into my teens, I began to look around my world, to search for a wider path to travel on, and to find a community of friends who supported me. At seventeen, my friend Paul used to put his arm around me and give me a little shove, and say that he could tell me anything because 'I was just like one of the guys.' I was never sure just what he meant, but it always made me smile. When Paul was killed in Vietnam in 1966, I realized that he would never tell me that again. I did not protest the war or Paul's death, but simply let him go in silence. Feeling powerless to change the course of my life and the political struggles of my generation, I learned to watch events. I missed my conversations with Paul, and thought of him often as I wandered about waging my own wars, and stepping on land mines, some that I placed myself, that disrupted the course and direction of my life.

In 1976, after an unsuccessful marriage, I placed myself in the position of needing to find my feet once again as I stepped into an abyss of the unknown. Now, having a family to support, I reluctantly took the advice of a rehabilitation counselor to become a special education teacher. Since there was an apparent need for them in the job market, I was assured that I would have a lot to offer. I assumed that teaching, as a career choice, would make it possible for me to have a respectable enough position to claim a place in the working world. So, I wandered into the university somewhat blindly, not having any particular expectations other than to prepare for employment.

I found that learning my role as a teacher in the real world of education was difficult. I could usually deliver the lines for the expected performance, but I did not want to talk about it after work. Somehow, I did not feel like a good teacher. Even though my administrative evaluations had been positive, I had a need to prove that I was strong, capable, and smart enough to handle the job.

After seven years of teaching, I felt overwhelmed by the growing body of research in the area of learning disabilities that I was supposed to absorb and felt ill-equipped to keep up my act as teacher. I was frustrated with my self-identified inability to create new directions for my teaching. I had trouble getting up in the morning, and felt like a graying, shell-shocked, battle-fatigued warrior weary from facing the daily resistance my students offered me. The vast technical base of information in my field helped me to describe my students, but it did not help me prescribe successful strategies or interventions. More importantly, these descriptions did not help me develop positive relationships with my students. Despite the comments from friends and family members that indicated that I was a good teacher, and that my career 'surely must be rewarding,' I was on the verge of quitting. The prospects of being the beaten down teacher going the distance until retirement was so unattractive that I sought some release or new direction.

When I entered the ERP in the fall of 1988, I saw myself as being apart from other teachers. Initially, I thought that revealing my sense of isolation would only expose my timid sense of professionalism. I was reluctant to speak to anyone for any extended length of time because of this fear of revealing myself, but, intuitively, I knew that I had to change my life even if it meant disrupting my old routines. I suppose the fear that I might never set out to tackle my dreams or to find my place in the world, both paralyzed me with a consuming fatigue, and encouraged me to move; to go somewhere even without a direction or a road map. Perhaps, my first response in joining the ERP was like that of a tourist in search of a travel guide. I assumed that the other teachers knew where they were going. I decided to get lost in the crowd with them, and head for this unknown destination. My attitude was quite simplistic: 'What did I have to lose by just taking one class?'

LEARNING TO BE A STUDENT AGAIN

When asked to write a personal history, it took me a long time to confront writing about my reasons for becoming a teacher. I viewed the exercise as being an invasion of my privacy. Would I tell the truth, or should I construct myself in such a way that I could not really be recognized? Finally, I just began to write, and the result was a description of myself as a student.

> I have always viewed education as a positive endeavor from the first time I pressed my five year old palm into a mound of gray clay and made that 'handprint' to give to my parents as a Christmas gift. School was a good place for me where I basically felt comfortable, but as the years went by, certain subjects would be difficult. Math was especially hard for me at first, and I was slow to finish my work, but I learned to cope and maximize my strengths. I found ways to hide those fingers counting under my desk. I drew wonderful pictures, and I learned to clean-up.
>
> (Personal History)

These self-revelations brought an awareness that coping and deception had perhaps been lifelong companions. Could it be that my experiences as a student influenced my behavior as a teacher? I began to notice that my speech reflected a definite separation in my thinking about students as 'them.' I was not comfortable being with 'them' for very long periods of time. In fact, I sometimes felt suffocated by students when I could not cope with or understand their needs. The real world of teaching was much different than the one I had created in childhood when I 'played school.'

> As I look back to that early time, I think I enjoyed the control, and I got to be the one to put the 100%'s on the papers. Everybody got an 'A' in my school, and they loved me.
>
> (Personal History)

Was my dissatisfaction with teaching the result of my inability to control my students, to help them become successful, or to have them love me? Admittedly, a few of my students did not see me as a benevolent ally, and I was feeling some emotional detachment from them as well. As a teacher, I viewed school as work; it was not play and I painfully identified with the description offered by Jackson:

> The daily routine, the 'rat race', and the infamous old grind may be brightened from time to time by happenings that add color to an otherwise drab existence, but the grayness of our daily lives has an abrasive potency of its own.
>
> (Jackson, 1968, p.127)

I wanted to create something. I wanted to find more color and life in my teaching experiences, but finding the way alone had not been productive. Asking for help had never been easy for me in my long pursuit of self-importance and expertise, but I knew that I needed to take a different route if I wanted to learn to participate in events instead of watching them.

INVITING PEOPLE IN

Evaluation has always been an inevitability in the school system, but I had not found a need to ask for it beyond the yearly requirements. Consequently, I reluctantly opened the door to participate in Horizontal Evaluation with another teacher in the ERP. At first, I was not willing to share extensively, and sought to comply only by fulfilling the course assignment. However, even when the process was quite new, the things I said, that just tumbled out in fragments, were so revealing that I felt caught by my own statements. The following excerpt illustrates how revealing my own words were to me. Eeva, who had observed a student who was acting out in one of my instructional groups, posed this question to me:

Eeva: Do your students act this way much of the time or . . . ?

Karen: Yes, they do. John had a really rough morning. I'll talk about him first. His teacher brought him in earlier saying that he had a difficult time being in class. He was being destructive with peers and refusing to work. So, a lot of the time, what he says is, 'I quit! I'm not doing this anymore!'

Eeva: I also notice that when you work with the students, you encourage them with statements that indicate that they have 'almost got it.' Is almost better than not at all?

Karen: You know, I've had to struggle with what I expect from the students. It seems like I've had to really slice-back my expectations about what success is for the students I work with. It's something I work on every day to find responses that even approach what I'm asking them to do.

Clearly, my discussion of success was incomplete and fragmented. With a certain embarrassment, and some degree of personal squirming, I came to the realization that a significant part of my educative journey, and the development of my research question, would need to involve defining success.

When I began to do research at the library, the bombardment of issues and layers related to this question were overwhelming. I could see that there were no black and white answers. Yet, my interest continued, and I decided to go forward despite the grandness the topic suggested. I knew that success was most probably viewed as a state of mind and very individualistic with many cultural boundaries, but I wanted to find some personal clarification so that I could complete a sentence about what success in school meant to me, and to formulate some kind of a study to investigate what success meant to my students as well. The developing trust with Eeva was a key factor in encouraging me to risk asking my questions, and venturing out to find new possibilities and understanding.

Competing voices

I began my research to define success from a perspective of genuine confusion. It was as if I was standing on some shore looking out at a wide expanse of water. I was agreeing to go in for a swim, but I did not know how far out I would go. As I began to wade into the literature, I first looked to the philosophers to help me with my existential quandary. I wanted to find out where the gaps were in my historical understanding by reading the enlightenment and wisdom of the past. Developmentally, my approach was much the same as going to the dictionary to find the meaning of a word. In addition, I had always found some aesthetic appeal in philosophical inquiry and the language used to describe the dilemma of the self yearning for expression in the world. Perhaps the 'technicalese' of behaviorism had not addressed my need for the human connection, and I was desirous of another voice that spoke in terms different from those of stimulus and response. Maybe I was just hungry for poetry. Starting with Plato's quest for 'the good life,' and traveling through time with philosophical zeal, I was enamored with the grand conversation. I had difficulties, however, connecting with these male philosophers because their voices did not reflect my experience as a woman. Consequently, I was drawn back to the more familiar world of the practical as I examined readings that focused on teachers and students. In my search through this practical literature, I found myself in the middle of a continuing tug of war between the concrete and the theoretical. Initially, I looked for research that offered some proof and verification based on observable results, but, later on, I was pulled to more theoretical studies that offered summaries of societal concerns that, at times, challenged empirical evidence.

Within the practical literature, I found research that indicated the importance of teacher expectations on student achievement and student/teacher relationships (Cooper and Good, 1983, Good 1987). Teacher expectations were defined as being the inferences that teachers make about the future behavior or academic achievements of their students, based on what they know about their students. Since my relationship as a special education teacher began with the expectation of disability, I wondered how these expectancy studies related to my being able to change the behaviors or raise the skill levels of my students.

Rosenthal (1974), in reviewing Brophy and Good (1974), suggested several factors that could counter the effects of the self-fulfilling prophecy. Specifically, I thought that these identified factors could possibly become beginning guidelines to help me find a focus for research with my students. I was particularly impressed with four suggestions outlined in this study:

1 Create warm social-emotional relationships with students.
2 Give students more feedback about their performances.
3 Teach students more (and more difficult) material (input).
4 Give students more opportunities to respond and to ask questions (output).

(Rosenthal, 1974)

Even with this newly found encouragement to provide an environment for success through improved communication efforts, I was also attracted to the more abstract and theoretical voices within the family of education that did not demonstrate faith and confidence in the institutional ideals of schools to deliver success.

Examining the more theoretical literature, I found some unexpected agreement. Illich (1971), for example, in *Deschooling Society*, reinforced my own beliefs that schools should be re-made to meet the needs of humans in terms more complex than just the physical environment.

> Many students, especially the poor, intuitively know what the schools do for them. They school them to confuse process and substance. Once these become blurred, a new logic is assumed: the more treatment there is, the better are the results; or escalation leads to success. The pupil is thereby 'schooled' to confuse teaching with learning, grade advancement with education, a diploma with competence, and fluency with the ability to say something new. His imagination is 'schooled' to accept service in the place of value.
>
> (Illich, 1971, p.1)

I was also intrigued by Illich's retelling of the story of 'Pandora', who allowed all the ills of the world to escape from her box, closing the lid before the one positive attribute, 'hope,' could be released. He called educators to rediscover the distinctions between hope and expectation, and, moved by his eloquent words, I found myself saying, 'Yes.' I agreed with Illich in spite of my search for concrete answers, and personally acknowledged that my survival as a teacher was probably dependent on the discovery of hope. Just how the teacher voices and the student voices with their opposing expectations could bond together in hope was a mystery, but it seemed a fertile, untilled field for further study and research. From both the personal and professional perspectives, I wanted to find alternative ways to communicate with my students, and to discover for myself the difference between hope and expectation.

Another important influence on my thinking about success was Freire's *Pedagogy of the Oppressed*. He inspired me with his commitments to emancipatory interests for education. I was intrigued by his ideas on critical reflection and his conception of 'teachers-learners' who, with their students, could examine their actual situations through dialogue:

> [Teachers and students] . . . can develop their power to perceive critically the way they exist in the world with which they find themselves; they come to see the world not as a static reality, but as a reality in process, in transformation.
>
> (Freire, 1970, p.7)

Freedman *et al.* (1983) also provided their encouragement, and pointed to a need for teachers to take risks so that they could begin to analyze the implications of their actions. By learning with their students in a relaxed environment, they suggested teachers could find hope and begin to develop student and teacher voices committed to hearing each other. With one foot in the practical, and the other in the more theoretical literature, I was inspired and committed to abandoning fear so that I could create new visions for my teaching.

THE FIRST YEAR STUDY: LEAVING TERRA FIRMA

I chose to focus on two girls and five boys who had been enrolled in special education programs for three or more years for academic remediation in reading, language arts, and math. My assumption was that these students who had experienced little success in school would not be able to communicate adequately their possibilities for success. My intentions were to help them become more aware of their own possibilities for success by learning to talk specifically about their strengths and weaknesses.

My training as a special education teacher had involved learning to deliver high rates of reinforcement, as well as to find multiple ways to say, 'Good for you!.' The methods I relied on to question students and to provide feedback to them had been primarily used to elicit the correct response. If the correct response was not given, I knew techniques to shape the responses toward that end. Signaling and cuing were all prompts to get at desired results. I rarely asked for student opinions, or allowed any extended time for student reflection. After years of snapping my fingers, slapping my leg, and 'keeping them all together,' I became aware that any shift to participate in student–teacher dialogue would be a challenge for me. In fact, I was somewhat resistant to change, feeling that I was abandoning the familiar equation I had memorized from my training that indicated that the rate of 80 percent correct responses was correlated to optimal learning experiences. I had been schooled to believe that the statistical relationship was the only one that mattered in the world of remediation.

My first investigative session with the students was a departure from my usual instructional arrangement and style of presentation. I often had the lesson's outcome well in mind, and was ready to fire away at students the moment they sat down so I could keep to my time schedule. On this day, I told the students that we were going to do something different, and invited them to sit where they wanted to sit. This seating arrangement was so informal that some of the students sat on the table, and some on the floor. As we began, I told them we would not be doing our usual skill lesson, and that this activity would not be graded or assigned points. This shift to a more relaxed environment was not immediately understood by the students. As a result, there was an initial lack of enthusiasm evidenced by audible sighs and moans.

I started this beginning discussion by writing SUCCESS on the chalkboard, and then asked them to brainstorm with me, what this word meant. At first, the students appeared unmotivated. Chris and James stretched themselves out on the floor and started playing some kind of a pencil and paper game. I was uncomfortable with the silence, and feared that the activity might not be engaging because no one said anything, or even looked at me. Finally, James said, 'So, why are we doing this instead of work?' I asked him if he would rather do work, and he replied that he didn't care, but he just didn't know what I was getting at. I then redirected the question back to him, 'So, James, what do you think success is?' His response was, 'You mean like when you get a raise?' From this point, a discussion began, and eleven student responses were offered:

1 You're good at things.
2 You win.
3 You're rich.
4 You get a prize.
5 Like you get it when you're older, and have a job.
6 Somebody's lucky.
7 You get away with something, and don't get caught.
8 You get a vacation.
9 You don't have to come to school.
10 Like when there's an assembly or a field trip, and you get to miss math or something.
11 Some people are lucky and other's aren't.

I was curious about the students' perceptions of success being related to luck and getting out of something, so I questioned them further. Coincidentally, I started to cough a little, and broke away to get a drink of water. James said, 'Like when you get to waste time and don't have to do stuff. Like now, when you have to get a drink, we can do what we want.' He went on to tell me that the wasting time did not upset them as much as it apparently upset me. With my curiosity piqued, I asked them to tell me what they thought most teachers would say about success in school, and the following six items were suggested from the students' point of view.

1 Getting 100 per cent.
2 Being good and nice, and not getting into fights.
3 Not passing notes, and not getting into trouble with the principal.
4 Getting all your work done.

5 Getting all A's.
6 Being nice to them (teachers).

James asked me what I thought success was, and I just told him I was trying to figure that out. No one questioned me further, which I found interesting. Andrea spoke up to say that she was not worried about it, and that she would probably think about it more in high school. Ron clowned around imitating a stand-up comedian; using his pencil like a microphone and introducing himself as the world's best comedian, 'even better than Eddie Murphy.' This event was light and fun for all of us. I thought we had reached some level of success in that three of the students wanted to talk more with me at the recess break. This first conversation was not as I had envisioned it would be, but I felt pleased with the outcome. The following months would prove to be more difficult as I struggled to balance my direct instruction curriculum, and our open-ended discussion times.

There was one significant event with this math group that proved to be particularly insightful and challenged my understanding of success. The topic for study was the addition and subtraction of unlike fractions. I was trying to teach them how to find the lowest common multiple so that they could convert the unlike fractions into fractions with common denominators. I was frustrated because we had been studying this for several days, and I was discouraged with the lack of progress I observed. Truthfully, I think my expectations were: 'These kids are never going to get this!' One student, Ron, said, 'These are hard, I hate this! Can't we do these kind on the calculator?' Without hesitation, I said, 'No! This is something I want you to be able to figure out in your own head.' I used egg cartons, and folded and tore-up pieces of paper to show equivalent amounts, but Stewart and Chris exhibited even more resistance by poking holes in the cartons with their pencils. Finally, out of a sense of desperation, I drew a numberline on the chalk board with numbers from zero to ten. I said, 'Look, I need to know what you know and understand about this.' I wanted them to compare for me, their present knowledge and understanding from the beginning of the math lesson to the end of the lesson. The responses were honest, and I found that there were no responses at ten. The range of understanding was from two to six. Andrea said, 'You don't have to get mad about it. You give us too hard of work.' I paused and then asked quite defensively, 'Why do you come to my class?' The answers I received from Andrea were particularly thought-provoking. She indicated that the work upstairs (in her regular classroom) was really hard, but my class was 'supposed to be easier.'

Andrea's and the other students' responses concerned me. I had assumed that something was missing in my instructional approach given that these fifth and sixth grade students were still having so much difficulty with adding and subtracting fractions. What I was trying to teach them should have been easy, I thought. Also, I was concerned about the things they called easy and said were a 'cinch' because I still wasn't convinced that any of the math concepts I had been trying to teach were mastered by any of the seven students.

The student laughter during the time we were discussing the math lesson confused me as to who was frustrated by the difficulty of the task. Were the students upset or just me? James told me that I shouldn't get so 'worked-up about this stuff,' and Nancy told me, 'You're so funny.' It appeared that the students' adaptive skills were well-developed to discount and minimize the frustration of difficult tasks.

At the beginning of my literature search, I had been introduced to Willis' study of working-class high school 'lads' who resisted learning and their teachers in school. Eddie, one of the lads, says, 'The teachers think they're high and mighty 'cos they're teachers, but they're nobody really, they're just ordinary people ain't they?' (Willis, 1977, p.11). The students' comments about me being 'all upset,' 'worked-up,' and 'all mad at us' made me think that my students might share Eddie's perceptions. This new awareness helped me to look at student resistance from a new perspective that I had not thought about previously. I was curious if the students thought of me as 'high and mighty,' and if so, what implications would this have for the possibilities of our developing meaningful teacher–student relationships?

Brophy and Good had suggested teachers could be thought of as being on a continuum from 'proactive through reactive to overreactive' (Brophy and Good, 1974, pp.40–1). Their conclusions pointed to the need for teachers to believe that they could teach their students, regardless of the students' current performance. This reminded me of my expectation: 'These kids are never going to get this!.' I wondered how I could develop a more confident belief that I could teach students in a successful way. My interactions with these students led me to question if their refusal to learn was an avoidance of task difficulty, a fear of failure, a native deficiency, a result of reacting against an 'overreactive teacher,' or as Erickson points out the negative stereotyping of their ethnic identity:

> Consistent patterns of a refusal to learn in school can be seen as a form of resistance to a stigmatized ethnic or social class identity that is being assigned by a school. Students can refuse to accept that negative identity by refusing to learn.
>
> (Erickson, 1987, p.350)

The students' apparent refusal to learn influenced me to ask what I was refusing to do. Often, I caught myself hearing students' comments only superficially, and I often had to ask students to repeat what they said. Increasingly, I consciously had to prompt myself just to hear them out. I also wondered how I could learn to listen so as to reduce this need for student re-explanation. It was becoming more apparent to me that my own view of success was undergoing some reconstruction as I reappraised my ability to interpret student responses in a different light.

As I contemplated how to increase the opportunities for listening to students more specifically, I came to the realization that maybe, if I invited more people into my classroom to help me with one on one student communication, I could create a greater forum for students to be heard, and I could move into a position of being more of an observer. On one particularly difficult day, I expressed to a colleague, in frustration, that if I had one person for every student to help me listen, maybe I would see more evidence of progress, and find some answers on how to work with 'these kids!' I felt encouraged to take a leap in this direction, and was soon to find more help than I had bargained for.

Our school had embarked on a project with university student volunteers who were eager to work in the schools. My beginning proposal requested volunteer help in listening and providing more tutorial support for the students. This invitation to have a greater number of helpers in my room was very complex in terms of organization. However, it was through relinquishing some control to the volunteers that I began to feel a greater sense of movement for the students, and a beginning shift in my own perspective as the teacher 'in charge.' I felt that my whole concept of teaching was undergoing some kind of reconstruction. At some level, I was now the coordinator of this environment, rather than the teacher. I felt a little perplexed about what I was learning from this sharing of students. Yes, the resistance was greatly reduced, but there were genuine moments of not feeling connected to the students as much as I would have liked. The positive side to this situation seemed to be that there were more visible smiles from the students as I sensed they felt some increased freedom, and a different sense of participation than they had experienced in my classes before. I watched the volunteers develop relationships with the students but felt discomfort in my own increasing emotional detachment.

The students' investment in these relationships was evident when they asked if they could plan a party for the volunteers and all the other students in my classes. With amazing speed, the students set out planning the menu, assigning the potluck items, and deciding who should be cooks, waiters, and clean-up persons. This event turned out to be one of the most disorienting, 'successful' events I had experienced in a long time. Before the party began, James had offered to cut-up the carrot sticks for the relish tray. I was reluctant to agree to this because he was often careless, and I was worried about him hurting himself. He took the knife and cut the carrots into 'rounds' and said, 'It's easier that way.' I had assumed that the only way to make carrot 'sticks' was to cut them into strips. Eeva laughed when I told her, and replied, 'It looks like you're letting go of a little control, and allowing the students to be successful.' 'Yes,' I confessed, 'control does seem to be one of my issues.' As I remember the party, I stepped out of my usual zone of comfort, and, at least, learned how to cut carrot sticks another way.

My personal ambiguity about this first year success was to continue. I felt at a loss to articulate clearly the exact location of my confusion, but I know now that the fact that I did not know my place in my own classroom was bothering me. On the other hand, some new knowledge had been won. I now had the beginnings of a definition of success: success was connected to relationships.

THE SECOND YEAR STUDY: FOUR LESSONS OF CRITICAL REFLECTION

Sometimes it is hard to face the beginning of a new school year. The first two weeks of school are always stressful for me as I try to arrange the time in the day to accommodate the students in my case-load. The teachers in our school are flexible and work very hard with students, but I can get really anxious when any one of them asks, 'When are you going to take students?' I have often chuckled to myself that I would like to ask them, 'Where should I take them?' This defensiveness is usually a product of too much for everyone to do at the beginning of the year.

The classes I had registered for at the university would soon begin, and a group from the ERP, of which I was a part, was preparing papers to present at a curriculum conference. It was a very busy time as many of us were preoccupied with getting ready for this, along with teaching and taking classes at the university. Frankly, I just felt tired. I closed the door to my classroom, just to rest for a bit, and returned to the status quo.

A few students were not settled into the idea of being in school again either, and it seemed that the frequency of behavioral episodes escalated, especially with three eleven-year-old boys in one of my instructional groups. I felt annoyed that I had to settle their arguments, and it was unpleasant as I looked to the year with all of them in the same group. As a student myself, I felt that I just wanted to study, and to ease off on the battle, but my students' insistence to be noticed persisted, and I found myself writing about them at the end of the day just to let off steam. This field journal was to become a record over the remaining year that would provide a thick description of my hopes, fears, confusions, and enlightenments that surfaced from the relationships with Ramon, Nick, and Ben. At this time, I had only one volunteer once a week for one hour, so I decided that this was a chance to experiment with my own capacities for making relationships. I also secretly hoped that I might gain the satisfaction I had missed from the first year study in terms of developing stronger connections to the students myself. I was coming to the recognition that I needed to do my own listening, to make my own relationships with the students. Although it had been a place to start, I was not willing to remain in the more distanced role of the observer. However, the combination of limiting the volunteer program and my more remote approach to these boys at the first of the year contributed to a growing conflict between all of us.

All three students were close in terms of academic skill levels, as well as having somewhat similar competitive, attention-seeking personalities. They had frequent fights with each other out on the playground, in the lunchroom, and before and after school. It appeared to me that they were bonded together in dualistic chains of love and hate. When they were separated from each other, they were miserable, and when they were together, they fought and argued constantly, blaming each other for wounds both seen and unseen. After having completed the schedule and trying to meet the time and subject requirements of student and regular classroom teacher needs, I was reluctant to suggest any grouping readjustments or schedule changes. But I felt I was in the middle of a war zone and expressed some pessimism, as is illustrated in one of my earliest journal entries.

> September, 1989: I guess it is too much to hope that the year would begin without 'a hitch.' I feel so tired today. I don't know what to do with the constant turmoil the boys supply. Today, Ramon swore at me in Spanish, and all I did was to ask him to join the group. I'm afraid I scowled at him a little. I dread 9:30 – I can feel the boys close – coming down the hall – and hearing the 'burst' of the opening door. I don't know what direction to aim for. Maybe, I should get a volunteer for each one just to 'divide and conquer,' and to reduce the amount of time I have to spend with them!

Ramon, an attractive dark-haired boy with a winning smile, had returned from Texas after an absence of about a year and a half. His parents were divorced, and the custody arrangements for him and his sisters changed frequently back and forth between the mother and father. The difficult thing for Ramon was that he had not been able to stay in one place for the duration of any school year since entering kindergarten. His family had moved in and out of our school, as well as many other schools in our district. He had not learned to read beyond a beginning second grade level, and he was embarrassed about it. He was defiant, and verbally abusive to peers as well as to adults. Everything was a confrontation, and his ability to argue was impressive. At other times, when he would get agitated, he would just mumble in Spanish, and make unpleasant facial expressions. But, he had another side to him as well. Sometimes, when recess was difficult, he would come into my room and ask if he could help me, and would erase the chalkboard, or play a game on the computer. The change in him was puzzling because his treatment of me would switch from ally to enemy within minutes.

Nick, an imaginative talker, with spiked blond hair, always had a pencil or colored markers in his hands or stuffed into the pockets of his blue denim jacket that he rarely took off. He would bargain for paper almost every day as he was always wanting to paint or draw. His cartoons were often controversial, and sometimes explicit for the shock value, but I soon learned that his self-confidence was grounded in his ability to draw. His competitiveness often got him in trouble when he boasted about being the best, but he would seldom back down even under threat of physical harm or pressure. Being somewhat small for his age, he made up for it in terms of speed and determination. His reading ability was lower than expected, and many oral reading sessions were difficult, as frustrated attempts could cause explosive results.

> October, 1989: The substitute teacher came in this morning at 8:30 holding Nick by the arm, saying that he had thrown a tantrum, had torn-up his worksheet, and had written on another student's paper causing it to be ruined. The teacher's response was, 'What shall I do with him? He's too disruptive to be in class'. Nick has a way of making his presence known, but I don't know what to do with him either. The principal was at a meeting, so what was I suppose to do? He came into my classroom, sat down at the table with the second graders in my group, and worked with them very peacefully. I felt bad for him, but by the time his group started at 9:30, he was right back mouthing off, and competing for his share of the attention.

Ben, a good-looking Navajo boy, dreamed of being a boxer and challenged many students to fights at recess to show them that he was the strongest and toughest. His inability to converse quickly enough with peers was a source of frustration for him. Often, while he was trying to express a thought, others would lose interest, turn, and walk away from him. The offending person would then receive a blow from behind. Because of his size and strength, he was capable of causing physical harm. Ben could read first grade material with a few prompts provided that it was done in private. His sensitivity to criticism was so keen that it seemed many students 'walked on eggshells' in awe of his bully reputation. But, he too, had a different side that was artistic and creative:

> September, 1989: Today, Ben came in during lunch recess to talk. I did not go to the faculty room for lunch because I had a headache, and had just wanted to turn out the lights and 'regroup.' Ben came in and asked, 'Are you sick?' I told him I just needed a little break. He asked me if I had seen the clouds outside because they were 'real pretty.' I looked outside, and it appeared that it might rain. Ben said, 'I love to watch clouds. When I'm in Gallup, I love to lay on the ground and look up at them. It makes me feel real good.' The bell rang, and Ben ran to wash his hands telling me, 'I hate to get my hands dirty.'

The windows these students opened for me as to who they were, always left me reeling. Just when I thought I had a hold on them, they would show me a new direction for my learning. The following events are representative of the major lessons that Ramon, Nick, and Ben contributed to my education during the 1989–90 school year. These experiences will convey the difficulties we faced together and apart, as we struggled to hear each other's voices and forge relationships.

Facing the facts: the teacher talks too much

My feeling of overload at the beginning of the year was due, in part, to my anxiety over presenting my paper at the conference in Ohio with the other members in the ERP. The push and stress of completing the paper was a stretch for me as I tried to integrate my experiences, and understand the research literature I had read. My paper focused on the teacher as a student, confronting my educative doors of confusion, opposition, and hope. The conflict for me was that I wasn't really hopeful, I only wanted to be. My experiences at school with the boys were, at best, tense. I often felt distracted and bothered with having to deal with their daily conflicts, or even to teach at all. A few days before leaving for the conference, there was an incident that should have alerted me to my own levels of incongruency, lack of understanding, and fear.

Ramon and Ben were involved in a fight at recess, and the playground aide brought them into my room to talk it out. I was impatient as it was the last thing I felt I had time in which to participate. As it turned out, I jumped in and talked too much and completely lost the students with too many words. The following journal entry is still painful as I remember back:

> October, 1989: I was asked to intervene in a conflict between Ramon and Ben. The outcome was that Ramon yelled at me defiantly, 'You're

not my real teacher!' I do feel like a fraud sometimes . . . Does that come from not being the real teacher? These students are driving me crazy! I don't think I can stand their insolent, abusive behavior for a whole year. Ben is like a buffalo to me. He pushes up against me, and pushes and pushes, and I feel like I'm about to be stampeded. His language skills are such that I can't really talk to him. He doesn't always understand what I say and doesn't care, for that matter. He told me today, 'Oh, you're just a woman, I don't have to talk to you!' And Ramon! I feel like pulling that tail of his hair, the little shit. He kept getting into my desk drawer, looking for God knows what, all the time I was trying to talk to him. It's hopeless! These kids have no respect for me, and they have no respect for each other, either!

I left for Ohio with these angry feelings, and tried to convince myself that everything would work out if I could just relax. The moment the plane landed, I felt out of sync with myself and the members of the ERP. The presentation of my paper was not a pleasant experience for me, and certainly was not a success. As with the boys, I talked too long and got very disoriented due to the stress and my need to perform. I did not accomplish this performance, and relived an old dream as I walked naked in a crowd of strangers.

After stumbling through this difficult afternoon, I found a glimmer of hope from hearing another paper at the conference later that same day. Still not sure of my feet, I didn't want to be with the others in the ERP because I was embarrassed and feeling that I had let them all down in some way. I heard this Japanese flute music somewhere down the hall, so I followed it, and went in and sat down. I cannot honestly say that I understood all that was said, but I was in this self-absorbed mood, and the presenter's words just washed over me. From his paper, *A Bell Ringing in an Empty Sky*, Jardine read the following passage:

This piece of music and its evocative title call up a sense of openness and spaciousness; images of echoing and resonances; images of the space for the natural affections of speech, its kindness, its interweaving and living kinships or 'family resemblances' to come forth. Our aspirations are strangulated into an unearthly discourse that must always have something new and notable to say at a moment's notice. We live, it seems, in a relentless proliferation of speech which leaves us neither time nor place for a settling word, for quietly shepherding the mystery of our earthliness which is no mystery at all, which is right at our fingertips no matter what.

(Jardine, 1989, p.3)

Jardine's paper was very complex in its own right with his references to more philosophers than I'd heard of, but I found a strange comfort in hearing the words. When he later made reference to a quotation from Piaget's *The Construction of Reality in the Child* (1971, p.15), it was a piece that somehow helped me to transport my thoughts back to my students and my challenges with them.

> The real work is what we really do. And what our lives are. And if we can live the work we have to do, knowing that we are real, then it becomes right. And that's the real work: to make the world as real as we are within it.

> (Jardine, 1989, p.23)

For a time, I sat quietly, lost in my own thoughts, and realized that 'the living kinships,' or 'family resemblances' had not come forth for me at this conference. I had wanted to connect, 'to be one of the guys,' but I was not ready, and my understanding was fragmented in this exotic environment. I had found it difficult literally to find a place at the table to eat my lunch, and found only a few people with whom I could risk a simple conversation.

Upon my return to school, I was surprisingly anxious to see the boys, and was committed to being real. My first encounter with Nick when I returned was both illuminating and comical. He came up to me in the hall before school started and said, 'You're back! Did you have fun?' Before I had a chance to answer, he added, 'I hope so, because you were really a grouch before you left.' With this opening for dialogue now closed, I feebly answered, 'Yeah, I had fun.' I really wasn't ready for the next lesson, but I got it anyway.

Face it: life isn't fair

Later on in the day, when Nick came to my class, he was teasing and hitting Ramon from behind trying to get a fight started. Ramon told me, 'Make him stop! You never do anything to make him stop!' I tried to get them to sit down so that we could get started with the lesson, but they wouldn't have it. Ramon took Nick's hat and began tossing it back and forth to Ben who had come into the room by then. I stood in the middle of the room and just watched them. Nick recaptured his hat, and yelled something at Ramon who exploded and started to cry. His outburst surprised me because I had not seen this display of emotion in him before. I moved toward Ramon, but he pulled away, telling me he knew that I didn't care about him, and that I always took Nick's side, and I was like all teachers who said they cared but didn't. I tried to suggest that he calm down, and give me a chance to talk to him to see if I could help, but his response was to leave the classroom, and tell me, 'I'm never coming to your class again!'

The next morning before school started, Ramon knocked at the window of my classroom to say 'Hi' as though nothing had happened. Even though it was early, I invited him in to have that talk. He quickly came around to the door, and seemed calm and willing to have a conversation.

The multiplicity of feelings this conversation created for me would continue to offer a focus for the next several months. I started the discussion with something like, 'So, what happened yesterday? You seemed pretty upset. Can we talk about it now?' His response was, 'Talking never helps.' I asked him why he'd come in then if he didn't want to talk? Right away, I knew I had created some defensiveness and felt, myself, that talking might not help. The following journal entry would be one that I would read over and over, trying to make sense of it:

> October, 1989: This morning, Ramon came in to talk about his outburst yesterday, I thought, but instead he just kept flitting around the room telling me things about his family, the new pierced ear he had that was now infected. Then, he took a yard stick and started making fencing moves, and asked me if I knew how to play pool – told me he was a good pool player, etc. Then the bell rang, and he asked if he could stay with me for the morning. I promptly told him, 'No. You have to go upstairs.' He mumbled a derogatory remark at me, and said, 'See, you don't care.' I grabbed his arm, and told him, 'Look, you can think what you want, but you can't say what you want around here!' The minute this was out of my mouth – well, where did this come from? I must have said things like this a lot of times before – but here I invited Ramon to talk. He says talking doesn't help. So, he talks, and what do I say? 'You can't say what you want.'

It seemed to me that Ramon's byline in life was, ' That's not fair!' It drove me beyond frustration sometimes as I thought it was also his supreme manipulation of me: a button he could push somewhere in me to get me to let up on him. It was so disappointing that, on many days, he would greet me with a smile but would leave swearing.

I was at a point of 'living contradiction' (Whitehead, 1985). I wanted to create a warm, successful environment for my students and develop relationships with them to enhance their chances for success, but I didn't like them very much. In many ways, the class was a negation of my stated values and the very intentions I advertised for all.

The subsequent literature I read, interestingly, focused on women and moral development. Gilligan (1982) challenged both Piaget and Kohlberg on their justice perceptions of moral development, and introduced a perspective of care. My feelings of detachment from Ramon, in particular, elicited an uncomfortable recognition for me as I read the following passages from Gilligan's later work:

> Since everyone is vulnerable both to oppression and to abandonment, two moral visions – one of justice and one of care recur in human experience. The moral injunctions, not to act unfairly toward others, and to not turn away from someone in need, capture these different concerns. . . . The strength of women's moral perceptions lies in the refusal of detachment and depersonalization . . . The promise in joining women and moral theory lies in the fact that human survival, in the late twentieth century, may depend less on formal agreement than on human connection.
>
> (Gilligan, 1987, pp.20 and 32)

The paper I had presented at the Ohio conference was about reaching for the human connection, but in my practice, there was this enormous gap that I wanted to close, and did not know how to do it. Ramon seemed to be helping me learn about issues of equality and justice. My challenge, I thought, would be to figure out how to care authentically and not abandon him. However, this opportunity would be taken from me as his parents pulled him abruptly out of school, and moved him back to Texas by the end of November. This left me with a sense of having unfinished business, and a lost sense of control as I had to let go of him after all, and could not make my peace with him.

Face against face: conflicting identities

Wanting to change and changing are not the same, obviously, but sometimes it is hard to accept the difference. The complexity of dialogue is certainly more difficult to understand than I had imagined. Gadamer (1975) provided me with the following insight:

> The art of dialectic is not the art of being able to win every argument. On the contrary, it is possible that someone who is practicing the art of dialectic, i.e. the art of questioning and seeking truth, comes off worse in the argument in the eyes of those listening to it . . . The art of questioning is that of being able to go on asking questions, i.e. the art of thinking. It is called 'dialectic' for it is the art of conducting a real conversation.
>
> (In Lomax, 1989, p.40)

Nick also provided me with an opportunity to learn about real conversations early in January. He was two weeks late in returning from the

Christmas holiday break, and openly expressed his displeasure about being back in school. When he came in at 2:00, he burst through the door, and announced, 'I'm not doing any of this crap, and you can't make me!' Within a few minutes, he was pushing chairs over, dumping out blocks, and ripping up other students' papers. Ben got involved, and had a strangulation hold on Nick, causing his face to go red. It was toward the end of the day, and I'd had it. I went over to Ben and pulled him off Nick, but Nick just laughed and was off and running again. I went after him, literally cornered him, and demanded that he stop. It was one of those moments that escalated beyond reason. The following journal excerpt describes this unraveling event:

> January, 1990: I did something today that could get me fired if anyone found out about it. I think that maybe I ought to quit. I can't seem to get a grip on my feelings. Nick was really wild today, and I don't know why. It was his first day back after the vacation and he was really out of control. I wasn't pressing him to do anything – this is the hard part – but I got so angry, I was out of control. I pushed him against the wall and told him to stop or else the consequences wouldn't be good. He pushed his face up to mine and said, 'Cunt!', and like a reflex, I slapped him on the face. Ben, Candace, and Leslie all watched without a word while I told him with more rage than I've felt in years, 'No one gets away with calling me that!'

The instant I slapped Nick, I was jolted back to reality. Nick's face was flushed as he yelled, 'Why don't you slap your own kids around?' I instinctively knew I couldn't let him go just yet, so I maintained my balance as I looked him directly in the eye, and tried to restore the natural rhythm of my breathing. It was one of those moments that was frozen in time. As I looked at Nick's face closely, and saw the little bubbles of perspiration on his upper lip, my heart pounded. This was an eleven-year-old boy. I realized that I was responding as a woman would to a man, not as a teacher to her student. I did not feel proud of this intervention strategy. I knew what it was like to be cornered and wanting to fight back. But here I was, doing the cornering, and the fighting back. I felt Nick relax a little, so I stepped back from him. There was a moment when neither one of us said anything and we just looked at each other. I wanted to say something that would smooth this over, but I had no words to describe my feelings. The tears started to well-up in my eyes, but did not spill out. I think Nick saw this, and reached out his hand. We made a feeble handshake. He didn't say he was sorry, and neither did I. I felt a strong connection to Nick that was much different than I had hoped for, but I couldn't deny the power of the moment. Things were amazingly quiet in the room and Candace simply asked, 'You were really mad, weren't you?' The intensity of this confrontation left me feeling drained. I felt exhausted that last hour of the day. Both Nick and I left soon after the bell rang. I suppose it is strange that we never talked about this event again, but as I think back on this moment, my response mirrored my personal history. My usual style for facing the reality of conflict was to back off when threatened or pressured. Though this episode literally threw me off my center, I know that because of this experience, Nick helped me learn the value of otherness, and the tremendous creative challenge involved in dealing with diversity. This moment with Nick is one that I will never forget. In a way, it brought to my awareness some painful roots of who I am. Gurevitch consoled me with this encouragement:

> One assumes that by striking up a conversation and by declaring a will to overcome differences and to lay down a basis of understanding, dialogue will succeed. Every attempt at understanding requires, therefore, not more explanations, but first the power to not understand, to restore the other party's freedom as other to participate on an equal basis as a free, independent party to a dialogue. Only when two parties grant each other the power of presenting themselves as other origins of truth and justice, can dialogue begin.
>
> (Gurevitch, 1989, p.162)

Nick helped me push through my ambiguity about the conflict of difference so that I could begin to confront my own capacities for being a 'conflicting identity' (Gurevitch, 1989). However, my behavior for the next few months was very low-key as I searched for ways to enhance my own sense of self-esteem and productivity.

Facing success: celebration and collapse

As a result of an overload of third grade students in our school for the year, I was given the opportunity to teach the science and social studies curriculum for sixteen students. Eight students were considered to be regular education students while six were considered academically at risk. Only two students were identified as special education students. The time commitment in the day was one hour, and I really began to look forward to it. It was not a time of war, but one of enjoyment and even laughter. Some of the students were behaviorally challenging, but there was a good feeling in the classroom. I enjoyed learning about science with these third graders. The students gave me feedback that they liked coming to my class, that 'it was fun.' I found that I was thinking about the third grade group more and more. It was a creative time for me as I thought of what projects to try next. I sometimes let the projects spill-over to the other students who came to my classes during the day. When we were making papier mâché animals for individual reports, Ben, Nick, and a number of other students asked if they could also make animals. The result was a wild monster from Nick, and a large white swan from Ben.

By the end of May, there was a school-wide event that was a sharing and a celebration of individual class projects that related to our year-long study of Japan with our exchange teacher, 'Toshi.' Many classes wanted to demonstrate their newly acquired skills for writing Japanese characters, creating poetry, and mastering many Origami patterns. However, Toshi had asked if some classes could display typical subjects and projects that American students study in elementary school. He wanted to complete a slide presentation to take back to Japan to represent his experience with our school.

The third grade group who had been studying the solar system at the end of the year decided they wanted to turn my room into outer space. They made models of planets, rockets, and space stations, and labeled them in their best Japanese lettering. They welcomed Japanese and US astronauts, as well as those from Jupiter and Mars. Their intent was to create a universe belonging to everyone. The structure for school-wide sharing was an open house for all students to parade through each of the classrooms to see the various projects. I had not seen students so excited in a long time. Other teachers who came with their students to my room said, 'This is wonderful! How did you get the students to do all this?' My response was that they just wanted to, I guessed. I was elated and feeling good. Then the recess bell rang and the parade was over. Ben burst into the room, and started knocking things off tables, batting the rockets that hung tentatively by string from the overhead light fixtures, and pulled sheets from the various stations that had been pinned together to designate different worlds and planets. The noise was tremendous, as many students implored me to 'Make him stop!' I cleared everyone out except Ben, and grabbed him firmly by the arm, and demanded angrily, 'What's going on with you?' Ben's response was, 'My real dad died.' I let go of his arm and moved toward him to give him a hug. This gesture was refused vehemently, as he pushed me away and told me, 'Navajos don't give hugs. Don't you understand anything?', and then he left, leaving me with a significantly trashed room. Some of the third grade students came in the room again and were quite upset about their ruined projects.

I felt a sense of loss and collapse. I didn't know any more about success with these students at the end of the ERP, than I had known at the beginning. I interpreted this event as a defeat, a battle lost. The following journal entry describes my feelings.

May, 1990: I wanted things to turn out so differently than they did, but even today, I can't exactly articulate the source of this lump in my throat. I almost cried when I talked to Ben and asked him how I could touch him to let him know I care. I probed him, I guess, because I wasn't really convinced that 'Navajo's don't give hugs.' Have I really made a big cultural mistake, or is he jerking me around, playing this little game with me? . . . Ben told me today that we could shake hands, so we created a special-coded handshake. I asked him if he hugged his family, his mother. He said, 'Sure, but you're not my mother.'

With Ben, I was on the outside, trying to get in, and felt badly that I did not know how to help him. I later acknowledged that I had wanted a hug from Ben that day he trashed the room, and was beginning to see that I did want to find a place for love in education. The intensity of my feelings for Ben opened me to new understanding of the possibilities and limitations of developing student and teacher relationships. One such possibility is described by Noddings.

What the giver hopes for is genuine response in the receiver – the more confident growth, more open communication, more joy in companionship, more serenity in trouble and stress . . . All this means, I think, that teachers must find ways to be with their students: to talk with them (and not at them) about their own lives and about great intellectual ideas, to solve problems with them rather than merely setting the problems, to share cultural delights with them without testing the joy out of the shared event.

(Noddings, 1989, p.192)

CONCLUSION: THE BEGINNING AND THE END

As I look back on my two year study to define success, I can find laughter and I can find tears. Like Carlos Castaneda, in *Journey to Ixtlan* (1971), I had wanted to 'stop the world and see,' but this did not happen. If I remember his story correctly, each of us has a place we are hunting for in the world of power. As a woman and a teacher I have found it difficult to 'be one of the guys.' It has also been a struggle to develop my voice and seek personal empowerment. I have lived long enough to have many of my illusions shattered, and feel the gendered differences that have restricted my voice. I have found it difficult to find my place in the many cultural worlds in which I am asked to participate. But, as Wise (1980) suggests, looking at any culture in the 'whole' is not possible. I would like to add that looking at 'success' in the whole is not possible, either. I find his notion of 'taking the strategic journey through concentric fields' to be more within the range of my learning style as I am not a particularly linear thinker. I feel I have been successful in finding a focal point that has identified a series of 'concentric fields' for my education as a teacher, as a woman, and as a human reaching for connection to other humans who are trying to find their feet on different paths than my own.

'The circle of understanding', as Gurevitch explains, involves the ability to not understand. He suggests that the notion of the 'common' is necessary for understanding, but understanding also values the contributions of the strange.

> Dialogue requires understanding, but it never overcomes the strange. The strange remains a creative challenge, a source of possibility and vitality, and a seed of alienation, opposition, and war.
>
> (Gurevitch, 1989, p.162)

At times, I have felt that I have gone around the world and back with no improvement in my understanding, and have been disappointed in the resiliency of my war metaphors. I have wanted to replace them, and to become someone else. I have always been a kind of wanderer, and I have been encouraged since childhood to watch where I was going. I suspect that I will not become someone else and suddenly have my directionality problems cured. The fact that I focus on narrow paths, and look down at my feet is really the 'good news' and the 'bad news' about who I am. In the real world of teaching and education, one could not get through the day if one did not focus on the here and now. Teachers are not often expected to inaugurate new knowledge and scholarship, but are expected to absorb such a vast base of information that apathy is often the result of the overload. The pursuit of abstract knowledge can be a propelling direction toward possibility, but if education only addresses the race for competitiveness in the world, we will all lose. The assumption that all knowledge is digestible is a step away from reality. My view today is that teachers must be allowed to prioritize their commitments, and to protest some of the requests aimed at them to deliver more than society can. It is impossible to support every good educational cause or argument with equal passion and scholarship. One 'Elementary Axiom' from Wise (1977) suggests an approach that I find helpful now.

> Scholarship is a serious business, but we must not take ourselves too seriously. We should remind ourselves that 'play' of mind as well as 'work' of mind is necessary to understanding. Besides, it is healthier!
>
> (Wise, 1977, p.530)

I have admitted that my experience as a teacher has reflected work more often than play, but if there is any culture where 'play of mind' should be encouraged, it is the culture of teaching. My step into Educative Research has been a step into a difficult concentric field that has helped me to move in the direction of wanting to play.

I have also learned how to be a participant with other teachers, with a greater sense of reciprocity and purpose, and have come to a real beginning pride in calling myself 'teacher.' In allowing some pieces of who I am out into the world, I have started to examine my own attributes and limitations for teaching, which has given me the courage to continue on my journey. Stenhouse (1979) expresses simply what I distill my experience to be in the ERP.

> We shall only teach better if we learn intelligently from the experience of shortfall both in our grasp of the knowledge we offer and our knowledge of how to offer it. That is the case for research as a basis of teaching.
>
> (In Lomax, 1989, p. 21)

The current language of strategic planning for success in education is enticing for anyone who has such well developed war metaphors as I do, but my hope is now more grounded in my growing ability to voice my protest of any mission to which I cannot authentically contribute. I yet have other concentric fields to travel through in order to understand the success question, but if Eeva were to ask me what success involves today, I would tell her that it has a lot to do with love, and learning the difference between hope and expectation just as Illich said in the beginning of my search for understanding.

> Hope means trusting in the goodness of nature, while expectation infers the reliance on the results produced by man. Hope centers desire on a person from whom we await a gift. Expectation looks forward to satisfaction from a predictable process which will produce what we have a right to claim.
>
> (Illich, 1971, p.152)

My hope is that when I again find myself on a narrow path, and my gaze is down on my feet, there will be another student like Ben, who will love me enough to ask if I've seen the clouds.

8 Computers: the link to tomorrow or the reproduction of today's inequalities

The first computer arrived at my elementary school in 1982. After a brief mandatory teacher training session which dealt with the fundamentals of Apple Basic programming, my interest in computers started to develop. In the weeks that followed, I spent hours in a small crowded room trying to figure out very simple programs. The principal was duly impressed with my dedication. Over time, I became very interested in the mechanics of the technology and attended district computer workshops whenever they were offered.

At this point, my curiosity about computers had little impact on my classroom practice in part because the school had only one stationary computer. However, as the school acquired more computers and different types of software, I started to use the computer in my classroom. My first attempts to implement this technology primarily involved students taking turns using drill and practice programs for math, spelling, and language arts. I enjoyed the activities, as did the students, and felt confident that I was part of the vanguard of educational practice.

After using the computer for about two years, I firmly believed that this technology would revolutionize schooling by enabling teachers to meet the individual needs of students. Computers would be, as Thompson and Cloer noted, 'the link between yesterday's proven learning theories, today's learner, and tomorrow's world' (Thompson and Cloer, 1982, p.84). I had discovered the answer to the problems of large class size, high and low achievers, and students' lack of interest in school. All students would be taught through this medium, with the gifted students doing problem solving and higher level thinking skills, and the low achievers spending their time 'catching up.' Endlessly patient, this technology would move the student from one level to another with ease, thereby making it possible for teachers to serve large numbers of students more efficiently.

In my view, the only problem with using the computer was trying to gain the needed technical expertise. To overcome this problem, I signed up for computer training sessions which focused on, among other topics, 'user-friendly software.' These sessions reinforced my beliefs about the importance of computers. No questions were raised about the politics of computing or the more specific concerns about which groups of students might benefit most from this technology.

A RESEARCH QUESTION

As might be expected, when I decided to pursue a Masters Degree in Education, I chose computers and technology as an area of specialty. However, due to university cutbacks, this area was no longer an option in the Cooperative Masters program. This was a serious disappointment for me, for I had hoped a degree in educational technology would enhance my expertise and knowledge of computers. I envisioned myself as the first teacher in my district to become a full-time computer director in an elementary school. My disappointment, however, was quickly overcome when I realized that in the ERP I could continue to pursue my personal interest in computers. At this point, the only research question I could think of was whether it was better to put computers in the classroom or to develop a computer laboratory. My personal goals were to promote educational computing and to find the knowledge that would help me use computers more effectively in the classroom.

As I reviewed the literature as part of the Educative Research process, I found validation for what I already believed to be true: the problem with computing was how to implement these machines as quickly and efficiently as possible. Dwyer, for example, supported my view that computers could accomplish what no other technology had before.

> We have found that computing, placed in the hands of well-supported teachers and students, can be an agent for catalyzing educational accomplishment of a kind that is without precedent. We believe that there has been no other tool like it in the history of education.
>
> (Dwyer, 1980, p.113)

Mullan (1984) reinforced my assumption that computer technology would enhance learning. Specifically, he viewed the computer as an electronic blackboard that could deal with the 'what if' situations better than through traditional methods. A child could use a program and the machine would be endlessly patient, giving praise and moving the child to the next level of difficulty. Gross (1989) relieved any doubt I might have had about the impact of computers on low achieving students by explaining that a good

CAI (computer-assisted instruction) system could be a crucial part of a program to keep these youngsters in school by improving test scores and enhancing self-confidence.

Rizza (1982) furthered this line of thinking by suggesting that gifted education could also be served by computer systems which provided access to a wide array of challenging instructional materials. And Papert (1980) removed any lingering doubt I might have had by suggesting that computers could give students more control of the curriculum by having them do the programming.

The question: a reconsideration

In spite of this confirming literature, my beliefs about computers were not to remain fixed. As I continued to read, I also found arguments which refuted those that supported my position. For example, there were critical concerns raised about drill and practice software. If the computer is simply a substitute for the worksheet, it was argued, this technology would do nothing more than increase the endless repetition pervasive in schools and surely do nothing to increase students' control over the curriculum. These concerns, which I had not previously considered, encouraged me to examine the question of computers from a different perspective. In particular, I started to look at the relationship between computers and society. When I did so, I found authors such as Bowers arguing that the proponents of educational computing were 'strengthening the connections between schooling and a technological social order' (Bowers, 1988, p.95) by centering educational experiences on simulated situations as opposed to real world problems. Teaching, in his view, should be about the formation of educational communities in which students act on their environment, not about figuring out abstract possibilities. Broughton (1984), on the other hand, criticized Papert's advocacy of educational computing because it valued systems over cultural understanding. And Sardello (1984) felt computer use would completely remove the student from concerns about life and the environment. Personal feelings and beauty in nature would be de-emphasized as this doomsday device was implemented.

My review of the literature produced an internal struggle. I felt that the computer might serve the needs of low achieving students, allowing them to learn the skills which could help them advance, and challenge the gifted with problem-solving programs. I was concerned, however, about the repetitious nature of schooling, the need to have students act on their environment, and the importance of appreciating the aesthetics of the natural world. I was not convinced that any of the views I encountered in the readings represented the total position that I, or any teacher, should take. I did not accept new arguments without question, but I also could not keep my previous beliefs without some reservation.

While this process of rethinking the use of computers began with arguments which questioned computing, my concern about gender was the one factor which initiated the most powerful reason to refocus my approach. Issues about gender and equity were addressed in a general sense as part of the ERP. I found these readings and discussions to be of great personal interest, but at first did not see how they related to the question of the implementation of computers. As I reflected on my personal history, however, I began to see connections between issues of gender and computing.

My experiences as a child were strongly influenced by divisions between boys and girls. It was neither fashionable nor acceptable to be interested in sports as a young girl in the fifties. The typical label of 'tomboy' was not one I accepted without internal protest. It was painful to watch from the outside while my peers were able to participate in Little League, and I, knowing that my skills were comparable, if not superior to some of these boys, had to accept this sideline position. I recall sitting in the stands watching my neighborhood friends enjoy the competition while I was limited to cheering. Boys my age were making substantial money caddying while the girls were relegated to poorly paid babysitting jobs. The drum and bugle corps was also divided along gender lines: only boys were allowed to actually play the instruments while girls carried the flags. Even here the girls were silenced and obviously too inadequate or ladylike to handle the manly art of blowing into metal or beating something with a stick.

In contrast, my experience as an undergraduate allowed me to see women in positions of authority and power. In the late sixties, I attended a small Catholic women's college that reflected the religious, educational, and political freedom movement of that time. There were women professors and leaders who took controversial stands concerning civil rights. Students were encouraged to be compassionate and involved in community struggles with poverty and injustice, even if their beliefs challenged the religious practices of that time. There was a compelling sense of community where individuals felt concern and empathy. These strong women helped me realize that I could combine the traits of leadership and power with those of caring and nurturing.

In large part, because of these contrasting images, I wanted to avoid the artificial divisions of my childhood and promote wider opportunities for girls in my classroom. In 1979, the media center in my elementary school used sixth graders as audio-visual helpers. These students were allowed to be in the projection booth during assemblies, and go to different classrooms to run the movies for teachers. Historically, all these helpers had been boys, so I made changing this practice my goal. Although it took two years to convince those in charge that the change would not cause educational havoc, girls were finally allowed to be audio-visual helpers. In addition, requests from the office for 'some strong boys' to carry or deliver boxes were now filled with a mixture of strong girls and boys who complied with equal enthusiasm to breathe the air of freedom in the halls.

Even though this good faith attempt seemed to satisfy my quest to challenge divisions between boys and girls, my experience as part of the ERP encouraged me to ask further questions about gender. Did I challenge boys more often, give them more time to respond, and encourage them to stick with it? If girls were quiet, did I move on to others, the boys? If a boy didn't respond, would I prod him more, expect more, and therefore give him attention I would not give a silent girl? With these concerns in mind, my research question could no longer remain bound by issues of effectiveness, such as whether or not to implement a computer lab. Gender bias and equity were clearly concerns in my past that needed to be linked to my everyday school life.

To begin to integrate these concerns into my research question, I decided to ask initially why computing should be included in the school curriculum. I then focused on who had access to computers and whose interests were served by their use. In particular, I wanted to know if students had equal access to computing and if they were challenged in similar ways by the experience. These issues were pursued during the first year in the ERP and provided the framework for new questions about gender differences and student perceptions about computing. Do girls perceive their abilities differently than boys? Do boys and girls believe that gender is a factor in deciding who is competent in using the computer? I realized that I had neglected these questions as I rushed to implement computers in my classroom. In addressing my first query about why we are using vast amounts of resources, both human and financial, to promote computers, I came across some literature that confronted some of my assumptions about this technology. I had assumed that if computers are perceived as the future, then we, as teachers, need to prepare students to meet that future. Prior to my involvement in the ERP, I was convinced that computer jobs were the new wave of future employment. Once I explored the computer literature, however, I discovered that there was a significant amount of research that refuted this notion. Jobs in high-tech industries, it appeared, would account for only a small percentage of the total people in the workforce. Apple (1986) stated that current research indicated only 15 percent of projected jobs would be in high-tech areas and of the people employed in these industries less than 25 percent would have jobs requiring advanced computer knowledge. The vast majority of workers would be doing assembly or data processing, jobs which paid workers the least. Jobs such as computer engineers or analysts would be well paid, but these would account for only a small minority of workers. Apple argued further that the workers at the lower end of the pay scale would be predominantly women.

These arguments made a tremendous impact on my vision of computing in schools. I began to realize that my zeal for computers might run counter to my beliefs about equality. I needed to find out more about the implications of computer practice.

THE FIRST EXPLORATION

One way to explore computer practice was to understand how teachers in my school were using the computer. Having only one computer in a classroom required the teacher to manage the movement of students to and from the single machine. I wanted to find out how teachers arranged for students to have a turn on the computer, and whether these times were equal for all students. I also wanted teachers to describe which groups of students were using the computer most often. Finally, I asked teachers to explain what types of software were being used. I felt these issues were important because they would help me to see how computers might have connections to my concerns about gender and strengthen inequalities between students generally.

To research these issues, I interviewed five teachers, one from each grade level, second through sixth (see Appendix A).[9] I chose an interview approach because it was more personal than, for example, a survey. Through interviewing, I could learn more about the teachers. Because teachers are accustomed to being treated as a large, homogeneous, and often faceless group, I believed that interviews would also place value on their opinions.

Issues of equity

When asked to respond to the question of who most frequently requests computer time, Jean (all names used in the study are fictitious) noted that in her class there was an equal amount of requests from both the girls and boys. However, she stated that boys were 'more competitive' than girls in their utilization of software. Another teacher, Kelly, stated that boys more frequently requested computer time. 'The first name that comes to mind is Jake.' Betty, on the other hand, described the most dominant users as 'aggressive, smart boys.' She felt that at times these boys 'intimidated' the girls, encouraging them to hang back. Hence, the girls would not use the computer when boys were around to watch them. She responded that the girls would rarely mix with the boys and stated that there was 'too much competition' for the girls to feel comfortable enough to participate with boys. These examples suggested that boys and girls interacted with the computer in very different ways. When I looked at how teachers scheduled computer time, I could see why this sort of inequality and others were encouraged through taken-for-granted classroom practices.

One such practice is the tendency to allow students who finish first to use the computer. This type of selection process seemed to be favored at my school. For example, according to Kelly, during the interview, the students who most frequently requested time were high achievers. Betty commented that the frequent users were, 'the ones who are getting finished . . . the ones getting A's or high B's in the class . . . that pushed themselves . . . expected a lot of themselves.' In my own classroom practice, I had often tried keeping a list and having students take turns. However, I too would allow students who finished first or those who finished assignments accurately to take extra turns. This practice tended to be a convenient way to keep the computer in use. But at the same time, it also gave advantages to those who are already high achievers. The fact that other teachers used this same technique was not unexpected, but still disturbing given its implications for those less successful students who need the most attention in schools.

I began to realize that software choices, while seeming to individualize instruction, also strengthened inequalities between low and high achievers. This difference appeared to be related to the common practice of using rote, workbook-type programs with low achieving students, and problem-solving ones with high achievers. Four of the teachers interviewed used some drill and practice software with low achievers, while only two teachers used a problem-solving approach. My own classroom practice and these findings support O'Connor's position that drill and practice is given more frequently to low achievers. As O'Connor states:

> Students who are achieving at a high level are typically given computer experiences in which they are in control of the situation. Those who are having difficulty seldom experience anything, but drill and practice.
>
> (O'Connor, 1986. p.234)

However, a few teachers did allow specific times when all students could use any available software. It cannot be concluded, therefore, that drill and practice is used exclusively with low achieving students. Instead, the findings of this study suggest that often teachers use different types of software for low and high achieving students.

These findings indicate that the assignment of particular students to certain kinds of software based on their academic achievement, and the allotment of computer time according to who finishes first, are common practices that further inequities between students. Clearly, the issue of computing was more complex than I had thought.

THE DEVELOPMENT OF A NEW DIRECTION

Since teachers were the focus of the first year's study, I was determined to involve students in the second phase. I also wanted to make sure my classroom practice reflected my beliefs about gender and the appropriate place of women in society. To consider the relation between my beliefs and practices, I gave thirty students in my fourth grade class a survey to ascertain their understandings and attitudes about computing (see Appendix B). They were asked to give a response ranging from strongly agree to strongly disagree. Included in the survey were questions concerning who owned computers at home and to what extent they were used. Preferences about choosing the computer over other choices during free time were also sought. The children were asked to name students they perceived as experts in computer technology. The same survey was given at the end of the year to discern any changes in student opinion. In addition, students were asked to keep a journal and with each computer turn include an entry that expressed their feelings about how the session on the computer affected them. Did they feel confident, confused, anxious, relaxed, or worried? I asked them to express their feelings freely and explained that I wanted to try to alleviate problems, if possible. Finally, ten students chosen randomly were interviewed at the end of the year for their opinions about the differences between boys' and girls' expertise on the computer (see Appendix C).

Myths, beliefs, choices: two perspectives

The girls in my class did not feel they knew much about computers and often named boys as being the computer experts. They also indicated that they resisted the challenging programs and were concerned about making mistakes. In some cases, these concerns were intensified when the boys competed with the girls for computer time. Monica, for example, noted that, 'Ben was using it all the time . . . I thought he was really good.' Mary Ann observed, 'We could use it when we wanted to, but the boys would get there first and make fun of us if we lost at 'Math Blaster'.' When boys and girls used the computer together, boys tended to dominate. One girl stated, 'He wouldn't let me do anything . . . he took up the whole time.' Another complained, 'Sam kept telling me what to do the whole time . . . my turn was a disaster.' These comments reinforced the assumption that the boys were the computer experts.

This domination by the boys seemed to increase the girls' doubts about their ability to use the computer. For example, one girl commented that, 'My computer turn was horrible . . . I couldn't get it to work.' Another said, 'I felt stupid . . . I made too many mistakes.' Still a third remarked, 'It was terrible. I couldn't get it right.' These statements reflect a sense of self-blame for not understanding the program. If something went wrong, it could not be the fault of the machine or program, the problem must lie with the user.

As the year went on, however, girls gained confidence in their abilities. One girl remarked, 'My turn on the computer was really fun. I figured it out by myself. It was easier than I thought.' Still another girl who expressed dissatisfaction with computer use in the initial survey remarked, 'This was great . . . my turn turned out better than I figured . . . it was neat.' When Alicia was interviewed, she related how well she did when the task became difficult, 'I just about quit . . . but then I figured it out . . . it was neat.' It seemed that some of the previous apprehensions were alleviated as the girls acquired more skill through experience.

In contrast, right from the beginning of the year the boys expressed little apprehension about this technology. In the first survey, all the boys agreed that they 'knew a lot about computers.' Performing tasks which were challenging to them was not a deterrent in their self-evaluation of computer skills. Nine of the boys could definitely see themselves in the computer programming profession. Unlike the girls, who named both boys and girls in listing those who were experts, the boys named only boys.

In their journals, some boys had negative experiences similar to the girls, but with fewer occurrences. One boy commented, 'It was fun, but I worried something would go wrong and I would get in trouble.' When there was a computer experience which turned out to be less than pleasant, several boys blamed the program. 'It was stupid . . . the dumb stuff wouldn't work right . . . ' 'It was dumb . . . I hated it.' These comments reflect the boys' feelings that the fault lay with the machine or the program; it did not seem to be internalized. Unlike the girls, there was little blame put on themselves.

By the end of the year, some of the students' beliefs started to change. For example, when the students were asked if they thought the boys or the girls were better at using the computer, Josh commented, 'I really think the girls were actually a little better . . . Alicia and Bonnie were real good at the math problem solver.' Monica also stated that, 'Neither the boys or girls were better . . . we're both good!' Still another girl remarked, 'I don't think one was better than the other . . . there's no difference.' The girls also demonstrated a significant decrease in their anxiety, illustrated by their acceptance of making mistakes on the computer without worry. Furthermore, while not one boy named a girl as having expertise in the earlier survey, in the second survey, four boys included girls' names. Clearly, the experience of using the computer for a year altered both girls' and boys' attitudes about the ability of girls to be computer experts.

While these findings are encouraging, the past socialization of these girls may have already limited their views of themselves and their role in the world. In their journals, for example, girls expressed the belief that they would choose the traditional occupations of teaching and nursing. Many put marriage as their top priority for the future and quite a number saw large families as desirable. There is nothing inherently wrong with these choices; however, many of these girls will find themselves needing to work in the public sphere in jobs that require some computer skills, such as retail clerks, bank tellers, and data processors. These jobs are not the ones paying the best wages, as both Apple (1986) and Weiler (1988) indicate. As a teacher, what this suggests to me is that while it is desirable for girls to gain confidence in their ability to use the computer, it is also necessary to expose the students to the political implications of gender that are inherent in this technology. This would include an awareness of how women are relegated to lower paying, lower status jobs, and the fact that work in the home is devalued. If such a curriculum could be implemented, some of the political implications of computers could be illuminated and, hopefully, challenged.

CONCLUSION

The journey that has led me to gain technical expertise has also led me to examine the political dimensions of computing. In particular, when I looked at computer use, it became apparent that instructional techniques, such as 'open computer time,' provided advantages for the boys in the class as well as those who finished their work first.

In many ways, these results are not surprising given that teacher training sessions and other computer forums tend to emphasize the mechanics of computing to the exclusion of the political dimensions. If computers are to do more than serve the interests of those who are already advantaged, computer education must be expanded to include the politics of computing. It is significant to note that the one teacher in the study who used techniques which fostered equal access to the computers, attended a computer workshop in which the idea of equity was stressed. Teacher practice should reflect a concern about equity if the computer curriculum is to avoid silencing particular students. As Tittnich and Brown note, this responsibility lies solely with those who develop and use this technology.

It is time then, to look at the development of people. . . . The obligation for responsible social and moral uses of technology must come from the individuals who develop and use it because the technology itself does not possess those human characteristics.

(Tittnich and Brown, 1982, p.21)

However, even if teachers used instructional techniques that allowed equal access to computing, inequities between students would still be likely. This is so because students come to the classroom having had different opportunities to use computers at home. Obviously, those families who have the economic resources to buy computers will have an advantage over those who cannot purchase this technology. Furthermore, socialization may also play a role in encouraging boys to use computers more often in the home than girls. Since it is likely that particular groups of students will enter the classroom with certain computing advantages over others, it is essential that teachers view this activity as something that happens not only in schools, but also in the home. By viewing computing as an experience that goes beyond the school context, teachers are more likely to act on inequities that may be hidden if the focus is on equal access in the school. One specific way to confront this type of inequality, as Kepner (1986) states, is to increase computer time for girls and those who do not have the resources to buy computers for the home. Terry (1987) supports this position and suggests that schools provide an extra twenty minutes of computer time for groups of students who have limited access to computers at home. My current view is that I will provide extra computer time for those who have limited opportunities in order to challenge the viable gap between the computer 'haves' and 'have nots.'

Understanding that computer inequities start long before students enter school was an important insight for me. I have, however, also come to realize that inequities connected to computing are not totally explained by concerns about computer access. The type of knowing fostered by computers also plays a role. For the most part computer programming reflects a linear, sequential form of knowing. If this form of knowing is accepted without scrutiny, other forms of knowing are likely to be de-emphasized and/or devalued. In particular, it is likely that the linear, sequential form of knowing furthered by computers will devalue a more feminine expression that tends to be holistic and integrated. The ways of knowing fostered by computers, therefore, must be understood as *one* way of dealing with knowledge, not *the* way, if particular groups are to benefit equally from this technology.

Finally, my study of computers has also helped me see that the politics of computing involves understanding computer decisions within the wider context of other educational decisions. In my school, for example, there was a choice between a music program and a computer system that uses a particular type of software. The system was seen as desirable, but its cost required that we cut our music program and reduce our athletic classes. Part of the politics of computing is considering the value of computers in relation to other programs in the school. For our school, we felt the 'cost' of the new computer system was too high.

One of the most significant results of my struggle is that I've learned something about my unquestioned acceptance of computers. What was at first a simple issue about computers became a complicated one. I now believe that issues in education are extremely complex and involve varied layers of understanding. I have acquired a new frame of mind with regard to computers and other educational issues. Initially, it was easy for me to jump on the bandwagon and try to find opinions which agreed with my own. Through the ERP, however, the question of whose needs are served and who benefits from computing has become a consistent educational concern.

APPENDIX A: QUESTIONS FOR TEACHER INTERVIEWS

1 Describe the method of classroom management used to access students' use of the computer.
2 Are there any periods of time when the computer is available to requests from students?
3 Can you recall any specific students who requested time more often than others?
4 Describe the types of students who made these requests.
  a Was there a dominance of boys?
  b Describe their level of achievement.
5 Describe the types of software you use.
6 Have you assigned specific software to particular students?
  Explain the situations under which this occurred.

APPENDIX B

Name _____

	Strongly Agree	Neutral	Disagree	Strongly Disagree	
1 Computers are easy to operate.	1	2	3	4	5
2 Computers are easy to understand.	1	2	3	4	5
3 I know a lot about computers.	1	2	3	4	5
4 I want to learn more about computers.	1	2	3	4	5
5 I like to do challenging things on the computer.	1	2	3	4	5

		Strongly Agree	Neutral	Disagree	Strongly Disagree	
5	I like to do challenging things on the computer.	1	2	3	4	5
6	I sometimes worry about making a mistake when using the computer	1	2	3	4	5
7	When I am older I would like a job as a computer operator or programmer					
8	I would stay after school to work on the computer if I could	1	2	3	4	5

9 I have used the computer at school   Yes   No

If yes, how often or how many times
did you use the computer?
this year? _____
last year? _____

10 I have my own computer at home.   Yes   No

11 My family has a computer which I
may use.   Yes   No

12 I use the home computer.   Yes   No

13 If I had some free time in school I would choose to:
Check one. __ read __ do a science experiment __ write stories __ use
the computer __ draw

14 When I use the computer at home or school, I like to use these games or
software.

_____

_____

_____

_____

_____

15 Name some students who are good at using the computer._____

_____

APPENDIX C: QUESTIONS FOR STUDENT INTERVIEWS

1   Do you believe the boys or the girls are better at using a computer this year?
Explain why.
2   Who did you believe was better at using computer skills last year? Explain why.
3   Did you prefer working alone or with a partner when you took a computer turn?
Why?

9 A community of learners: developing student voice through personal history

After nineteen years of teaching, I chose to go back to school to obtain a higher degree. Why? Certainly not because I thought university professors could teach me anything; I considered myself an innovative teacher who was up to date with current trends in education. Rather, my reason for returning to the university was that I had no way to increase my pay substantially without seeking a Masters degree. I anticipated two more years of meaningless philosophy, a lot of unimportant readings, and the usual tests and written papers that would have little relevance to my classroom practice.

At first, the program lived up to my expectations. We read articles that 'experts' had written telling me what I already knew was lacking in education. None of these experts offered concrete solutions, so what was the point in reading about the dilemmas all teachers face on a daily basis? I played the game and did the assignments because I sought the monetary reward.

Over time I began to view the ERP in a different light. The writing of my school and personal history, for example, helped me understand why I teach the way I do and what structures impose restrictions on my educational goals. Horizontal Evaluation furthered this reflective process by helping me see the ways my classroom practice conflicted with my intentions and goals. Monetary rewards were no longer my sole concern; instead I started to see that the ERP could make a difference in my understanding of schools and my life as a teacher.

To trace in detail this change toward an educative orientation and illuminate the types of insights and questions that were a part of Educative Research, I will describe the process of question posing, provide an account of the study I conducted, and reflect on this study to suggest what it means for me as a teacher, for schooling in general, and for educational change.

QUESTION POSING

The process of question posing began with the writing of my school history. As I started this text, I was able to see that some school structures were in place purely because, as I was told by many teachers, 'That's the way we've always done it.' What is taught in school is not always the result of reflective decision making, but rather the result of traditions that have not been questioned. Dividing the school day into subject areas is but one instance of a structure born out of tradition that continues year after year with little or no discussion. As I continued to analyze school structures, I was also able to differentiate these structures from others which were imposed. Homogeneously grouping math students by ability, for example, is imposed and strictly enforced by my school district. Even though many teachers disagree with this and other imposed structures, we often do not challenge them because we assume that edicts from the hierarchy must have educational validity. Finally, I found that some structures are kept in place because teachers are either satisfied with the status quo or fear the process of conflict and change.

Understanding that quite a few school structures were justified by tradition rather than articulated beliefs was very empowering for me. Changes that seemed to be impossible were now open to question. In particular, I could seek alternatives to structures that contradicted my educational philosophy.

Writing my personal history also provided insights that would aid in the identification of my question. Prior to examining this history, I never considered why I consistently chose to teach students with learning disabilities and behavior problems. After doing so, I realized how important my brother's school career was in shaping my orientation to teaching. My brother never learned to be compliant and was labeled a trouble-maker from first grade on through high school. As Eisner notes, his experience is typical of many who do not learn the importance of compliance:

> rather than cultivate initiative, schools foster compliant behavior. One of the first things a student learns – and the lesson is taught throughout his or her school career – is to provide the teacher with what the teacher wants or expects.
>
> (Eisner, 1979, p.75)

The system had failed him until he encountered a high school teacher who realized his potential, encouraged his artistic talents, and made him aware of his value as a human being.

Involvement in my brother's experience encouraged me to teach children who, like him, have not been adequately served by schools. I gravitate toward children who have not mastered the system, who need more than just a textbook and a teacher. I want to recognize children for what they are and what they wish to become without labeling them or judging them from their reputation as 'failures.'

In the process of writing my personal history, I also discovered that my student teaching experience had a major impact, not only in the way I teach, but on the way I view differing cultures. I grew up in an upper middle class suburb of San Francisco that was 100 percent Caucasian. Following graduation from San Jose State University, my student teaching assignment was at a school with 98 percent Hispanic children. I was suddenly immersed in unfamiliar territory. Not only was this my first encounter with non-English speaking adults and children, but it was also my first exposure to families affected by poverty.

During that year I learned much about teaching. I was involved in all aspects of the day-to-day life of teaching. I helped set up the classroom in August, attended faculty meetings, helped plan daily lessons, and participated in conferences. I discussed and debated curriculum issues, discipline, and cultural diversity, including its impact on classroom practices. However, all these discussions and practical experience did not prepare me for the emotional investment that would need to be forthcoming as a teacher. I found myself wanting to take these children home with me, to wash their hair, to feed them, to care for them. In retrospect, I suppose I wanted them to have the same middle class experience I had, without fully understanding their lives.

The analysis of my personal history also exposed contradictions between what I believed and what I practiced in the classroom. Even though I embraced change, for example, I accepted without question many of the school structures imposed on teachers, as well as school norms. Realizing that contradictions existed between my beliefs and practices, and examining the roots of these contradictions were important first steps toward addressing these tensions. Berlack summarized my feelings at this time when he noted that:

> Only as we come to view our own actions and preferences as products of historical as well as biographical forces, rather than as natural or inevitable, can we escape the ideological assumptions that underlie teaching practices, and engage in reflective teaching.
>
> (Berlak and Berlak, 1981, p.175)

Upon further analysis of my personal history, what was left out became significant. I had outlined my life as a student and a teacher, but had not made any connections to my life outside the classroom. I treated my personal life and my teaching life as separate entities, as if they had no relationship to one another. Reflecting on the separation of my home and school lives encouraged me to ask: 'How important is this home–school connection for my students and for me, as their teacher?'

Through dialogue with my Horizontal Evaluation partner, I came to see additional discrepancies between my goals and practices. One point became obvious: I knew little about my students. I also knew that the writing of my own personal history had a significant effect on my understanding of self. Combined, these two insights encouraged me to use student personal histories as a beginning point to revise my reading curriculum and increase my understanding of the children I teach. Through personal histories I hoped that a home–school connection could be made and a classroom community might evolve in which we would share goals and interests, while gaining respect and understanding of one another. In particular, I posed this question and challenge for myself: can the use of personal histories promote further understanding of self and others, build trust and develop a sense of community in the elementary classroom?

THE STUDY

To address this question, I decided to use personal histories with my reading students. Eight of these students were designated as learning disabled, one was labeled as having a behavior disorder, and still another child was taking Ritalin to control his hyperactivity. Two of the students were Hispanic, one was Black/Puerto Rican, and the rest were Caucasian.

These students had been identified as 'failures' by their former teachers. In keeping with my prior experience and interest, I chose to work with this homogeneously grouped class, realizing their need for 'more than just a textbook and a teacher'.

After the first few months of school, it became obvious that my usual teaching techniques and curriculum were ineffective with this group. These students were not willing or able to participate in discussions, did not possess the skills to make informed choices, constantly fought, and were not relating well to the school experience in general. By all appearances, this group had no commonalities, except that they could not read and seemingly had no interest in learning. At this time I chose to change my methods and teach them as a whole group, hoping to command their attention and, in so doing, force them to learn. Discipline was strict, attention was demanded. Reading skills were not improving. Everyone was miserable. I knew that everything I was doing was in opposition to my philosophy, but I could not go back to the fighting and total chaos that existed before I became dictator and they, the unwilling slaves. For three and a half hours, Monday through Thursday, I hated what I was doing and saw no way out. The knowledge that my practices contradicted my beliefs only served to increase the stress level.

In an attempt to change the educational climate in my classroom, personal histories were solicited from my students. With parental assistance, children were asked to record their childhood experiences on audio tape. General themes were suggested (i.e. infancy, pre-school experiences, school and family life, special vacations, and memorable events in their lives), but these could be expanded on if students so desired. When the audio tapes were returned, they were transcribed and multiple copies of all histories were made available to the students. The completed tape recording became part of our classroom listening center where a tape recorder and several sets of earphones were provided.

Simultaneously, we began making daily journal entries to extend our histories and use them as springboards for discussion and study. Most often, students were encouraged to write about anything of their choosing. Those students who did not possess any writing skills, drew pictures to illustrate their thoughts. Spelling, punctuation, and correct grammar were not stressed, as emphasis was placed on the writing process and the content of the extended histories. Possible themes for journals were suggested only if students felt they had nothing worthwhile to write. Following journal writing each day, the children and I sat in a circle to read and discuss their entries. Students chose whether to share their journal entries with others or keep them confidential.

To better understand this process, I conducted one indepth case study. The case study utilized the student's personal history, journal entries, comments, and actions observed over a one year period. My Horizontal Evaluation partner and I did all the observation. These observations were then discussed to examine the relationship between my intentions for the use of personal histories and journal writing, and the actual changes that were occurring in my classroom.

Interviews were conducted with all students who had submitted and used personal histories in class. Questions were developed to determine what, if any, insights were realized by the students themselves (see Appendix A). I did not want to ask specific questions for fear that I would 'bait' the children into giving the answers they thought I anticipated. I hoped by asking for general information regarding the use of personal histories and journals I would indirectly get answers related to my own questions concerning the understanding of self and others.

The student chosen for the case study was selected in light of his low self-esteem, lack of trust toward teachers and peers, his aggressive behavior and his inability and unwillingness to learn in the traditional school setting. What follows is a description of what I learned by having Jacob (fictitious name) do a personal history and write journal entries. Throughout the case study, my impressions will be intertwined with Jacob's story.

JACOB – A CASE STUDY

Jacob's background

Jacob is an eight-year-old male, with a Black father and a Puerto Rican mother. At the time of this study, he lived with his aunt and uncle because his mother agreed to commit herself to a drug and alcohol rehabilitation program after many years of substance abuse. At this time, she chose to give temporary guardianship of Jacob to her brother and sister-in-law. She resided locally in a live-in rehabilitation center where Jacob was allowed to see her on Sundays, for two-hour visitations. She was expected to be in the program for about two years. Jacob's father had not been present since he was a baby. His step-father and half-sister lived in California. He had not seen them for at least one year.

Throughout his early years, Jacob was exposed to his mother's heavy drinking and drug use. He took care of her when she was 'sick' and accompanied her while she would steal to support her drug habit. He was a witness to and suffered from physical and emotional abuse by the man he called his step-father.

Jacob was assigned to my reading class because of his low reading skills. He did not seem to relate well to students or teachers. Jacob seemed to have a chip on his shoulder and acted as if he needed to protect himself from everyone in the class, including me. I perceived his self-esteem to be low and he rarely talked to me or other students in the class. His method for solving problems with other students was usually physical. His attitude was hostile toward his peers, his teachers, and the entire school culture. Jacob's anger and hostility were expressed by using physical violence. Verbally, he was silent. His only friend seemed to be his cousin, but they also fought. Classroom and school rules had little or no meaning for him. He often responded to assignments by putting his head down on his desk and refusing to talk. Jacob was routinely involved in playground fights and would often come in from recess angry. Although he never chose to discuss what had transpired, the expression on his face indicated his anger and inner hostility.

My first insight into Jacob's history was in November at the parent/teacher conference. His aunt shared with me his mother's drug and alcohol problems and indicated that Jacob would be living with their family for as long as was necessary. At that time, his aunt indicated that she felt his mother was, and would continue to be, unfit to care for him. She said if she had anything to say about it, Jacob would remain with her family permanently. She informed me of his difficulty in many schools he had attended and said that his attitude at home paralleled what I was observing at school.

Jacob's views on his prior school experiences were negative. He talked of teachers who did not like him, saying, 'I could tell they didn't like me because they never talked to me, but only to other kids.' He eventually revealed through his journal writing and conversations, that children called him names. He said he sat alone in many of his classes, looked around a lot, and did minimal work. He also said he talked to himself.

Jacob stated in a May interview with me that he had lived in about fifteen houses. Although that may be an exaggeration, his aunt confirmed the fact that they moved frequently and that Jacob had been in at least five different schools while he was living with his mother. In his personal history (see Appendix B) his mother describes her view of his schooling:

He had kind of conflicts with his teacher so we ended up moving a lot. We moved quite a bit and I think that was a little hard for him at times changing from school to school. He seems to adjust all right. At times he falls back with his reading. I ended up holding him back one year because I felt that the school he was at didn't teach him well enough and I didn't spend too much time with him with reading and writing, but Terry took an interest in him and taught him quite a bit. It was a hard decision to make, but I felt it was a real good one because now he knows how to read and write a little better. I'm still really kind of concerned with him in school. Sometimes I feel that what he's going through right now is interfering with school.

Jacob had historically not assimilated well into the school system. He had not acquired many academic skills, except perhaps how to 'slip through the cracks.' He went from one school to another, never feeling that any one teacher cared about him. What follows are the changes I observed in Jacob when personal histories became a major part of the reading curriculum.

A metamorphosis

Although Jacob resisted most assignments, he was visibly excited at the prospect of doing his personal history. He was concerned, however, that his mother might not participate in the process. I assured him that his aunt could help him, but he was adamant that his mother was the only one who knew him well enough to recount his history. His uncle arranged for him to see his mother over a weekend in February to tape his history. He returned his tape on the following Monday and waited in anticipation for it to be transcribed. In the interim, his excitement was evident. Every day he would ask, 'When will I get my personal history back?' and when we received the transcription, Jacob was visibly thrilled. He sat down on the floor and tried to read it. This was the first time I had seen him read without coercion. Obviously, he had found an interest . . . himself. Jacob, with my assistance, read his personal history over and over. He also spent time listening to the tape. He seemed to savor the connection it provided with his mother.

As more transcripts were made available, we began using them for reading material, rather than the basal text that I had used previously. Jacob would read alone or with a partner, and began talking with me and his classmates about his life. On one occasion, while the rest of the class members were busy with their reading activities, Jacob and I talked about his personal history. I asked him who Terry was. He replied, 'Terry is my dad, not my real dad. I hate him.' I asked why he hated Terry, since his mother had indicated that Terry helped him a lot with school work and that his mother felt that Terry cared about him. He said Terry called him 'Ju-Ju lips' because he doesn't have the same color skin as Terry does. Jacob went on to tell me about his sister, how Terry took her away to California, and how much he missed her.

As part of the reading choices, Jacob illustrated his personal history. Others became interested in listening to and reading Jacob's history. In time, a curriculum evolved using personal histories for reading, listening, questioning, role playing, and, most importantly, initiating dialogue between members of the group.

During this period of time, the class also wrote in journals to provide an ongoing history of their lives in and out of school. At first Jacob chose not to discuss any of his journal entries with the class, but as time passed and other students shared their experiences and concerns, he began to expose his on-going personal history and discuss his feelings and fears. He told of his mother's drug and alcohol abuse and how she was trying to overcome her habit at the rehabilitation center. Because Jacob introduced the topics of drug abuse and living away from one's parents, the class discussed these issues at length.

As the issue of peer relationships, and later adult/child relationships, surfaced in our discussions, the topics of fighting, arguing, name-calling, friendship, and child abuse were addressed. Jacob found that he was not alone in his feelings, or his experiences. He told of a variety of incidences where he was called 'the N word.' He didn't know why it made him mad, but his reaction was to defend himself against anyone who called him 'that bad word.' Although Jacob is of Black and Puerto Rican descent, his appearance is characteristically Black. In registering Jacob for school, his mother listed him as Hispanic. He and his mother both denied that he had any connection to the Black culture. There were no other Black children among our second graders and only four or five in the entire school of over 700 children. His identity was also a topic of conversation among students because he resided in the home of his Puerto Rican uncle and Caucasian aunt with their three children whose appearance is Caucasian.

Since peer relationships were strained because he was called 'Nigger,' and other children questioned the fact that he and his cousin were related, it became an issue that needed to be discussed in class. The following describes one such incident that led to a dialogue on individual differences, specifically those dealing with skin color.

Jacob was crying as he came into class after recess. A student from another class had seen a picture of Trent (his cousin) and him together with Trent's family and had asked if they were brothers. The student said that they couldn't be related. Since it was journal writing time, I asked Jacob to write how he felt. He wrote, 'I hate that name [nigger] and they always ask me or they ask Trent, "Are you Trent's brother?" and I say "No." And they say "Oh."' He expanded on this entry stating that, 'The kids won't leave me alone, they keep asking me questions,' adding that he wanted to run away when they questioned him. The class discussion that resulted from Jacob's entry led us to role-play alternatives to running away from an uncomfortable situation. Accepting who we are as individuals was another issue addressed in light of Jacob's problem in dealing with other children. The group pointed out differences and similarities among them and expressed their concern for his feelings and his problem.

Upon hearing of another child in the class whose 'real' father used to beat him and his mother, Jacob related stories of physical abuse by his step-father. This, too, became a topic of discussion.

Jacob continued to reveal his history and his daily journal entries to the group and, as a direct result of this dialogue, his physical aggression diminished. Instead, his anger and frustration came out in his journal writing and classroom discussions. As I was also sharing my journal writings, the children began to understand that adults, even teachers, also felt anger, frustration, joy, pride, and all the other emotions that they, as children, experienced.

As a result of this interaction, we discussed commonalities and differences and the importance of gaining an understanding of and respect for physical differences as well as an appreciation for alternative viewpoints. Gradually, the students began communicating with each other in a more caring manner. Friendships emerged where there had seemingly been no previous common ground. Students acknowledged each others' strengths and verbally commended improved reading skills. They began to work together cooperatively; they read histories with partners and in groups, openly discussing and helping each other. Jacob, no longer silent, dialogued with friends as he answered questions about his personal history and in turn probed their histories. He confided in me and the students when he had a problem, as well as when he was particularly proud of an accomplishment. He openly talked about his mother's drug and alcohol abuse and how it had affected his life.

As I began to facilitate, rather than lead discussions, I listened to the students pose various solutions to problems that they felt were important. I, too, voiced my concerns. They learned to compromise, to discuss without shouting, and to listen as others spoke. The group established mutually agreed upon classroom rules which they enforced with minimal help from me. These changes occurred gradually over a period of four months. Arguments did not cease, but were solved in more humane ways.

It is interesting to note that as the trust level in the class increased, some students extended that trust to other teachers and students outside our classroom. But for Jacob, trust was limited to the confines of our group. After a week of illness, for example, I returned to class to discover Jacob had saved his journal entries to relate to me. He said, 'I didn't know that other lady, so I waited 'til you came back to read my journal. Can I read it to the class now?'

Another example of Jacob's growing, but limited, trust came in May when Jacob brought a letter to show me. He waited until we were alone and handed me a neatly folded, single sheet of paper that was obviously very special to him. He smiled as I read the letter his mother had written to him. I realized that it had been written before Halloween. Until now, he had treasured this letter unto himself. I felt I had finally earned his trust.

Interviews conducted at the close of the school year also indicated that the students valued the writing of their personal histories. All respondents stated the importance of learning about each other, and identifying what they had in common. They found personal histories to be interesting and enjoyed discussing these to find out how others grew up. One child noted that the journal discussions helped the class to 'get along better, instead of fighting like before.' Jacob's comments revealed what he saw as the benefits of personal histories.

Kathy: Why do we do personal histories and journals?
Jacob: Because to get to know the children a little more better, and to hear how your feelings are, like if you are mad at somebody else, or if like you are happy. Like if you got a new bike, and you thought it was neat. Or if you had something sad, like your dad got thrown in the hospital. Then you could write about it and tell them about it.

Kathy: You said something about telling people about your feelings. Do you think that's important?

Jacob: Yeah.

Kathy: Why?

Jacob: Because . . . well when you don't tell anybody about . . . you sit around and you are all sad, and so people ask you, and you go, 'I don't want to talk about it.' Then they beg you and beg you, and then they will tease you because you are sad and you won't talk, and you are crying sometimes. So that's a way . . . and it is good to write in your journals to tell people about your feelings.

Kathy: What kinds of things have you learned about yourself and others?

Jacob: That some people are like me. That they have an ex-dad . . . I used to eat dirt (laughs) . . . that was in my personal history . . . that some people feel bad and some people don't. Some people see that they are sad, and some people see that they are happy.

Jacob also told me about his experience with a friend that attended a different school:

> I think journals are cool, because telling people about yourself is really neat because people get to know you better, because I had a best friend that I thought was my best friend, but we didn't really talk to each other very much. We were usually playing, and we didn't know each other very good. So he is still my friend, but it is hard for me to get to know him. Now when I go up to my Grandma's, I go up to his house and we talk a lot. We don't always play. We just go down to the school and we just do 'cherry drops' and talk to each other while we are swinging on the bars . . . Because now I learned about doing histories and journals and talking about people, so I wondered if he wanted to talk about me and I talk about him. So we started talking about each other, and then we started talking about old times, and I told him about how I've been feeling, and since all these years how I haven't seen him. He told me about all of the stuff about how he missed me, and he didn't have very much friends, and he remembers the first time that we met.

Jacob had developed a caring for others that he had not exhibited in school before the introduction of personal histories. Not only was he sharing in the classroom, but his curiosity about others had extended to those beyond our class. Jacob's aunt and I met just prior to the end of the school year. I told her of the many changes that had taken place over the last four months. She agreed that she had also observed changes at home indicating that he was much happier and more accepting of his present situation. She was also pleased with his increased reading skills. She attributed these changes to his mother's rehabilitation efforts. Although Jacob was proud of his mother's accomplishments, I believe Jacob's transformation was more directly linked to an understanding of himself and his worth, his increased self-esteem, a developing trust of others, and the realization that students and teachers could care for him despite his differences.

Jacob and I developed a relationship of trust, understanding and mutual friendship which would never have been possible without my under-standing of his personal history and his of mine. Jacob told me at the conclusion of our May interview, 'You are my best teacher because you care about me and don't think I'm dumb.'

Prior to Jacob entering third grade, I met with his teacher, Susan Spilsbury, to inform her of Jacob's family situation and to discuss academic needs. Susan expressed an interest in personal histories and asked how I had used them in the classroom. We discussed personal histories at length and the changes that had occurred. She relates:

> At the beginning of the year, I read children's books about family problems to the class. As the children discussed them, Jacob also volunteered information about his step-father, his mother's drug abuse and suicide attempts, and the time he was taken to the police station. He seemed to trust his classmates and was willing to risk with me, his teacher. Jacob and I talk privately everyday about what he does at recess, and how his mother is doing in rehabilitation.

In January of the 1989–90 school year, Susan initiated the use of personal histories in her classroom. Jacob was the only child in her class who was familiar with personal histories and so, before beginning, she talked to him. While reflecting back over her concerns, she said:

> I was worried that he wouldn't want to do this because he had already worked on this most of last year. But Jacob was really excited and volunteered to tell the rest of the children about how they first recorded the history, then waited for someone to type it and then read them and how he answered questions about his history. He was very proud that his mother could remember things about him.

Susan felt that personal histories were integral in helping Jacob further develop his own identity.

> I also think it helped him build a better relationship with his mother, who is so often too caught up with herself to care for Jacob. Jacob is a 'fair'

reader and reads with the class. He is a good citizen in the classroom and has many friends.

Susan and I discussed Jacob's progress throughout his third grade school year. Her reports of his continued success served to reinforce my belief in and commitment to using personal histories in the classroom. Jacob was a sullen, violent, and angry child void of any strong school relationships when he entered my classroom in September. I felt that Jacob had made great progress in the year he was in my class, but feared that he would revert to his prior behaviors when faced with new peers and a different teacher. I was never so pleased to be wrong. A year later he was described as a 'good citizen' who had many friends. Jacob had come a long way. Perhaps I had really made a difference in his life. I knew that he had made an impact on mine.

Unfortunately Jacob's story does not have a . . . 'and he lived happily ever after' ending. Jacob's mother checked herself out of the rehabilitation center close to the end of his third grade year. She took him back to live with her, for the remainder of the year. His attitude changed as soon as he was back with his mother. He became secretive, angry, and no longer wished to discuss his life with me or Susan. He did tell me that he was glad he was living with his mother and that she was only taking 'little drugs.' He warned that I better not tell the cops.

Jacob is now in fourth grade at the school where he had previously been so unhappy. I asked Jacob's cousin how Jacob likes school this year. His reply was, 'He hates it and wants to come back here.'

I wish he were here, too.

REFLECTIONS

I never intended that my study deal with the issue of individual differences, but it became a matter that could not be ignored. My college experience put me in contact with other cultures, and through my student teaching year I thought I had developed a knowledge and understanding of differences. I believed that being cognizant and tolerant of cultural and physical differences was all that was needed to teach in an unbiased manner. I was mistaken. Teaching units about handicapping conditions, Black Americans' contributions to society, and celebrating holidays such as Chanukah and Cinco de Mayo was my way of bringing differences into the classroom curriculum. What I did not realize was that within the personal histories of the students was a curriculum of difference. Understanding differences is not just being aware of them; it involves changing the role of teacher. I did not have to 'teach' these children about differences; they taught me and we learned from each other. My teaching role was to facilitate dialogue that was initiated by the students.

I also started to see my role more in terms of teaching individuals who come to me with their own knowledge and separate histories that need to be understood as opposed to a supposedly homogenous group. We can learn together about our differences as well as our similarities and use this knowledge in conjunction with our interests and goals to develop a curriculum that fits our needs. If we, as teachers, take the time to investigate the lives of the children we teach, make that important home–school connection, we would know what impact the children's prior experiences have had on their view of the world in which we live. From there, the teacher's task would be to question, to investigate interests, to establish common goals and to learn together what is most important for the individuals as well as the group. Rather than taking the typical stance of disseminating information, I would prefer to see myself posing problems, asking questions, and, perhaps most important of all, listening.

Listening was an important lesson for me during that year with Jacob. By listening, I was able to make more meaningful connections with my students' lives outside the classroom. Before personal histories became a part of my curriculum, I felt that Jacob's mother was a parent that did not care much about her child's schooling. I was wrong.

> We moved quite a bit and I think that was a little hard for him at times changing from school to school. He seems to adjust alright. At times he falls back with his reading. I ended up holding him back one year because I felt that the school he was at didn't teach him well enough and I didn't spend too much time with him reading and writing . . . School-wise I'm not really sure what's going on with him because he doesn't really say too much about it and I would like to know how he's doing on it . . . but I'm really kind of concerned with him in school. Sometimes I feel that what he's going through right now is interfering with school.

This is not the voice of an uncaring parent. If a home–school connection is of importance, and my view is that it is vital, finding the time and opportunity to listen to parents as well as students is crucial.

Unfortunately, altering the role to listen, facilitate dialogue, and understand the separate histories that students bring to the classroom is difficult given the structures found in my school. School structures are now set up for teachers to tell, talk, and disseminate information to parents and students. For example, one structure that facilitates this one-way communication is the parent/teacher conference. This structure limits parents involvement in the school and does not provide a forum for them to help inform teachers about students and schooling. They are, after all, conversations structured primarily from the viewpoint of the teacher. The students and parents are the object of these communications, but their voices are not heard. To foster a more reciprocal communication, parents need to be continuously involved with the school, thereby enhancing home–school relations. This connection can be achieved if the school day is rearranged so that teachers have time to make this essential link. Meeting with groups of parents, and students during the school day or evening might provide a forum for all to explore educational goals. For working parents, we might initiate programs whereby the parent(s) could be released from work to come into the classroom to participate in their child's school experience. Parents need to be involved in meaningful ways to create a broader sense of community. I would like to see more cooperation between teachers, parents and students. Using parents as volunteers in the classroom is certainly a step in the right direction, but is it enough? Ideally, I would like to see parents have full participation in the schooling process. Their input and understanding is essential if a true home–school connection is to become a reality in the classroom. Unless a conscious effort is made, the home–school relationship will continue to be limited to ten minute conferences to discuss report cards or notes relating primarily to the academic or social problems the student is having in the classroom.

Another structure that limits the reciprocity encouraged through personal histories is the system of evaluating students. Currently, grades focus on the product rather than the process of learning. As teachers, we make judgments about our students and what they have learned, rather than make judgments on the process of learning. I have discovered that we tend to give the lowest grades to those students that we do not understand. A grade given by a teacher is not only a reflection of the student, it is a reflection of the teacher's characteristics, background, and personal history. Learning needs to be thought of as a process based on the histories of the students, rather than a product based on 'correct answers.' Grades, if we use them at all, need to be more process oriented. An evolving portfolio of the student's work shared with the student and parent might illustrate the process of learning more so than grades based on culminating tests.

Yet another structure that runs counter to the establishment of on-going reciprocal relations between students, teachers, and parents is the tradition of dividing students and teachers by grade levels. According to Goodlad and Anderson the tradition of dividing students by grade has little significance.

By the fourth or fifth year of school, more than half the achievement scores in a class are above and below the grade level attached to the group. There is, then, no such thing as a fourth-grade class or a fifth-grade teacher, regardless of the labels within our conventional graded structure.

(Goodlad and Anderson, 1987, p.28)

So, why continue using a system that does not accomplish its presupposed purpose? A nongraded approach might better meet the needs of students and teachers. The traditional horizontal grouping model (grades) could be replaced by flexible horizontal and vertical groupings created to meet the needs of both the students and the teachers. Groups could be formed to meet specific interests and goals and disbanded when such goals are achieved. Children of varying ages could come together to pursue a common interest with a teacher who shared that interest. Children would have the opportunity to work with groups of many sizes, formed for different purposes. Interests, prior knowledge, and goals would replace age as the major factor in determining placement.

Children do not come to the classroom as empty vessels to be filled. They possess experiences, skills, knowledge, and preconceived ideas of what learning and schooling are all about. Unfortunately, these personal experiences and the existing knowledge of students is often ignored. The consequence is that students go through the motions of mastering separate knowledge without ever making the connections that would help make this knowledge their own (Belenky *et al.*, 1986). Personal histories are one way in which the learners can re-experience the events, persons, and forces in their past.

Through the use of personal histories, I have only begun the process of learning about the students I teach. In doing so, a door has been opened for me to continue to pose problems for myself and my students, to make attempts to strengthen the home–school connection, and to take action to change structures that do not further my goals for schooling.

Although we cannot say what will happen to Jacob from this point on, the writing and sharing of his personal history opened a door for him. He learned that his knowledge was valued and worthy of discussion. He no longer felt isolated and alone and realized that his experiences were shared by other members of the class. He experienced a sense of belonging and, most importantly, had the opportunity to tell his story. The following seems to capture what personal histories meant to Jacob:

It is good to tell about my family . . . and sometimes I feel really bad, so I guess I just need to spread it out instead of keeping it a secret for days and days and days, and you just can't get it out of your head, and so you just finally got to tell somebody.

APPENDIX A: INTERVIEW QUESTIONS

1   Why do we do personal histories and journal writing?
2   Do you like doing personal histories and journal writing? Why or why not?
3   Did you learn anything about yourself and others? Explain.

APPENDIX B: 'JACOB'

Jacob: The year I was born was 1980. Momma, what did I do when I was little?
Mom: You did lots of different things.
Jacob: I learned how to walk and all that stuff at a very young age.
Mom: You learned how to talk at a very young age. You were interested in colors and you liked dirt. You liked to eat dirt. We had a hard time with that. You were potty trained real early, and you didn't get teeth for a long, long time, until you were about two. You started walking real young, about ten months, and you could feed yourself. You were a pretty loving kid. You liked to hug on me a lot and follow me around the house.
Jacob: Why did I do that?
Mom: Because you like to play with me and you like me holding you. You loved your grandma and you used to try crawling out of your bed a lot. I remember one time I came in there and you were stuck up on the crib, by my waterbed, and you were sitting there screaming and screaming because you almost fell, but you wouldn't move. You just stayed there until I got there. You like blocks, the real colorful ones. You were good with the shapes. We used to teach you stuff like that. I remember when you were born you got sick and I had to put you in the hospital for about a week. You had intestinal flu and you were always throwing up and stuff. We finally got that taken care of, but it seemed like you always had stomach problems. Then I met Terry.
Jacob: But, Mom, what was good that happened to me?
Mom: What was good? You learned how to ride a bike really fast. I was really surprised with that.
Jacob: All by myself?
Mom: Yes, on that BMX bike. You learned how to talk really fast at an early age and I was really proud of that because most kids that young didn't know how to talk or walk. You got a little sister and you guys were really close. You got along really good. I remember one time, for your birthday when you were a year old, we gave you a cake and we let you eat it by yourself. You liked that and you ended up sitting in it. You seemed to like that a lot. We met Terry. Do you remember Terry?
Jacob: Yes.
Mom: He liked to play with you a lot and pat you on your head. He was always playing with you and stuff. I remember one time – do you remember he accidentally dropped you? We had to take you to the doctor. Your nose was bent and you ended up having a black eye. He used to hold you up on his hand and try to balance you. I remember a few times when you used to eat on your high chair and you'd fall asleep.
Jacob: Mom, remember when I got hit by a car?

Mom:	Yes, but you didn't get very hurt.
Jacob:	I know, it didn't hurt that much.
Mom:	Tell what happened.
Jacob:	I was at the store with my friend, I mean my cousin, and this lady – I looked both ways – and this lady didn't put on her blinker and I thought she was going to stop. It was a red light, and I peddled off across the street and the lady hit me. I was alright, it scared me a little bit. The police brought me home and everything.
Mom:	I remember one time we put Jacob in a baby contest and he was really good because he used to like to sing and dance when he was a baby. He was pretty talented that way, but when we got him into the baby contest and everybody saw him he got really shy and started crying. He didn't want to be up on the table in front of everybody. I remember I had to take him down because he was really shy to be around a lot of people. I still feel that he's like that a lot. In school out in West Valley, he got straight As. He was doing pretty good out there. When he went to the school, Nibley Park, he didn't seem to do too well out there. He had kind of conflicts with his teacher, so we ended up moving a lot. We moved quite a bit and I think that was a little hard for him at times changing from school to school. He seems to adjust alright. At times he falls back with his reading. I ended up holding him back one year because I felt that the school he was at didn't teach him well enough and I didn't spend too much time with him reading and writing, but Terry took an interest in him and taught him quite a bit. It was a hard decision to make, but I felt it was a real good one because now he knows how to read and write a little bit better. His relationship with his sister was really unusual. They seem to be really close, really bonded together. I know since what's happened, that he hasn't been able to see her, that he has been having problems with that. We've been trying to work through it because I know he misses her a lot. Just with me being here and trying to be rehabilitated from alcohol and drugs has been kind of hard on him and just the life that he's led with that. I've tried to explain to him that it's time for us to be a family again. A good family, too, where we can do a lot of things like going to the park and the zoo and spending a lot more time with each other. I spend a lot of time with him now, every Sunday, and I feel we've gotten a lot closer. We're talking and communicating, which we never have. He still seems to have that bond which is really nice, considering what he's been through. My most concern is how he has a tendency to shy away from talking about his sister. I feel he's having a problem with that. School wise I'm not really sure what's going on with him because he doesn't really say too much about it and I would like to know how he's doing on it. As a baby he was always pretty affectionate and loving. He used to throw temper tantrums when he didn't get his way. He eventually grew out of it. He seems like he has a good capability of learning things, when he has an interest in it. You have to make him be interested in it instead of making him feel like he has to do it. I know this because even as a baby trying to teach him something I had to make it be kind of fun and not make it a chore, like he had to do it because then he wouldn't do it. If I made it to where it was fun he'd seem to take an interest in it or if it wasn't expected of him.

I think a lot of it lies with I never really expected him to clean his room or pick up after himself. I always did it for him, but I realized in the long run I should have taught him how to do things for himself. As he got older I made him clean his room and he didn't seem to like it too well. He was really rebellious and got mad at me for making him do that. When he cleaned his room he did a really nice job at it. I feel the relationship with him and Terry wasn't exactly like his real father. He's seen his real father once or twice, but I feel that Terry loved him a lot and still does. He still sends him presents and stuff. I know he misses him a lot. He still seems to be really close to me. He has a lot of passion, a lot of interest in what I'm doing. He talks about his cousins, that he stays with right now, quite a bit. He has kind of a problem getting along with the fact of not being with me. Learning wise I'm not really sure how he's doing in school because he says he's doing really well. His birthday seems to be good for him and Christmas. All holidays he seems to be pretty content with it. He seems to pick up things really easy, an easy learner. When you explain something to him, or even when you don't, he catches on really quick. As a child he still liked to be alone. He didn't ever really play with kids too much. He would occupy himself really good. He didn't need too much attention. As long as I was in sight or he knew I was around he would be content. He wasn't really too demanding as a baby. My mother helped out a lot with him, raising him and stuff. I've always gotten really close with her. He listens to her really well. She has a way of teaching him about school stuff. She has a lot more patience with him. Even when I brought him home from the hospital, she took care of him quite a bit because I was kind of scared of him because I didn't know how to raise him. She showed me a lot, so I think he's got a pretty good relationship with her and he listens to her really good. As a child, he used to always like to stay with her and she took him a lot. She'd teach him things. She said that he always picked up stuff really well and that he memorized things really well. I don't know about the relationships with males. I have some brothers that used to take him quite a bit. He was pretty happy with that, but I'm still really kind of concerned with him in school. Sometimes I feel that what he's going through right now is interfering with school.

Part III

Reflections on Educative Research

10 A turning point

Our primary criticism of traditional research methods is that they do not take into account issues of power. When issues of power are raised, it is clear that those studied are silenced, that their experiential or practical knowledge is discounted, and their potential claims of expertise are denied. Instead, it is only research knowledge that is seen as legitimate and researchers who are seen as the experts. Furthermore, because the 'subjects' in an educational context are often teachers who have generally been denied opportunities to speak out and participate fully in shaping the nature of schooling, research acts to strengthen what are already alienating and oppressive relations found in the educational community.

RECIPROCAL RELATIONSHIPS

To challenge the way research strengthens these alienating relations, we structured our practice around the evolving concept of Educative Research. In particular, our challenge was to enable those who have been traditionally silenced to speak out and use their voice to protest and act on narrow and oppressive notions of schooling. The development of voice, therefore, is linked to personal empowerment and a larger process of school change. Inherent in both these related aims is the establishment of reciprocal relationships between researchers and 'subjects' such that no group is silenced and change can become a process contributed to and influenced by all community members.

Unfortunately, as we reflected on our desire to establish more reciprocal relationships, it became clear that our original assumption, that alternative methods alone can foster new relationships between the researcher and the 'subject,' was faulty. What we discovered is that the research context and commonly held ideologies have as much to do with these relationships as does the method itself. For example, what is considered legitimate knowledge, and the work conditions of those housed in particular institutions, has a dramatic effect on the research participants and who is considered to be the expert. Because Educative Research could only suggest the need to expand notions of what is considered legitimate knowledge and did little or nothing to change the basic working conditions of teachers or those housed at the university, our attempt to alter relationships among research participants in the ERP was limited from the outset.

These limitations became more prominent given our lack of attention to the issue of gender. In the ERP, as is true of many other research situations, the researcher is a male and the teachers primarily female. Establishing some sort of reciprocal relationship between a male researcher and female participants requires a method that not only gives 'subjects' a voice, but also acts on patriarchal assumptions about authority, competence and role. Unfortunately, these issues were not adequately addressed because our generic approach to voice de-emphasized the particular problems associated with altering relationships between men and women.

Our inability to alter the research context, to establish broader notions of legitimate knowledge, and to address the gender of the participants constrained our attempts to transform the relationship between researcher and 'subject.' We can now see that accomplishing such a change requires a project that reaches well beyond the limits of the ERP. Nevertheless, we did make strides in understanding the boundaries of our current relationships and in providing a foundation for a more reciprocal relationship between the research participants.

Participants in the ERP, did, for example, take into consideration the way gender acts to strengthen hierarchical authority relationships. In particular, Robyn noted how important it was for her to confront Andrew and challenge his authority as a researcher and as a male.

> It has been helpful for me to get angry with Andrew because he is an authority figure. It was a risk for me, but it was one I felt I could take. I started to trust that we could work it out. Since then, we have had a lot of open clashes and I still come away feeling the relationship will survive.

Karen also stated that she is no longer willing to enter into relationships with men where she has no choice but to wait for the 'next blow.' Instead of simply replicating such behavior as a member of the ERP, Karen spoke out and, in more than one instance, told Andrew off. By doing so she challenged her own history of compliant behavior as well as authoritarian relationships between men and women.

> Sometimes I have been really angry with Andrew for his declarations about the amount of personal sacrifice that he went through and his

assumptions that our [the teachers'] sacrifices were not commensurate with his. As I sit here I hesitate to bring this up, but I think I need to have the courage to say that my participation in this group has helped me to confront some very negative feelings about men . . . I have gained some insight into my own communication style as I have confronted conflict. 'Andrew you just don't know how important it has been for me to just tell you off and have an argument with you' . . . For me I think there is an inherent struggle for power between men and women that has been an issue with me since childhood.

Naming the way women are silenced by men within a research context led to further insights about relationships taking place outside the ERP. Gender operated in the privacy of one's home as well as in the public domain of research. For those in the ERP the public and private spheres were clearly linked. For Beth, this linkage became apparent when her need to be involved in the ERP conflicted with her role as a mother.

Now I am home and my husband is working. His interest and his career take precedence in a lot of ways. It is hard for me to leave Lindsay, so I had planned to bring her to the ERP meeting. And then I thought, 'No, it is going to be difficult to bring her', and I said to him, 'Can you rearrange your schedule a little bit? Do you think you could go to your appointment a little later?' Well, in the middle of the afternoon he called and said he would rearrange his schedule. He recognized that I had something important to do even though I'm not getting paid for it. It was important for him to say, 'Well, you need some time; so I will stay home.'

Robyn is also unwilling to remain silent in her relationship with her husband. What she found, as was true of Beth, was that speaking out altered some long standing traditions taking place in her home.

As we were reading more and discussing more, my voice increased in my own house. It wasn't a loud, blaring voice, it was simply that some things were no longer acceptable to me and they were dropped. It was amazing to me how suddenly I would see something we had struggled with for years in a new light and then it was resolved.

By speaking out, and no longer accepting traditional relationships found in the public and private domains, the women members of the ERP called into question what is commonplace about the researcher's relationships with other participants as well as men's relationships with women. Understanding the layered dimensions of these relationships not only exposed their hierarchical nature, but also made it difficult for those involved in Educative Research to remain in their accustomed roles.

For Karen, this meant that she was no longer willing to be a 'watcher'. She wanted to take a more active role in her relationships with others and participate in the ongoing educational discourse.

> I have always been more of a watcher than a participant. So I think if I were to distill what this project means to me it is that I have made gains in learning how to participate . . . to say what I think even if I find that my views change the very next day.

Andrew, who entered the ERP from the privileged position of the university researcher, also started to see his role in different ways.

> I have still dominated the conversation and still played the role of a teacher. There are differences among us that will not easily disappear . . . The type of research that I did before, the type of projects that I was involved in were basically about self-interest. They just do not seem all that worthwhile anymore. There will surely be times in the future when I will slip into those roles again, but fundamentally, my view of the world and what is important has changed forever. The split in the educational community [between professors and teachers] is something I will continue to address.

While reciprocal relationships were not established, Karen and Andrew's statements suggest that those traditionally silenced have begun to play a more active role in shaping their relationships with others, and those in positions of authority are more aware of how commonplace research practices are part of a process of maintaining privilege and status.

VOICE

Because reciprocal relationships are only possible when all involved have the opportunity to speak out, a significant part of establishing these relationships is the development of voice. In many cases, involvement in the ERP strengthened the voices of those traditionally silenced. Beth talks about this process of developing voice in terms of transforming her orientation to knowledge from that of a 'sponge' to that of a 'creator.'

> Most significantly for me, was the fact that I realized through the encouragement of the ERP, that I could create knowledge . . . that contrary to how a high school teacher once labeled me, I was not a 'sponge.' I had a story to tell . . . stories to tell – that had value and from which I could construct new knowledge. But up until the ERP, my 17 years of schooling had never shown me, or given me the confidence to be anything but a sponge.

For Valerie, the development of voice was directly connected to her new-found confidence to express her views and, more than that, to feel that her practical experience had value.

> I look at myself, how I functioned this year in school and I feel empowered to give my opinion. To say, 'This is what we have to say about the direction of education and the lives of the children we teach.' I mean, why in all the decades is this a new idea, that being in the classroom and actually seeing it happen gives us something to say?

While these statements are encouraging, our focus on participants speaking out left many questions about voice unanswered. As Robyn clearly points out in her case study, voice is not only about speaking out, but also about whether one's voice is heard. Our lack of attention to audience created two problems in how we understood voice. First, we confused silence with a lack of an accepting audience and second, we underestimated the work that needs to be done to foster such an audience. Kathy provides a case in point. She had always spoken out to parents, administrators, and local policy makers. However, she was 'always getting in trouble for it.' Her seeming lack of voice, therefore, had more to do with how her arguments and opinions were received than whether she spoke out on educational issues. Furthermore, because we emphasized voice as opposed to audience, it was easy to overlook the important issue of why Kathy's voice was not accepted. It is true that within the ERP the voices of the participants were heard and that some administrators and other teachers listened. However, no explicit work was done to look at the relation between voice and audience, or to encourage those in positions of authority to take account of the knowledge produced.[11] Part of our future work, therefore, is to bring potential audiences into the Educative Research process so that they can hear what is said and contribute to this process. In many ways this book provides a modest first step in this direction by linking the ERP with a larger audience.

Speaking out and being heard is only part of developing voice as a form of protest. Enabling those who have been silenced to enter into public debates and to have influence is a necessary step in altering hierarchical relations and establishing a community-based approach to inquiry. However, because participants are likely to have some of the same blind spots, it is necessary to have all who contribute to the educational discourse look critically at their arguments as well as the structures and ideologies, that shape so much of what is thought to be desirable. Protests against school structures, wider ideologies, and self are essential if schooling is going to play a more important role in contesting oppressive societal relations.

In reflecting on this aim, it is apparent that members of the ERP did not simply speak out, but also lodged protests. Robyn, for example, was no longer content to accept her silence as a woman and a teacher. Her protest was directed at the school structures that keep teachers isolated and without time to examine and discuss educational issues. Kathy, on the other hand, directed her protest primarily at her own teaching. In particular, she tried to reconstruct her practice such that students were treated no longer as empty vessels to be filled with bits of information, but rather as individuals with histories that must be understood and examined. Karen also protested her teaching by raising questions about the meaning of success. By doing so, she challenged not only the framework she used to judge her success and that of her students, but also the practices that fit so nicely within that framework. And Pat protested what is clearly the most dominating technological influence of our age, the computer. After initially seeing this technology as a savior, the process of Educative Research illuminated the way this innovation could further the very type of gender relations Pat found so limiting as a youth.

What these examples suggest is that for many of the members of the ERP there was a linkage between speaking out and protest. By looking critically at self and context, these participants entered into an educative process that enabled them to pose questions and act on schooling in ways that had not previously been possible.

FOSTERING CHANGE BASED ON PROTEST

The development of voice is an important aim of the ERP. It is not, however, an end point. As opposed to other methodologies that exclusively focus on understanding, and then hope that this understanding will make some sort of difference, Educative Research attempts to link understanding and action by having those involved in the inquiry process act at the level of school practice. And, because understanding in Educative Research is centered around the concept of protest, it is possible that these actions will also challenge and even alter what one sees as limiting and constraining about schooling.

Given that the ERP started as a Masters class, one would expect that a large number of the participants would see their research as the 'cost' for a credential, not as a process that would lead to change. In fact, initially many of the participants viewed Educative Research in just this way. Kathy, for example, notes that, ' When I first started in the Masters program, I went into it so that I could boost my income on the salary scale, and for absolutely no other purpose.' Pat, reflecting much the same view, states, 'When I first began the project, I, like Kathy, was seeking a way to increase

my salary. I had a lot of hesitation about going into college work again.'
Over time, however, many of the participants of the ERP started to adopt a
more educative approach to the experience. Kathy explains the change in
her perspective this way:

> I think after coming into the program, when we started doing personal
> histories and school histories, and engaged in Horizontal Evaluation, my
> views slowly began to change when I found these experiences
> invaluable to my teaching.

Pat describes her change in perspective by saying:

> I had a lot of concerns about if I really had any potential, or was that just
> what people told you to get you to work harder? I think the process
> [Educative Research] has given me a lot of confidence in my own
> ability. So for me, it was of great value in giving me self-assurance
> academically.

As the participants' commitment and confidence increased, they often
stopped working for a grade or to please an authority and instead were
working for themselves. The strongest indication of this sort of change is
that, presently, the ERP has continued outside the class structure for almost
two years. There are no grades, credit, or financial benefits. In many ways
this developing commitment is foundational to the sorts of changes that are
apparent in the case studies.

For Karen, the change involved her understanding of 'what is success.'
Where initially Karen thought that success was something imposed from the
outside, she came to the conclusion that understanding success required an
examination of the teacher/student relationships that were made and remade in
her classroom. In place of the traditional hierarchical teacher/ student relationship, Karen desired more open, caring, and reciprocal relationships. Ironically,
as long as Karen wore the teacher mask of the 'good teacher' that had given her
a sense of worth, her ability to see the limits of her relations with students and
to act on them was constrained. With the mask off, she could question taken-
for-granted notions of success, and create a space which enabled her to see
students in a different light and begin to consider how alternative types of
relations inform constructed notions of success.

In contrast to the broad focus of Karen's project, Kathy's change was
more directly related to her reading program. What she found was that the
students were not reading as well as she would like and her relationships
with them had deteriorated to the point that the students were fighting and
disruptive on a regular basis while she was acting more and more in an
authoritarian manner. As the nature of this relationship came into focus,
Kathy acted to protest her role as teacher. As she notes:

Unfortunately, the personal experience and the existing knowledge of students are ofteń ignored. The consequence, according to Belenky, *et al.* (1986), is that students go through the motions of mastering separate knowledge without ever making the connections that would help make this knowledge their own.

(Case study)

She also redirected her educational aims toward the establishment of a community of learners. She began this process by trying to find out more about her students, through the writing of personal histories. In doing so, the pre-packaged traditional answers to teaching fell by the wayside and a more educative community started to emerge. Kathy's relationships with her students shifted as these 'non-learners' became teachers/students to and for each other. Importantly, Kathy was better able to understand and take into account the differences in students. This change in her approach to teaching, in time spread to other classrooms as other teachers could identify both with the constructed role that Kathy had found herself in and the types of new relations that were emerging. She summarized the changes made in her classroom by noting, 'It is my belief that the members of this class developed a caring and trusting attitude toward one another, were concerned for each other's well-being, and became connected in ways of knowing I never thought possible.'

Pat's protest regarding the gender implications of computer use sent her on a course of change within her classroom as well. Where initially Pat assumed that gender had nothing to do with computers, by the end of her study she was not only restructuring the way students used the computer, but also encouraging others in the school to consider how gender biases can be part of seemingly innocent decisions about the use of computers. Specifically, when the question of a computer lab was brought before the school, Pat was able to point out that the choice should take into consideration not only the advantages of a lab, but also the importance of computers in relation to other subjects that would be under-funded if the lab became a reality. As Pat stated, 'the choice of computers over other areas of the curriculum [is] a political one.' In part, Pat's arguments were influential in helping the faculty come to a decision to turn down a proposal to invest in a computer lab because the cost, in terms of other subjects that would suffer or be eliminated, was too high. The faculty would still like to have a computer lab, but they are unwilling to sacrifice other areas of the curriculum for it. They are left in much the same place as Pat when she stated, 'I still have strong convictions about the benefits of this potentially powerful tool. . . . However, this personal conviction is tempered with the same concerns that now will affect my classroom practice.'

While Pat's and Kathy's project went beyond the confines of their classrooms and fostered some change within the school, Robyn began her project with the desire to change her school as well as the teaching profession. Robyn's initial question considered how 'our schools, or even our profession, might change if discussion and reflection were made available and encouraged in a wider audience of teachers.' What she found surprised even her. Some school structures, such as faculty meetings, became less constricting as teachers articulated their values, first to each other and then to administrators. Where previously teachers had no control over the agenda, with the establishment of the dialogue sessions the discussion of professional issues became a regular part of the faculty's meetings. Even the district administration exhibited flexibility as the dialogue challenged the common practice of limiting teachers' curricular choice to the execution of educational aims determined by others. For example, instead of having to choose between several pre-determined science texts, teachers gained the right to center the science curriculum around an experiential approach that required manipulatives. Besides these sorts of changes, teachers also felt less isolated and gained the 'heightened sense of power a group can hold.' Robyn, on the other hand, learned through experience the difficulties and dilemmas of trying to organize dialogue sessions.

Looking across these case studies, we can see the possibilities of and limits to Educative Research. Educative Research had an important influence at the classroom level. For the teachers involved in this project, and the students with whom they came into contact, changes were made that challenged the way schooling acts to foster uncaring relations between students and teachers, to deny opportunities for particular groups, and to silence teachers. While these changes show how inquiry can lead to actions that act on what is oppressive and limiting about schools, it is also the case that much more needs to happen if these actions are to alter the nature of schooling significantly.

One limit of Educative Research is how to maintain the inquiry process and its link to action. If teachers are going to continue to practice Educative Research, resources need to be forthcoming that will enable these practitioners to leave their classrooms to do observations, collect data, review relevant literature, and write their assessments and stories. The beginning changes that have come out of this project will take root, even at the classroom level, only if the process can be maintained.

A second limitation of the changes made is that they were primarily confined to the classroom. While it is true that some changes started to occur at the school level, in general, school structures and the practices of most teachers remained unchanged. Given that our aim is to contest and alter confining aspects of schooling, ways must be found to enable this process to extend beyond individual classrooms. Not only must other teachers eventually join the educative process, but students, parents, and administrators need to have an opportunity to tell their stories, protest what is limiting about schooling, and act on these protests. This movement toward community-based inquiry is essential because only collective actions are likely to alter the structures and practices that define and shape so much of what happens in our schools. As Kathy notes from her personal experience:

> I was never able to change anything except in my own classroom on my own, even though I always expressed my opinion. But when we had five people from our school in the ERP, and we would talk about all these issues and bring things up at faculty meetings, things actually changed, and I couldn't believe that could actually happen. That if you got a group of teachers together, they could change something.

The movement toward collective action, however, is likely to produce contradictory effects: in the process of developing a sense of group, individuals are silenced. Differences must be acknowledged and valued at the same time that attempts are made to make collective decisions and changes.

A final concern we want to raise about the changes made by members of the ERP is that they were not linked in any way to the life of the community and society in general. For instance, Pat's work on computers has implications for those working in the computer field, for feminists struggling in the community to alter the opportunities of girls and women, and for other community members who are trying to understand the relation between technology and issues of gender. However, these connections have not yet been explored. While it would have been unrealistic within the boundaries of our project to expect these sorts of connections to be made, such work needs to be done if the inquiry process is to lead to a grassroots movement that is more diverse and broader in scope.

COMMUNITY

Before we could consider forming a wider community, a local community among the participants of the ERP needed to be established. Our challenge was not only to develop voice among those who have been disenfranchised and to have these participants act on and remake schooling, but also to establish relationships such that collective action would be possible.

From the beginning of our alliance, we have struggled with our aim to become a community. When we presented our work at a conference in October of our second year, the critic of our session asked quite pointedly,

'What is a community, and how do those in the ERP fit that definition?' We have been considering how to answer that question satisfactorily ever since.

In reflecting on this issue, our struggle both to acknowledge differences among individuals and to avoid hierarchical differences is of great significance. The hierarchical differences between the university researcher and those working in the public schools could not entirely be overcome. Our inability to accept differences among individuals in the ERP by holding all participants to common standards regardless of their histories, work conditions, and orientation, also limited our aim of creating a local community. It would be fair to say, therefore, that our ideal community did not occur. It should not be assumed, however, that the project totally failed in this regard. We have come to understand better the importance of difference and in many ways laid the foundation for the type of community we desire. Describing some of the significant events that occurred over our three years together may be helpful in tracing the winding path that has led us to our current sense of community.

We began the ERP with two aims that, on the surface, seemed to pull us in contradictory directions. The development of voice encouraged individuals to go their own way, to establish their own projects, and to speak authentically about their desires and hopes for schooling. We also wanted to develop a sense of 'group' where individuals would see areas of common concern and act collectively. Over time, we found that common ground could emerge without sacrificing the individual voices of the participants.

The exploration of self through the writing of personal and school histories, for example, was an important part of strengthening our individual voices. At the same time, however, these histories did provide a common terrain which connected all our work: the relationship of women and teachers to the outside world. In some sense, all these histories showed how self, norms, and material conditions act to set teachers apart, to deny them certain opportunities, and to silence their voices. What these teachers found in common, therefore, were both constructed boundaries placed before them and, importantly, the experience of bringing these boundaries into focus.

As the Educative Research process moved toward the formation of research questions, other areas of commonality emerged. We shared literature that might have application to each other's study as well as quotes of interest. It also became apparent that many of our projects were linked in surprising ways. Pat's discovery of gender bias in technology, for example, exposed how the socialization process that starts with young students can have implications for gendered professions, such as teaching, as Robyn clearly points out in her study of teacher dialogue. Furthermore, the participants in Robyn's dialogue sessions put together a proposal for a computer lab based, in part, on Pat's study of computers. The introduction of personal histories, a significant part of Kathy's study, not only changed the climate of the classroom, but also suggested that 'success' was a process that started with an understanding of the histories that students brought to the classroom. This perception had strong links to Karen's study which focused specifically on rethinking the common notions of success.

In time, we became a group of teacher/researchers, each following the study of his/her own interest, and yet sharing findings, support, dialogue, and a set of common goals: to understand education better and foster protest and change within ourselves and our environment. This is in direct contrast to the usual collaborative efforts that are organized around a single question or focus. In many ways, we were pursuing our individual interests for the benefit of us all.

This is not to say that there wasn't conflict. During our first two years, different philosophical 'camps' started to form and those camps did launch minor battles at times. This level of conflict found further expression within the group that gathered to write this book during the third year of the ERP. As Beth mentioned, 'I had no idea how much of our own histories we would bring to the writing of this book, and how they would influence, interact, and clash with each other.' Fortunately, our developing voices of protest not only addressed context and ideology, but also were directed inward at ourselves and the group. This 'inward' protest did not attempt to eliminate conflict altogether, but rather enabled us to acknowledge areas of unresolved crisis, search for an understanding of their roots, and act to reshape our relationships where deemed necessary. In short, we tried to treat conflict as a naturally occurring phenomenon which can lead to personal and collective growth rather than as a pathology (Nias, 1987, p.143).

Of course conflict is not always desirable. Conflict which reinforces hierarchy and silences participants by imposing one narrow standard of behavior on all participants can be destructive. While much of our conflict helped us rethink our relations and strengthen them, at times it represented a series of living contradictions; our personal relationships contradicted our aims for Educative Research. These contradictions were apparent even as we gathered to discuss the writing of this book. As Valerie states:

> Concerns about equal commitment to the project, and personal time constraints surfaced as we talked through the writing of the book. How were the credits of authorship to be decided? What if one person did most of the work and another did almost nothing?

In some ways, these concerns have hampered our sense of community. They have also, however, fostered consideration of more foundational issues such as how merit is determined. As Robyn notes:

There are certain values taken for granted in this society. The merit-ocracy is one of them, and I buy into it because I have been fairly successful in it. These conflicts [within the group] have made me re-evaluate all of that, and it has been really difficult. I come from a family that highly values the work ethic, and I have been able to see how that plays into everything I do and everything I am right now.

Despite the undercurrent of conflict and struggle, it was generally accepted that a stronger sense of community developed in the third year, during the book writing phase of the ERP. Those who chose to continue to work on the book did so out of a personal commitment. There would be no degree awarded at the end of our efforts. We all recognized the monetary reim-bursement would be minimal, and surely not enough to compensate for our work. We each had our own personal reasons for continuing, but what linked us together was the importance of engaging in an educative process. As Beth notes in talking about her commitment to the project:

My reason for wanting to be involved with the book was to keep my involvement [in education, reflection, and change] going in some way. I had finished my degree and I didn't want it to stop. When this book is finished, I still don't want that part of me to stop. I don't plan to go back to teaching any time soon, but it is important to keep it going in some way. I still look back at my personal and school histories and think, 'Boy, I would really like, even now, to sit down and do Horizontal Evaluation with somebody just on this paper,' because I think there is a lot there that I still should and could address.

This educative commitment encouraged us to support and critique each other's writing. It was as if we had become midwives to the other mem-bers' labors. Each person's progress in delivering up yet another revision was met with affirmation from the group. While this sense of family still had its problems and we have not established the type of community we had hoped for, Robyn describes well the collective we have become.

So how do we define ourselves within the larger backdrop of the edu-cational community? I guess the possible answer I have for myself is that we are people who are very deeply involved in question posing. We don't have many answers, but what we find are more layers of the question. I see us as a microcosm of the world at large. That world has conflicts, and people choose to work them out in all kinds of different ways, depending on their cultural and personal histories. The conflicts that we have had in this group have caused me to look back at my own personal history, to look at what, out of that past, has caused me to react the way I do. So I think we are continuing to define ourselves, individually, within the group. And I feel that within that struggle we are coming to a better understanding of ourselves as a group.

Our attempt to form an educative community will not come to an end, processes rarely do. We want to continue to challenge our professional and personal lives as we further define and re-evaluate ourselves as a group. The cycle of question posing, analysis, and action that we have experienced is about to begin anew. Our community, voices, and relationships did not turn out the way we thought, but we have noticed enough change to inspire further study and reflection. We are prepared to continue on toward our unknown destination. The journey, in itself, is enough.

Notes

CHAPTER 3

1 For example, in one school history conducted by three members of the ERP, the teachers had almost absolute autonomy over curriculum matters. Others in the group not only had very different stories to tell but, importantly, did not think that sort of autonomy was possible within their district.

2 Robyn, for example, can use her actions in the teacher dialogue meetings to fill out and analyze her personal history as the personal history may help her examine the origins of such behavior.

3 It should be noted that most anthropologists are critical of having researchers study a known culture because it supposedly limits their ability to see the deep structure of that culture.

CHAPTER 4

4 While we do not want to claim that the description of evaluation given is common to all schools, it is common to the local school system because the observation forms used and the general procedures described are mandated by the district.

5 This description is written by Karen Price and appears in a co-authored article with Andrew Gitlin. 'Supervision: An Empowerment Perspective,' (1992) in C. Glickman (ed.), *Supervision in Transition.* Washington, D.C.: ASCD Yearbook.

6 To practice Horizontal Evaluation, every time a teacher observed another teacher as part of the Horizontal Evaluation process, a substitute was brought in to cover the class. After both teachers had a chance to observe, substitutes also covered the teachers' classes as they conferenced with each other. Freeing up teachers in this way allows them to focus on the issues raised without adding additional burdens to their already over-scheduled day.

CHAPTER 5

7 It should not be assumed, however, that this shift in the quest for professionalism destroyed the values held by the normal school or the teachers college. Teacher educators continued to struggle to maintain at least some of the practices of these institutions; but the power and prestige of the university

compelled them to make some compromises. On a symbolic level, one such compromise involved taking the reference to teachers out of the institutional title. In some regards, this symbolic change was effective. The cost of this symbolic change, however, was quite significant. What these institutions were acknowledging was that prestige, status and legitimacy required a separation from teaching. However, the lack of research and published scholarship produced at the institution limited their prestige and legitimacy in relation to the newly established research programs.

8 Schools of education can simply ignore schools and those working in the educational community. There is a point where separating oneself from practice fosters such extreme criticism from the community that a modest shift toward practice or at least a symbolic gesture is necessary. For example, this may account for why schools of education that have a strong research orientation have of late become involved in developing professional development schools (Holmes Group, 1986).

9 The inclusion of women in the normal school was related to the expanding need for teachers (Wiles, 1967, p. 71).

CHAPTER 6

10 Twenty-one of the thirty-four distributed surveys were returned, representing about sixty-two percent of the teachers. Their teaching experiences ranged from three to twenty-nine years, with grade level assignments from kindergarten through sixth grade, one media specialist, and seven teachers from special programs, i.e. resource, self-contained learning, disabled, severely intellectually handicapped, speech, and gifted and talented. Eleven had graduate degrees, while three indicated that getting a graduate degree was a career goal. Two teachers were working on a "Master's Equivalency" offered through the district. Sixteen teachers indicated "Career Ladder" status, a district program devised to determine outstanding teachers for leadership positions.

CHAPTER 8

11 These teachers from the third and fourth grades each have had three years teaching experience. The second, fifth, and sixth grade teachers had fifteen years or more of teaching experience. No teacher from the kindergarten or first grade was interviewed because no one in these levels had computers in their classrooms or training in the technology.

CHAPTER 10

12 An extended audio-taped discussion was conducted at the end of the third year of the ERP to reflect on what the journey had meant to the participants. The quotes that are used in this section, unless otherwise labeled, came from this discussion session.

13 While no explicit work was done along these lines, we did present our work at two international conferences, as well as to the superintendent of the local school district. These events will have to become far more regular if the voices of teachers are to be heard.

References

CHAPTER 1

Apple, M. (1986). *Teachers and Texts: A Political Economy of Class and Gender Relations in Education*. London: Routledge & Kegan Paul.

Tannen, D. (1990) *You Just Don't Understand: Women and Men in Conversation*. New York: Morrow & Company.

CHAPTER 2

Agar, M. (1980) *The Professional Stranger: An Informal Introduction to Ethnography*. New York: Academic Press.

Apple, M. (1979) *Ideology and Curriculum*. London: Routledge & Kegan Paul.

Apple, M. (1982) *Education and Power*. Boston: Routledge & Kegan Paul.

Apple, M. (1986) *Teachers and Text: A Political Economy of Class and Gender Relations in Education*. New York: Routledge & Kegan Paul.

Bernstein, R. (1983) *Beyond Objectivism and Relativism: Science, Hermeneutics and Praxis*. Philadelphia: University of Pennsylvania Press.

Clifford, G. (1986) 'The formative years of schools of education in America: A five institution analysis', *American Journal of Education, 94*, (4), pp. 410, 434, 442.

Eisner, E. (1979) *The Educational Imagination*. New York: Macmillan.

Gadamer, H. G. (1975) *Truth and Method*. New York: Seabury Press.

Gitlin, A. and Goldstein, S. (1987) 'A dialogical approach to understanding: Horizontal Evaluation', *Educational Theory, 37*, (1), pp. 17–27.

Gitlin, A., Siegel, M. and Boru, K. (1989) 'The politics of method: From leftist ethnography to educative research', *Qualitative Studies in Education, 2*, (3), pp. 237–53.

Grant, C. and Sleeter, C. (1988) 'Race, class, and gender and abandoned dreams', *Teachers College Record, 90*, (1), pp. 19-40.

Habermas, J. (1976) *Communication and the Evolution of Society*. Boston: Beacon Press.

Kliebard, H. (1987) *The Struggle for the American Curriculum*. New York: Routledge & Kegan Paul.

Lather, P. (1975) *The changer and the changed* (record album) (produced by C. Williamson; co-produced by M. Adam, M. Christian and E.M. Dictorow). Oakland, CA: Olivia Records Company.

Lather, P. (1988) 'Feminist perspectives on empowering research methodologies', *Women's Studies International Forum, 2,* (6), pp. 569–81.

Leach, M. (1988) 'Teacher education and reform: What's sex got to do with it?', *Educational Foundations, 58,* (3), pp. 4–14.

Perry, I. (1988) 'A black students' reflection on public and private schools', *Harvard Educational Review, 58,* (3), pp. 332–36.

Sarason, S. (1971) *The Culture of the School and the Problem of Change.* Boston: Allyn & Bacon.

Simon, R. and Dippo, D. (1986) 'On critical ethnographic work', *Anthropology and Education Quarterly, 17,* pp. 195–202.

Spencer, D. (1984) 'The home and school lives of women teachers', *Elementary School Journal, 84,* pp. 283–98.

Weiler, K. (1988) *Women Teaching for Change: Gender, Class and Power.* South Hadley, MA: Bergin & Garvey.

Weis, L. (1988) *Between two worlds: Black students in an urban community college.* Boston: Routledge & Kegan Paul.

White, J. (1989) 'The politics of politeness in the classroom: Cultural codes that create and constrain knowledge construction', *Journal of Curriculum and Supervision, 4,* pp. 298–321.

CHAPTER 3

Apple, M. (1979) *Ideology and Curriculum.* London: Routledge & Kegan Paul.

Becker, H. (1970) *Sociological Work: Method and Substance.* Chicago: Aldine Publishing Company.

Canter, L. (1976) *Assertive Discipline.* Santa Monica: Canter and Associates, Inc.

Freire, P. (1970) *Pedagogy of the Oppressed.* New York: Seabury Press.

Goodson, I. (1988) 'Teachers' life histories and studies of curriculum and schooling', in I. Goodson (ed.) *The Making of Curriculum: Collected Essays.* London: Falmer Press, pp. 71–92.

Grumet, M. (1988) *Bitter Milk.* Amherst: University of Massachusetts Press.

Krall, F. (1988) 'From the inside out: Personal history as research', *Educational Theory, 38,* (4), pp. 467–79.

Kyvig, D., and Marty, M. (1986) *Nearby History.* Nashville, Tennessee: The American Association for State and Local History, p. 103.

Pinar, W. (1975) 'Curriculum: toward reconceptualization', in W. Pinar (ed.) *Curriculum Theorizing: The Reconceptualists.* Berkeley: McCutchan, pp. 398–414.

Sarason, S. (1971) *The Culture of the School and the Problem of Change.* Boston: Allyn & Bacon.

CHAPTER 4

Bullough, R. and Gitlin, A. (1987) 'Teacher evaluation and empowerment: Challenging the taken-for-granted view of teaching', *Educational Policy, 1*(2), pp. 229–47.

Gadamer, H.G. (1975) *Truth and method.* New York: Seabury Press.

Gitlin, A. (1990) 'Understanding teaching dialogically'. *Teachers College Record, 91,* (4), pp. 537–64.

Gitlin, A. & Smyth, J. (1989) *Teacher Evaluation: Educative Alternatives*. London: Falmer Press.
Habermas, J. (1976) *Communication and the Evolution of Society*. Boston: Beacon Press.
Whitehead, J. & Lomax, P. (1987) 'Action research and the politics of educational knowledge'. *British Educational Research Journal, 13*, (2), pp. 175–90.

CHAPTER 5

Bigelow, K. (1957) 'The passing of the Teachers College', *Teachers College Record, 58*, (8).
Borrowman, M. (1965) 'Liberal education and the professional preparation of teachers', in M. Borrowman (ed.) *Teacher Education in America: A Documentary History* New York: Teachers College Press, p. 24.
Bullough, R., Gitlin, A. and Goldstein, S. (1984) 'Ideology, teacher role and resistance', *Teacher College Record, 86*, (2), pp. 339–58.
Clifford, G. (1986) 'The formative years of schools of education in America: A five institution analysis', *American Journal of Education 94*, (4), pp. 410, 434, 442.
Clifford, G. and Guthrie, J. (1988) *Ed School: A Brief for Professional Education*. Chicago: University of Chicago Press.
Cubberly, E. (1909) *Changing Conceptions of Education*. Boston: Houghton Mifflin Company, pp. 67–8.
Goodlad, J., Soder, R. and Sirotnik, K. (1990) *The Moral Dimension of Teaching*. San Francisco: Josey-Bass Publishers.
Graham, P. (1978) 'Expansion and exclusion: a history of women in American higher education', *Journal of Women in Culture and Society, 3*, (4), pp. 759–74.
Haley, M. (1904) *Why Teachers Should Organize*. National Education Proceedings.
Herbst, J. (1989) *And Sadly Teach: Teacher Education and Professionalism in American Culture*. Wisconsin: University of Wisconsin Press.
Holmes Group (1986) *Tommorrows Teachers*. East Lansing.
Judd, C. (1929) 'Teachers colleges as centers of progressive education', *National Education Association Addresses and Proceedings, 67*, pp. 877, 879, 880.
Larson, M. (1977) *The Rise of Professionalism: A Sociological Analysis*. Berkeley: University of California Press.
Powell, A. (1971) *Speculations on the Early Impact of Schools of Education on Educational Psychology, 11*, pp. 407–11.
Steere, H. J. (1931) 'The developmental trends of teachers colleges', *Educational Administration and Supervision, 17*, pp. 192–94.
Strong, O. (1950) 'Some trends in teacher education', *Teachers College Record, 21*, pp. 83–84.
Wassermann, J. (1979) 'Wisconsin normal schools and educational hierarchy', in E. Rutkowski (ed.) *Papers and Proceedings of the Combined Annual Meetings of the Midwest History of Education Society and the History of Education Society*. Cedar Falls: University of Northern Iowa Press.
Whittemore, R. (1965) 'Sovereignty in the university: Teachers college and Columbia', *Teachers College Record, 66*, (6), pp. 266, 272, 274–75, 509–11.
Wiles, K. (1967) *Teacher Education and the University in American Association of Colleges for Teacher Education Yearbook*, (20), pp. 68–80.

Woodring, P. (1958) 'The new look in teacher education', *American Association of Colleges for Teacher Education, 11*, p. 14.

Wright, A. (1965) 'The new state colleges', *Improving College and University Teaching, 13*, p. 29.

Wrigley, J. (1982) *Class, Politics and Public Schools*. New Jersey: Rutgers University Press.

CHAPTER 6

Apple, M. (1986) *Teachers and Texts*. New York: Routledge & Kegan Paul.

Aronowitz, S. and Giroux, H. (1985) *Education Under Siege: The Conservative, Liberal and Radical Debate over Schooling*. South Hadley, Mass.: Bergin & Garvey.

Belenky, M., Clinchy, B., Goldberger, N. and Tarule, J. (1986) *Women's Ways of Knowing: The Development of Self, Voice, and Mind*. New York: Basic Books.

Berlak, A. and Berlak, H. (1987) 'Teachers working with teachers to transform schools', in J. Smyth (ed.) *Educating Teachers: Changing the Nature of Pedagogical Knowledge*. New York: Falmer Press, pp. 169–78.

Ellsworth, E. (1989) 'Why doesn't this feel empowering? Working through the repressive myths of critical pedagogy', *Harvard Educational Review, 59*, pp. 297–324.

Flinders, D. (1988) 'Teacher isolation and the new reform', *Journal of Curriculum and Supervision, 4*, (1), 17–29.

Foucault, M. (1980) 'Truth and power', in C. Gordon (ed.) *Power/Knowledge: Selected Interviews and Other Writings 1972–1977*. New York: Pantheon Books, pp. 109–33.

Freedman, S., Jackson, J. and Boles, K. (1986) *The Effect of Teaching on Teachers*. Boston, Mass.: Boston Women's Teachers' Group. (ERIC Document Reproduction Service No. Ed 85 63735.)

Gitlin, A. (1987) 'Common school structures and teacher behavior', in J. Smyth (ed.), *Educating teachers: Changing the nature of pedagogical Knowledge*. New York: Falmer Press, pp. 107–19.

Goodlad, J. and Klein, F. (1974) *Looking Behind the Classroom Door*. Worthington, O.: Jones and Co.

Gore, J. (1989) *What We Can Do For You! What Can 'We' Do For 'You'?: Struggling Over Empowerment in Critical and Feminist Pedagogy*. Paper presented at the American Educational Studies Association Convention, Chicago.

Grumet, M. (1989) 'Dinner at Abigail's: nurturing collaboration', *NEA Today, 7*, pp. 20–5.

Hargreaves, A. (1989) *Teachers' Work and the Politics of Time and Space*. Paper presented to the American Educational Research Association, San Francisco.

Hargreaves, A. (1990) *Cultures of Teaching*. Unpublished paper, Ontario Institute for Studies in Education, Canada.

Hooks, B. (1989) *Talking Back: Thinking Feminist, Thinking Black*. Boston: South End Press.

Jackson, P. (1968) *Life in Classrooms*. New York: Holt, Rinehart & Winston.

King, S. (1982) *Different Seasons*. New York: Signet.

Kliebard, H. (1987) *The Struggle for the American Curriculum 1893–1958*. New York: Routledge & Kegan Paul.

Nias, J. (1989) *Primary Teachers Talking*. London: Routledge & Kegan Paul.
Pateman, C. (1970) *Participation in Democratic Theory*. Cambridge: Cambridge University Press.
Rich, A. (1978) 'Cartographies of silence', In *The Dream of a Common Language*. New York: W. W. Norton.
Rorty, R. (1980) *Philosophy and the Mirror of Nature*. Princeton, NJ: Princeton University Press.
Sarason, S. (1971) *The Culture of the School and the Problem of Change*. Boston: Allyn & Bacon.
Thorne, B. (1984) *Rethinking the Ways we Teach*. Keynote address presented at Michigan State University.
Tiess, P. (1989) *Rethinking the Use of Computers in the Elementary School*. Unpublished paper, University of Utah.
Tye, K. and Tye, B. (1984) 'Teacher isolation and school reform', *Phi Delta Kappan*, January 1984, pp. 319–22.
Weiler, K. (1988) *Women Teaching for Change: Gender, Class and Power*. South Hadley, MA.: Bergin & Garvey.

CHAPTER 7

Brophy, J. and Good, T. (1974) *Teacher Student Relationships: Causes and Consequences*. New York: Holt, Rinehart & Winston.
Bullough, R. V. Jr (1987) 'Accommodation and tension: Teachers, teachers' role, and the culture of teaching', in John Smyth (ed.) *Educating Teachers: Changing the Nature of Pedagogical Knowledge*. New York: Falmer Press.
Castaneda, C. (1972) *Journey to Ixtlan*. New York: Simon & Schuster.
Cooper, H. and Good, T. (1983) *Pygmalion Grows Up: Studies in the Expectation Communication Process*. New York: Longman.
Erickson, F. (1987) 'Transformation and school success: The politics and culture of educational achievement', *Anthropology and Education Quarterly, 18*, pp. 335–56.
Freedman, S., Jackson, J. and Boles, K. (1983) 'The other end of the corridor: The effect of teaching on teachers', *Radical Teacher, 23*, pp. 2–23.
Freire, P. (1970) *Pedagogy of the Oppressed*. New York: Seabury Press.
Gadamer, H. G. (1975) *Truth and Method*. London: Sheed & Ward.
Gilligan, C. (1982) *In a Different Voice*. Cambridge, MA.: Harvard University Press.
Gilligan, C. (1987) 'Moral orientation and moral development', in Eva F. Kittay and Diana T. Meyers (eds) *Women and Moral Theory*. New York: Rowman & Littlefield.
Gitlin, A. D. (1987) 'Common school structures and teacher behaviour', in John Smyth (ed.) *Educating teachers: Changing the Nature of Pedagogical Knowledge*. New York: Falmer Press.
Good, T. L. (1987) 'Two decades of research on teacher expectations: Findings and future directions', *Journal of Teacher Education*, July–August, pp. 32–47.
Gurevitch, Z. D. (1989) 'The power of not understanding: The meeting of conflicting identities', *Journal of Applied Behavioral Science, 25*, pp. 161–73.
Illich, I. (1971) *Deschooling Society*. New York: Harper & Row.
Jackson, P. W. (1968) *Life in Classrooms*. New York: Holt, Rinehart & Winston.

Jardine, D. W. (1989) *A Bell Ringing in an Empty Sky*. Unpublished manuscript presented at JCT Curriculum Theorizing Conference, October, Dayton, Ohio.

Lomax, P. (ed.) (1989) *The Management of Change: Increasing School Effectiveness and Facilitating Staff Development Through Action Research*. Clevedon, Philadelphia: Multilingual Matters LTD.

Noddings, N. (1989) *Women and Evil*. Berkeley, Los Angeles, London: University of California Press.

Piaget, J. (1971) *The Construction of Reality in the Child*. New York: Ballantine Books.

Rosenthal, R. (1974) *On the Social Psychology of the Self-Fulfilling Prophecy: Further Evidence of Pygmalion Effects and Their Mediating Mechanisms*. New York: MSS Modular Publications.

Stenhouse, L. (1979) 'Research as a basis for teaching', in J. Rudduck and D. Hopkins (eds) *Research as a Basis for Teaching: Readings from the Work of Lawrence Stenhouse*. London: Heinemann.

Whitehead, J. (1985) 'An analysis of an individual's educational development: The basis for personally oriented action research', in M. Shipman (ed.) *Educational Research: Principles, Policies and Practices*. Basingstoke: Falmer Press.

Willis, P. (1977) *Learning to Labour*. Farnborough: Saxon House.

Wise, G. (1973, 1980) 'Appendix: Taking a strategic journey: Some questions for inquiry', *American Historical Explanations*. Minneapolis: University of Minnesota Press.

Wise, G. (1977) 'Some elementary axioms for an American culture studies', *Contemporary Approaches to the Study of America*. Papers from the 1977 American Studies Symposium, University of Iowa, pp. 517–46.

CHAPTER 8

Apple, M. W. (1986) *Teachers and Texts: A Political Economy of Class and Gender Relations in Education*. New York: Routledge & Kegan Paul.

Bowers, C. A. (1988) *The Cultural Dimensions of Educational Computing: Understanding the Non-Neutrality of Technology*. New York: Teachers College Press.

Broughton, J. M. (1984) 'The surrender of control: Computer literacy as political socialization of the child', In Douglas Sloan (ed.) *The Computer in Education: A Critical Perspective*. New York: Teachers College Press.

Dwyer, T. (1980) 'Some thoughts on computers and greatness in teaching', in Robert Taylor (ed.) *The Computer in the School: Tutor, Tool, Tutee*. New York: Teachers College Press.

Kepner, H. (1986) 'Communication skills with computers: Language arts, composition, and reading', in Henry S. Kepner Jr (ed.) *Computers in the Classroom*. Washington, D.C.: National Education Association.

Mullan, A. P. (1984) *Children and Computers in the Classroom*. Tunbridge Wells: Castle House Publications.

O'Connor, V. (1986) 'The computer in mathematics instruction, K-8', in Henry S. Kepner Jr (ed.) *Computers in the Classroom*. Washington, D.C.: National Education Association.

Papert, S. (1980) *Mindstorms: Children, Computers, and Powerful Ideas*. New York: Basic Books.

Rizza, P. J. (1982) 'Computer-based education (CBE): Tomorrow's traditional system', in Mary Frank (ed.) *Young Children in a Computerized Environment.* New York: Haworth Press.

Sardello, R. J. (1984) 'The technological threat to education', in Douglas Sloan (ed.) *The Computer in Education: A Critical Perspective.* New York: Teachers College Press.

Terry, P. (1987) 'Not enough computers? Fostering equitable access to scarce equipment', *Educational Technology*, March, pp. 22–4.

Thompson, B. and Cloer, T. (1982) 'A learning aid: Imaginative electronics applied to education', in Mary Frank (ed.) *Young Children in a Computerized Environment.* New York: Haworth Press.

Tittnich, E. M. and Brown, N. (1982) 'Positive and negative uses of technology in human interactions', in Mary Frank (ed.) *Young Children in a Computerized Environment.* New York: Haworth Press.

Weiler, K. (1988) *Women Teaching for Change: Gender, Class & Power.* Massachusetts: Bergin & Garvey.

CHAPTER 9

Belenky, M., Clinchy, B., Goldberger, N. and Tarule, J. (1986) *Women's Ways of Knowing: The Development of Self, Voice, and Mind.* New York: Basic Books.

Berlak, A. and Berlak, H. (1981) *Delemmas of Schooling: Teaching and Social Change.* New York: Methuen.

Eisner, E. (1979) *The Educational Imagination.* New York: Macmillan.

Goodlad, J. and Anderson, R. (1987) *The Non-Graded Elementary School.* New York: Teachers College Press.

Postman, N. and Weingarner, C. (1969) *Teaching a Subversive Activity.* New York: Dell Publishing Co.

CHAPTER 10

Belenky, M., Clinchy, B., Goldberger, N. and Tarule, J. (1986) *Women's Ways of Knowing: The Development of Self, Voice, and Mind.* New York: Basic Books.

Nias, J. (1987) 'Learning from differences: A collegial approach to change', in J. Smyth (ed.) *Educating Teachers: Changing the Nature of Pedagogical Knowledge.* Philadelphia: Falmer Press.

Index

positive reinforcement, *see*
  reinforcement
Powell, A., 71
power: and action, 93; and dialogue,
  109, 110; within educational
  community, 23–4; and
  professionalism, 84; in research
  process, 179; of students, 39, 48;
  and time, 101; and women, 84, 114
practical knowledge, *see* experiential
  knowledge
practice, *see* experience
prior knowledge, 65–6, 172, 186
process of learning, 70, 171–2
process orientation of research, 26, 28,
  32, 112
professional development schools, 194
Professional Dialogue Sessions, 106,
  113
professionalism of teachers, 69–85,
  111
professors, *see* academics
promotion, *see* career structure
protest: and change, 184–8; voice as,
  23–4, 27, 28, 29, 30, 84, 179, 183–4

questions, research, 7, 17, 26–7, 48,
  60–4, 69, 93

race differences in classroom, 16,
  164–5
readings on education, 13, 30–1, 91,
  157
reflection, 8, 35, 36, 105, 106, 113,
  130–3
reinforcement, 39, 43, 50–1, 125
reliability of research data, 27–8
research: 7; and action, 8, 21, 24–6,
  28, 48, 64–7, 83, 184–9; alienation
  of subjects, 19–21; conservatism of,
  25, 28; data organization, 27; and
  dialogue, 8, 15, 20, 28, 97; gender
  differences, 19–21, 78–9, 81–2,
  180, 181; hierarchical relationships,
  19–21, 25, 76, 84–5, 180; as
  legitimate knowledge, 1–2, 71, 80;
  objectivism of, 22, 26–7; power
  issues 179; and practice, 74–5,
  81–2, 83–4; process orientation, 26,
  28, 32, 112; questions, 7, 17, 26–7,

48, 60–4, 69, 93; reflection, 8, 35,
  36, 105, 106, 113, 130–3; silencing
  of subjects, 19–21, 179, 180;
  subject's role, 19–21; by teachers,
  7–8, 12, 15, 19–21, 26, 72–3, 83,
  97–8; teachers' access to results,
  20, 25, 74, 97; at teachers colleges,
  72–3; time available for, 75, 85, 98;
  and tradition, 25, 28; at university
  schools of education, 73–5, 83;
  validity, 27–8
researcher/subject relationships,
  19–21, 32–3
resistance to learning, 128–30
rewards, *see* reinforcement
Rich, A., 115
Rissa, J., 146
Rorty, R. 114
Rosenthal, R., 123

salary of women teachers, 78
Sarason, S., 13, 40, 91, 92
Sardello, R.J., 146
school histories, 13, 26–7, 28, 29–51,
  56–8
school structure: constraining
  dialogue, 101; and tradition, 23–4,
  39, 158; and voice, 93, 183–4
schools of education, 73–6, 80, 83
Seeds, C., 82
self, *see* personal histories
sharing by students, 165–8
Siegel, M., 20
silence and audience, 96–8, 183
silencing: of research subjects, 19–21,
  179, 180; of students, 153; of
  teachers, 6, 28, 90–2; by time
  constraints, 93; of women, 94, 112,
  147, 180, 181, 184
Simon, R., 22
Sleeter, C., 16
social class differences in classroom,
  16
socialization: education as, 47, 124; of
  girls, 153, 154, 189–90; role of
  computers, 146, 154; of women
  teachers, 77
software choices of students, 149, 150
status of academics, 32, 74
status quo, *see* conservatism